Take-Home Leveled Readers

Advanced Level

Science

PEARSON
Scott Foresman

Editorial Offices: Glenview, Illinois • Parsippany, New Jersey • New York, New York
Sales Offices: Needham, Massachusetts • Duluth, Georgia • Glenview, Illinois
Coppell, Texas • Sacramento, California • Mesa, Arizona

sfsuccessnet.com

ISBN: 0-328-19729-7

2 3 4 5 6 7 8 9 10 V004 13 12 11 10 09 08 07 06 05

Table of Contents

To the Teacher

Scott Foresman provides three Leveled Readers for every chapter of *Scott Foresman Science*, Grades 1–6: a *Below-Level Leveled Reader*, an *On-Level Leveled Reader*, and an *Advanced Leveled Reader*.

All three readers teach the same science concepts, same vocabulary, address the same target reading skill and contain the same graphic organizer as the corresponding student edition chapter, just at three different reading levels—providing access to important science content for all students. The On-level and Advanced readers also use additional examples to enrich the chapter and extend ideas

This book contains reproducible copies of the Advanced Leveled Readers for Grade 4. These are designed for you to reproduce and send home with your students as appropriate. Encourage students to share these books with parents or family members in order to practice reading skills and reinforce science content.

Online versions of these and other readers are also available through the Scott Foresman Leveled Reader Database.

Science

Genre	Comprehension Skill	Text Features	Science Content
Nonfiction	Compare and Contrast	• Captions • Labels • Diagrams • Glossary	Classifying Plants and Animals

Scott Foresman Science 4.1

PEARSON Scott Foresman

scottforesman.com

ISBN 0-328-13861-4

9 780328 138616 90000

Life Science

Science

REPTILE OR AMPHIBIAN?

by Laura Crawford

Vocabulary	Extended Vocabulary
cell	burrow
chloroplast	clutch
cytoplasm	ectotherm
genus	herpetology
invertebrates	mimicry
nucleus	molting
species	setae
vertebrates	

Picture Credits
Every effort has been made to secure permission and provide appropriate credit for photographic material. The publisher deeply regrets any omission and pledges to correct errors called to its attention in subsequent editions.

Photo locators denoted as follows: Top (T), Center (C), Bottom (B), Left (L), Right (R), Background (Bkgd).

5 (BL) Michael & Patricia Fogden/Corbis; 6 (CL) Michael & Patricia Fogden/Corbis; 7 "Jerry Young/DK Images; 11 (B) Philip Gould/Corbis; 12 Larry Williams/Corbis; 17 (TR) "Jerry Young/DK Images; 23 (TR) "Jerry Young/DK Images.

ISBN: 0-328-13861-4

2 3 4 5 6 7 8 9 10 V004 13 12 11 10 09 08 07 06 05

What did you learn?

1. What is mimicry?
2. Which animals use camouflage?
3. What is special about the chameleon's eyesight?
4. **Writing** in Science Most amphibians need water to survive, but they rarely drink water. Write to explain how amphibians take in water. Include details from the book to support your answer.
5. **Compare and Contrast** How are the roles of a female leopard tortoise and a midwife toad similar? How are they different?

Glossary

burrow to dig a hole or tunnel in the ground

clutch a group of animal eggs

ectotherm a cold-blooded animal

herpetology the study of reptiles and amphibians

mimicry an animal's resemblance to something in nature, which helps the animal to hide

3 **molting** the periodic shedding of an outer covering, such as skin

setae hairlike projections on the pads of a gecko's feet

by Laura Crawford

PEARSON
Scott Foresman

What You Already Know

All living things, or organisms, are made up of cells. A cell is the smallest unit of life. Each cell consists of many parts. At the center of a cell is the nucleus, which controls the cell's activity. The cytoplasm has everything the cell needs to carry out life processes. Plant cells have chloroplasts that trap energy from the Sun to make food.

Plants and animals are classified into groups called kingdoms. Kingdoms are divided into smaller groups. These smaller groups provide the scientific names for organisms. The first part of an organism's scientific name is its genus. The second part is its species. The animal kingdom consists of two main groups. Vertebrates are animals with backbones. Invertebrates are animals without backbones.

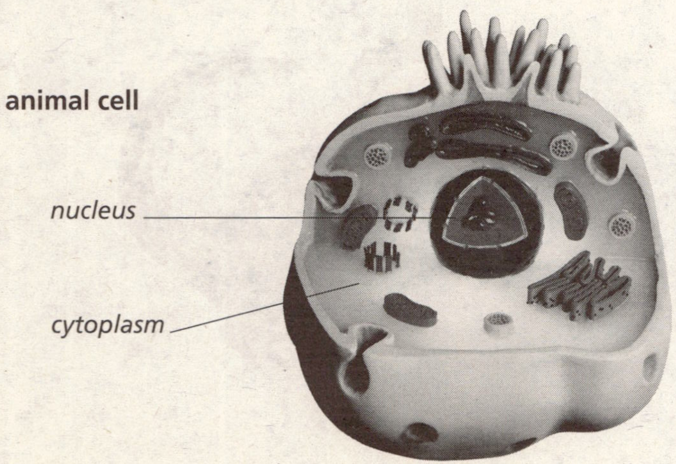

animal cell

Many amphibians and reptiles can hide from enemies because their skin blends into their environment. Some reptiles can even change the color of their skin to make it more difficult for predators to find them. Other species have poisons that give them added protection from predators.

paradoxical frog

Most amphibians reproduce by laying soft eggs in the water. Reptiles either lay eggs that have a protective shell, or they give birth to their young.

Scientists have classified thousands of species of reptiles and amphibians. The two groups of animals have many similarities. They also have many differences. Sometimes even animals in the same group seem quite different. Snakes and turtles don't look much alike, but they are both reptiles. The worm-like caecilians look almost nothing like frogs, but both are amphibians.

Scientists study the two groups to learn more about the relationships, adaptations, and behavior that have helped the animals survive.

corn snake

Similar but Different

There are similarities between reptiles and amphibians that cause confusion. Reptiles and amphibians are both cold-blooded vertebrates. Both reptiles and amphibians use their senses, such as smell and sight, to find food and stay away from predators. But when you compare the two kinds of animals, you will notice important differences. Amphibians have moist skin without scales. Most amphibians must live near water so their soft skin does not dry out. Reptiles have dry, scaly skin. Their skin does not need as much water as the skin of amphibians does, so they do not always live near water.

5

Different species of reptiles have different types of legs and feet. Some species, such as snakes, have no legs or feet at all! Most amphibians hatch as larvae, many of which do not have arms or legs. Many will grow limbs when they undergo metamorphosis.

chameleon

In the plant kingdom, vascular plants transport water and nutrients through vascular tissue. Nonvascular plants, however, pass water and nutrients from one cell to the next. Some plants reproduce with flowers or cones that produce seeds. Other plants reproduce with spores.

Animals have adaptations that allow them to survive in their environment. Some animals have adapted to blend into their environment. Animals have instincts, such as migration and hibernation, to help them survive. Animals also inherit and learn behavior from their parents.

The animal kingdom is very large and has many different groups. Two of these groups are reptiles and amphibians.

The crocodile is a reptile.

Introduction

Reptiles and amphibians are two animal groups that are often confused. They have many things in common. Both groups are cold-blooded vertebrates. Most of them hatch from eggs. But reptiles and amphibians also have important differences.

More than 3,140 species of amphibians live on Earth today. They range in length from 1 centimeter to 1.5 meters. Frogs and toads, with approximately 2,660 different species, make up the largest group of amphibians. They have powerful hind legs, which make them good jumpers. The next largest group, the salamanders, has around 320 species. Salamanders can be identified by their long tails. The smallest group of amphibians is the caecilians (suh-SIL-yuhnz). There are only about 160 caecilian species. These legless amphibians are sometimes confused with earthworms or snakes, but they are very different from both.

The European fire salamander is an amphibian.

Tortoise Reproduction

Tortoises are turtles that live on land. Before a female leopard tortoise lays her eggs, she digs a large hole with her hind feet. She later drops groups of five to thirty white eggs, called a clutch, into the hole. She then covers the eggs with dirt. Baby tortoises will hatch from their shells anywhere from six months to more than a year later.

The leopard tortoise breaks out of its egg.

Newly hatched leopard tortoises resemble their parents.

Frog Reproduction

Frogs lay eggs that mature outside of the adults' bodies. When frogs produce eggs, it is called spawning. Soon the tiny fertilized eggs become tadpoles. Tadpoles use gills to get oxygen. They have a tail to help them swim. As the tadpoles get older, they begin to grow lungs and legs. Their eyes move to a new position, and they lose their tail. Adults frogs don't need a tail to help them swim because they spend most of their time on land.

Frog eggs

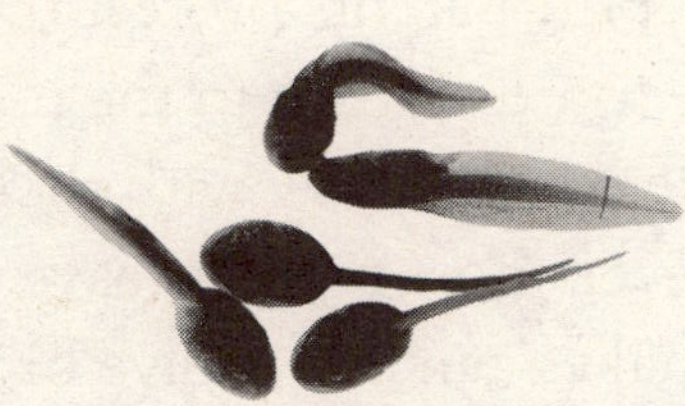

Newly hatched tadpoles

6–9 weeks

9 weeks

The tegu lizard is a reptile.

There are approximately 6,000 species of reptiles on Earth today. More than 3,000 of the species are lizards, the largest group of reptiles. Snakes make up the second largest reptile group. There are more than 2,500 species of snakes. Turtles and tortoises are next, with approximately 250 species. There are more than 20 species of crocodilians, including alligators and crocodiles. There is only one species of a very rare beaked reptile called a tuatara (too-uh-TAH-ruh).

Like amphibians, reptiles vary greatly in size. Some snakes and lizards are as small as 5 centimeters. But some crocodiles and snakes grow more than 12 meters long!

The study of reptiles and amphibians is called herpetology. This word comes from the word *herpeton*, which means "crawling things."

Caecilian

Amphibians

Amphibians live all over the world. They can live in water or on land. Since most amphibians have skin that must be kept moist, they usually live near water.

Frogs and toads can be found in every climate except polar regions and very dry deserts. Caecilians often burrow in the loose soil of tropical forests. They also live in rivers and streams. Salamanders live in ponds, swamps, wet mountain forests, and grasslands.

Frogs have large eyes that allow them to see in many directions.

The head and tail of a caecilian are hard to tell apart.

Salamanders are amphibians that keep their tails as adults.

This newt larva will live in the water until it becomes an adult.

Some reptiles lay eggs, while others give birth to their offspring. Reptile eggs have a hard or leathery shell. This helps keep moisture in. The eggs do not need to be laid in water. Unlike amphibians, reptiles look like their parents when they are born.

Reptile parents protect their eggs to varying degrees. Some lizards return to the nest to turn their eggs. Some female pythons stay with their eggs until they hatch. However, most reptiles leave soon after they lay their eggs.

Snakes can either give birth to live young, or they can lay eggs. In either case, when the young are born, they are independent and able to take care of themselves. They do not need very much help from their parents.

8

A snake emerges from its egg.

Reproduction

Amphibians hatch from jellylike, waterproof eggs. These eggs must be laid in water to prevent them from drying out. When amphibian larvae hatch, they go through a metamorphosis, or a change in looks and habits. Other amphibians lay eggs on land or give birth to their young.

After adult newts lay their eggs in water, the eggs hatch and the newt larvae stay in the water. Once the newts are adults, they live mainly on the land.

The male midwife toad has the job of carrying large strings of eggs. The male toad carries the eggs wrapped around his back legs for about four weeks. He often finds water to keep the eggs moist. When they are about to hatch into tadpoles, the male takes the eggs to shallow water and releases them.

Amphibian larvae vary from species to species. The larvae of frogs and toads, or tadpoles, look like little fish. Salamander larvae are very long. They have front and back legs. Caecilian larvae are thin and lack limbs, much like their adult form. After metamorphosis, all amphibian larvae change from plant-eaters to meat-eaters. They also go from breathing through gills to breathing with lungs.

A male midwife toad carries a string of eggs.

Reptiles

Reptiles can be found in just about any habitat except polar regions and tundras. Many reptiles have scaly skin, which holds in water and prevents their bodies from drying out.

Crocodiles and alligators tend to live near water. Turtles also live near water, while tortoises prefer dry land. Lizards and snakes make their homes on the ground or in trees. Tuataras often burrow.

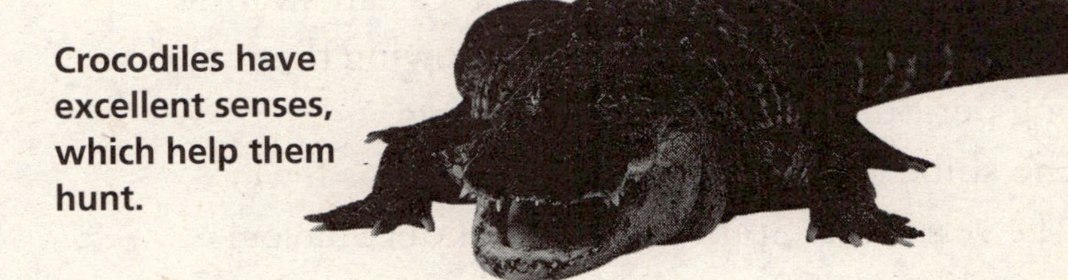

Crocodiles have excellent senses, which help them hunt.

A turtle's shell is made of bones, which are covered by plates called scutes.

Tuataras live only off the coasts of New Zealand.

Snakes contract their muscles in order to move.

Skin and Structure

Although all reptiles and amphibians are vertebrates, the number of vertebrae, or bony segments, they have varies greatly. Some snakes have as many as 400 vertebrae. But their jaws are what makes them different from amphibians and other reptiles. Some snakes are able to open their jaws wide enough to swallow their prey whole. The two halves of the lower jaw are connected by muscle and ligaments, rather than by bone. Snakes can swallow a huge chunk of food all at once, allowing them to go long periods of time without eating.

The spine of a frog or toad usually has fewer than 12 vertebrae. Spines of salamanders have between 30 and 100 vertebrae while spines of caecilians can have more than 200.

This salamander skeleton shows a flexible torso and long tail supported by many vertebrae.

Sight is an important sense in some amphibians. Frogs and toads have large eyes that stick out so they can see in most directions. The red-eyed tree frog can also use its eyes for protection. If something disturbs the frog while it sleeps, it opens its eyes and scares predators away with its bright red eyes.

Red-eyed tree frog

Caecilians spend much of their lives underground. Sight and hearing are not important senses for them. They rely on tentacles between their nostrils and eyes for information.

Since its eyes move independently, a Jackson's chameleon can judge distance accurately.

Senses

Smell is an important sense for reptiles. Snakes and lizards actually smell through their tongues! They flick out their forked tongues, which pick up scent particles. These particles are brought to a smelling organ in the roof of the mouth. From there the organ sends information about the scent to the brain. This helps snakes and lizards locate food, predators, and mates.

Most reptiles have keen eyesight. This makes up for their generally poor hearing. Chameleons can move their eyes independently of each other. That means each eye can be looking in a different direction. One eye can focus on the prey, while the other eye looks around to check that the chameleon is safe.

Some snakes, such as boas and pit vipers, have special organs on their lips or the sides of their head that can sense heat. This means they can hunt even in the dark!

A snake uses its tongue to detect scents.

Amphibians and reptiles are cold-blooded creatures, or ectotherms. They depend on the environment to regulate their body temperature. Some are warmed directly by the Sun. Others regulate their body temperature by staying on warm surfaces. Most reptiles and amphibians become dormant when it gets too cold. Some amphibians living in colder climates hibernate. Tuataras are the only reptiles that can stay active in colder temperatures. They have been known to survive in temperatures as low as 6°C (43°F) due to their slow heart rate and breathing.

White's tree frog has shiny, waxlike skin.

Amphibians have soft, smooth skin that is water permeable. This means that water can enter their bodies through their skin. Reptiles are covered in rough, dry skin that does not let water into their bodies. The skin of a snake does not grow with it. So snakes periodically shed their skin. This is called molting.

Notice the scales on this Madagascan day gecko.

Land or Water?

The word amphibian comes from the Greek word *amphibios*, which means "a being with a double life." Most young amphibians live in water. As they get older, they live both on land and in water. Some spend their entire lives moving between land and water.

Amphibians need water to keep their skin moist. Water passes through an amphibian's skin into its body. Amphibians might take in some water with food or gather it from wet surfaces, but they rarely drink it. They also need water when laying eggs.

The palmate newt is a kind of salamander. The webbing between its back toes helps it swim rapidly.

The collar of the Australian frilled lizard warns attackers to stay away.

Some reptiles and amphibians use methods other than hiding to protect themselves. An Australian frilled lizard has a large collar of loose skin that can be inflated when danger is near. By appearing larger and more intimidating, it frightens away predators. Mimicry can also be used in this way. Some animals' resemblance to another species helps them scare predators.

Other reptiles and amphibians have more active methods of protection. Some snakes have a venomous bite. The poison dart frog's colorful skin warns other animals that it is dangerous. If another animal touches the frog, toxins given off from glands in the frog's skin will poison it!

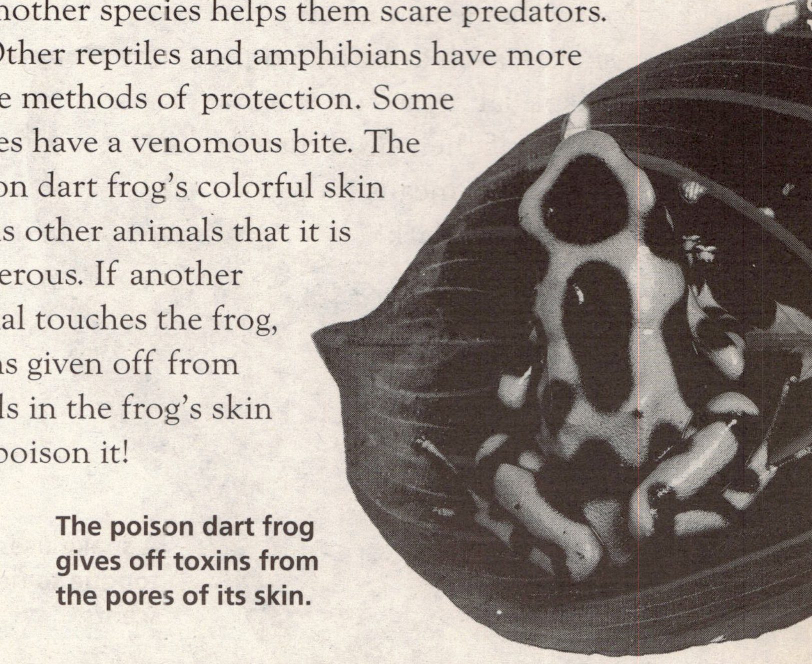

The poison dart frog gives off toxins from the pores of its skin.

Self-Defense

Amphibians and reptiles have different ways to protect themselves. Hiding is the most common form of defense. Snakes and lizards often hide in bushes, while crocodiles, turtles, and frogs may go underwater.

Some reptiles and amphibians have more advanced ways of hiding. Many lizards, such as skinks and chameleons, use camouflage to blend in with their surroundings. Camouflage can be anything that makes it difficult for other animals to find them. Chameleons even have the ability to change the color of their skin so that they can hide in many different places.

Mimicry is when an animal's body resembles something else in nature so that the animal is better able to survive. A leaf-tailed gecko's brown body looks very similar to the leaves in which it hides.

Can you find the hidden tree skink?

The mangrove snake spends most of its time looking for prey in the trees of Malaysia and other parts of Asia.

Unlike many amphibians, not all reptiles need to be close to water. Some reptiles, such as lizards, live in the desert.

Snakes live in many habitats around the world, both where water is plentiful and where it is hard to find. A few species of snakes are found on islands or in places that have cold winters.

Alligators and crocodiles live in large bodies of water where they swim and hunt for food. Crocodiles can also be found on land.

This alligator is crawling into the water, where it will wait for unsuspecting prey.

Legs and Feet

The legs and feet of reptiles differ from species to species. The basilisk is a lizard with long, thin toes on each foot. When frightened, it rears up on its hind legs and runs quickly across both land and water.

Sea turtles are strong swimmers. Their front limbs are shaped like paddles. These paddles help them move successfully in water, but they make walking on land difficult and awkward.

Small lizards called climbing geckos are equipped with pads on each of their toes. These pads are covered with thousands of thin, hairlike projections called setae (SEE-tee). The setae cling to any surface they touch, enabling the geckos to stick to the surface as well.

The huge front legs of this sea turtle act like paddles.

Tokay geckos have sticky feet.

The structure of amphibians' limbs also varies from species to species. When toads and frogs hatch, they do not have legs. As they change and develop, they grow legs that help them live on land.

Frogs and toads are able to hop due to their long and powerful hind legs. When they jump, they first push off the ground with their front legs and arch their back so they are facing upwards. Then they push with their hind legs, sending them flying into the air!

Like climbing geckos, tree frogs have pads on their toes. These pads allow the frogs to climb on different surfaces, including trees.

Most salamanders are hatched with legs, but their legs never develop to be very strong. They walk slowly in a diagonal path. Some salamanders, called sirens, live mostly in the water. These salamanders have no hind legs and very small front legs. They move by waving their tail back and forth like an eel.

A duck-billed tree frog grasps a tree with its strong legs.

Science

Science

Genre	Comprehension Skill	Text Features	Science Content
Nonfiction	Draw Conclusions	• Captions • Labels • Diagrams • Glossary	Plants

Scott Foresman Science 4.2

scottforesman.com

ISBN 0-328-13864-9

Life Science

Weird PLANTS

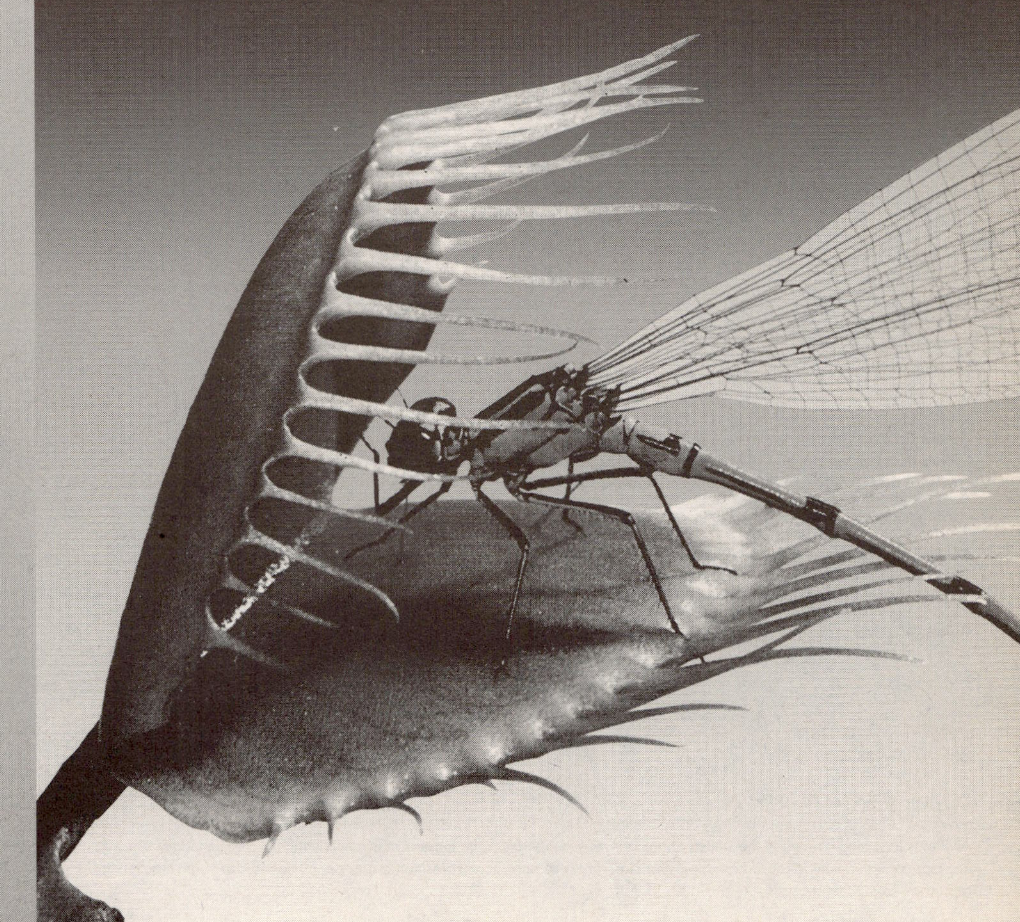

by Laura Johnson

Vocabulary	Extended Vocabulary
chlorophyll	cilia
dormant	debris
fertilization	epiphytes
ovary	nutrients
photosynthesis	pores
pistil	succulents
sepal	tentacles
stamen	

Picture Credits
Every effort has been made to secure permission and provide appropriate credit for photographic material. The publisher deeply regrets any omission and pledges to correct errors called to its attention in subsequent editions.

Photo locators denoted as follows: Top (T), Center (C), Bottom (B), Left (L), Right (R), Background (Bkgd).

4 (CR) Neil Lucas/Nature Picture Library; 9 (T) Hal Horwitz/Corbis; 13 (TR) Gary Meszaros/Visuals Unlimited; 14 Frans Lanting/Minden Pictures; 17 (TR) Artur Tabor/Nature Picture Library; 20 Joel Creed; Ecoscene/Corbis; 21 (T) Tim Fitzharris/Minden Pictures, (CR) Kathie Atkinson/Photolibrary.

ISBN: 0-328-13864-9

2 3 4 5 6 7 8 9 10 V004 13 12 11 10 09 08 07 06 05

What did you learn?

1. How do bromeliads get water?

2. Describe the relationship between ant house plants and ants.

3. How is the agave plant able to bloom in the dry desert?

4. **Writing** in Science Strangler figs begin life as parasitic plants before becoming independent. Describe how they are able to do this. Use details from the book to support your answer.

5. **Draw Conclusions** Think about the kinds of environments where the plants in this book live. Look at the pictures for clues. What kind of conclusion can you draw about where weird plants live?

Glossary

cilia	hairs along the edge of a leaf or other structure
debris	scattered pieces or bits
epiphytes	plants that grow on other plants
nutrients	substances that are required by living things for energy, growth, and repair of tissues
pores	very small openings
succulents	plants having thick, fleshy, water-storing leaves or stems
tentacles	long, slender, flexible growths on an organism used to touch, hold, or move something

Weird PLANTS

by Laura Johnson

PEARSON Scott Foresman DK

What You Already Know

No matter how big or small plants are, they are all made up of tiny cells. Inside some of these cells are structures called chloroplasts. They make sugar, the plant's food, through a process called photosynthesis. A chemical called chlorophyll gathers sunlight that provides the energy for photosynthesis.

Plants have many different kinds of cells. The cells form tissues, which work together. These tissues form organs. Flowers are plant organs that make seeds, which grow into new plants. Most flowers have four parts. Petals attract animals to the flower. Sepals are leaves that protect the flower while it grows inside its bud. In the center of the flower are the pistil, which holds the eggs, and the stamen, which holds the pollen.

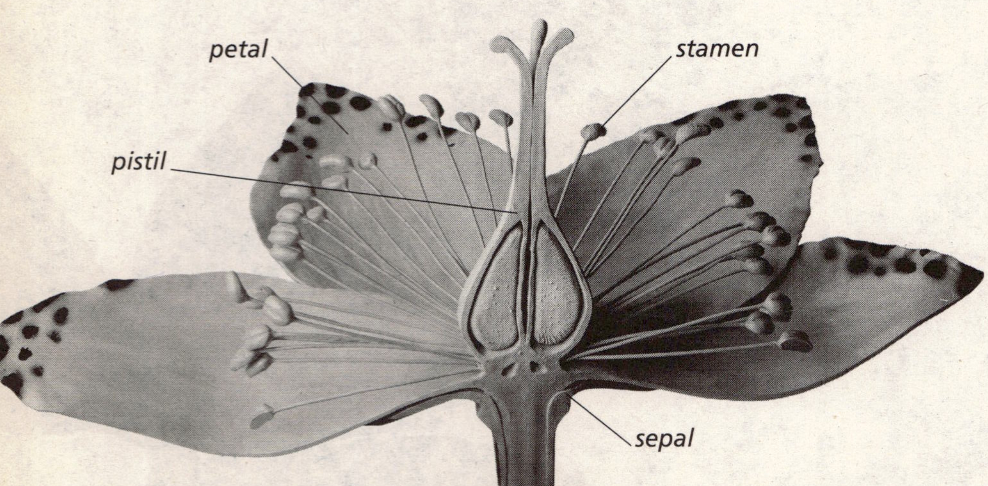

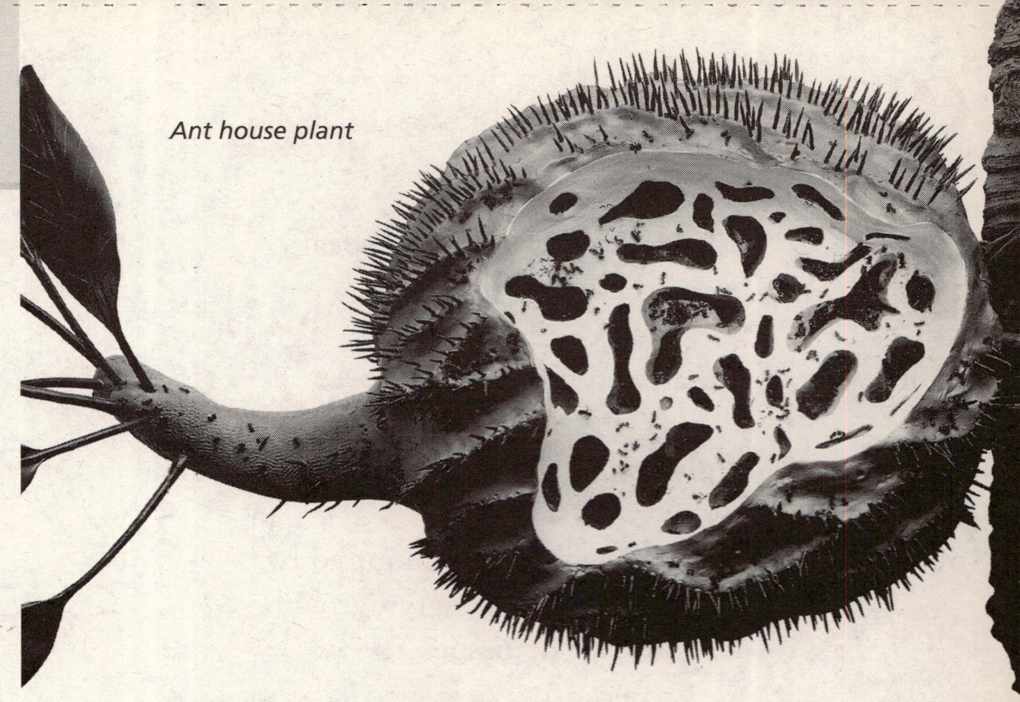
Ant house plant

The stings inject a chemical into the animal's skin that causes a painful reaction. Chemicals in some other plants give them a terrible taste and smell that animals avoid.

Still other plants form partnerships with animals. For example, ant house plants have hollow tunnels that ants can use as homes. In return, ants protect the plants and give them important minerals.

So plants can steal and share. They can attack and defend. They can survive with too little water or too much water. If you can't decide which plant is the weirdest, you might just settle for thinking that they are all quite amazing!

Plant Defenses

Plants can't run away from their enemies, so they have developed methods of self-defense. Some plants, such as cacti, have weapons such as razor-sharp spines and thorns. These not only keep animals from chewing on them, but they usually discourage the animals from even getting close.

Other plants use chemicals to defend themselves. For example, when an animal brushes past a stinging nettle plant, it is pierced with sharp thorns, called stings. But that's not the end!

Nettle stings are filled with chemicals.

The leaves of the nettle are covered with stings.

Stinging nettle plant

The pollen moves to the pistil in a process called pollination. Then the pollen moves toward the flower's ovary and combines with an egg. This is called fertilization. After fertilization, a seed forms and the plant's ovary grows into fruit. When the fruit is ripe, the seed is ready to become a new plant. It might be carried away by the wind or water. Or an animal might eat the fruit or get the seed stuck in its fur. The seed eventually lands on the ground, where it may lie dormant until conditions are right for it to start growing. Not all plants grow from seeds. Some grow from spores, which are like seeds, but made up of only one cell. Others can grow from a broken-off stem or a bulb. Strawberries send out special roots, called runners, that turn into new plants.

Venus's flytrap

Most plants have the same parts. But in some plants, these parts have developed into very strange shapes. Some even appear to have mouths and teeth! Read on to learn more about these weird plants.

Introduction

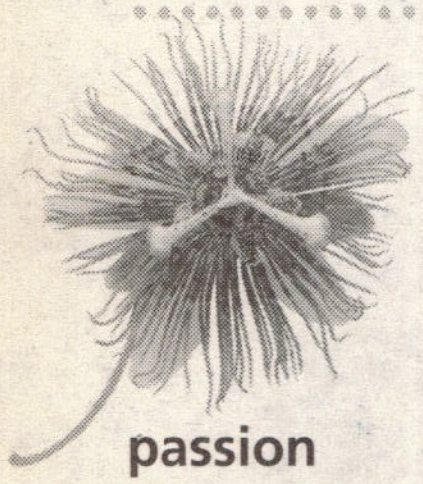

passion flower

You may have already heard about plants that trap creatures in their leaves and eat them. If so, you might think that these meat-eating plants are the weirdest plants of all. Well, have you ever heard of plants that actually steal from other plants? How about plants that strangle other plants so they can be closer to the sunlight? How about plants that snorkel for air? What about plants with really strange shapes? You are going to find out more about all of these kinds of plants. Then you can decide for yourself which one is the weirdest.

The bird of paradise looks like a bird that has landed on a leaf.

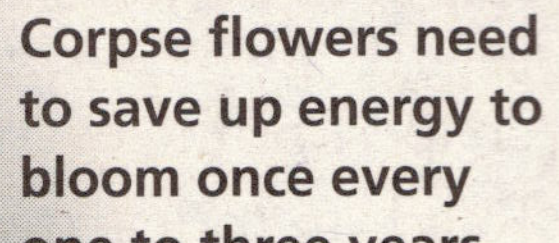

Corpse flowers need to save up energy to bloom once every one to three years.

Swamp cypresses

Swamp cypresses get oxygen to their roots in a similar way. They have large bumpy bases, called knees. These knees rise a few feet above the average water level of the swamp. Like the breathing roots of a mangrove, the knees take in oxygen and carry it to the plant's underwater roots.

Mangrove tree

Too Much Water

Too much water can be just as big a problem for plants as too little water. It's difficult for roots to breathe underwater and in mud. To handle this problem, some plants have developed special root systems. Some mangrove trees, for example, have breathing roots that stick up out of the water like snorkel tubes. These roots are covered with a water-resistant bark. Spongy cells inside these tubes take in oxygen and send it to the plant. Mangroves have many shallow roots that help them to stand in the soft mud. They weave together to form a surface that floats like a raft. They also have some longer roots that anchor them to the bottom of the swamp.

Thick, air-filled ribs on the undersides of Amazonian water lilies help them float.

Close your eyes and picture the strangest flower you can. Did you picture one that looks like a bird with blue and orange feathers? That's what the bird of paradise flower looks like. Its appearance tricks animals into thinking that it's another animal, not a plant. Did you picture a flower that's taller than a person? Corpse flowers, which give off an incredibly nasty odor, can grow almost nine feet tall!

You might have pictured a flower similar to the passion flower. It has colorful petals and green sepals. What you can't see is how parts of some species of the flower rearrange themselves to dust pollen on visiting insects and then collect pollen from other insects.

The passion flower is always busy spreading and collecting pollen.

Meat-Eating Plants

All carnivorous, or meat-eating, plants grow in places where the soil lacks some nutrients they need to grow. To get these nutrients, they feed on the flesh of insects and other small animals.

The Venus's flytrap is called an active meat-eating plant because its leaves actually move to trap flies. Flies are attracted to the plant by its red and green leaves and its sweet smell. In the center of the leaves are three or four sensitive hairs called trigger hairs. If a fly touches two of these, the plant's spiny leaves snap shut in a tenth of a second. It then takes about ten days for digestive juices to dissolve the fly into liquid that the plant can use as food. What if a non-food item, such as a pebble, lands on these trigger hairs? The plant can tell the difference and drops it out after twenty-four hours.

The leaves of the Venus's flytrap are bordered by 18 stiff spikes called cilia.

The flowering agave plant grows in the desert. It is also called the "century plant" because it flowers only once after many years. It usually takes eight to twenty years, not one hundred. In the years before it blooms, its fleshy leaves store food and water. When the leaves have gathered enough water and nutrients to produce flowers, it blooms. Once it does, the leaves and stem die and the roots produce a new plant.

In one season the agave plant can grow to its full height of 20 to 30 feet.

Too Little Water

No plants can live without any water at all. However, some kinds of plants, called succulents, can survive years between rainstorms. They have adapted ways of collecting and storing water. Succulents have very long roots that grow close to the surface of the ground. When it rains, these "rain roots" collect water from a very wide area. Some succulents store water in their thick leaves. Others store water in thick roots. Cacti are succulents that store water in stems covered with a waxy surface that seals in moisture. The pores, or tiny holes, in this waxy covering need to open to take in carbon dioxide. This happens only at night, when it's cooler and less water can evaporate.

Most of the inside of a cactus stem is water storage.

These succulents store water in thick leaves.

The most common pitcher plants have red, green, or purple vases.

The pitcher plant is called an inactive meat-eating plant because it has no moving parts. Its leaves form a pitcher, or jug, that holds rainwater. A sweet juice around the rim of the pitcher attracts small animals, such as insects and spiders. As they greedily try to reach into the pitcher for more juice, they slide down the slippery surface. When they land in the water at the bottom, thick hairs inside the pitcher keep them from escaping. Digestive juices then dissolve the animal into food that the plant can use.

The sundew plant is another example of an active, moving trap. Tiny red hairs, called tentacles, cover the sundew's leaves. Each tentacle is tipped with a sweet, sticky juice. Flying and crawling insects are attracted to the leaves by the sweet smell. When they land on the tentacles, their feet become stuck to the juice. The more the creature struggles to escape, the more juice the sundew produces. The tentacles near the creature begin to bend toward it. Then the whole leaf begins to curl around it. Finally, the creature is surrounded by sticky tentacles and the leaf sends out digestive juices. Animals are dissolved by the sundew leaf in just a few days.

Sundew plant

Sticky tentacles trap a fly.

The whole leaf begins to bend around the fly.

Roots grow stronger and spread around the host tree.

The host tree dies, and the strangler fig lives.

Mistletoe is growing in this white poplar tree.

Mistletoe is unusual because it is usually a parasitic plant, but it can also live on its own. When birds drop its very sticky seeds in trees, the seeds usually attach to a branch. Seedlings send their roots into the host tree's bark and take food from the tree. What about any seeds that do fall to the ground? It's not a problem. Mistletoe can also produce its own food through photosynthesis.

24

A strangler fig attaches itself to a host tree.

Its thin roots reach down to the ground.

As you have learned, the forest floor is a difficult place for a small seedling to grow. Strangler figs have developed a clever way to solve this problem. They begin life as epiphytes and then grow into independent plants. This is called being hemiepiphytic, or half-epiphytic. As animals eat the fruit of the fig tree, they drop seeds on tree branches. Strangler fig seedlings grow slowly, getting water and nutrients that collect on the host tree. The young plant sends many thin roots down the host's trunk. When they reach the ground, they begin to take nutrients from the soil. As the hanging roots become stronger and thicker, they squeeze the host's trunk. In time, they squeeze so hard that they cut off the flow of nutrients. Eventually, the host tree dies and the tall strangler fig stands on its own.

Pitcher plants grow in the southeastern United States.

Then the leaf uncurls and waits for more food to arrive. Individual leaves will live long enough to catch and digest about three creatures.

Like the Venus's flytrap, the sundew senses the difference between food and non-food. Not wanting to waste energy, only a few tentacles close around non-food items. This allows the items to fall out of the plant.

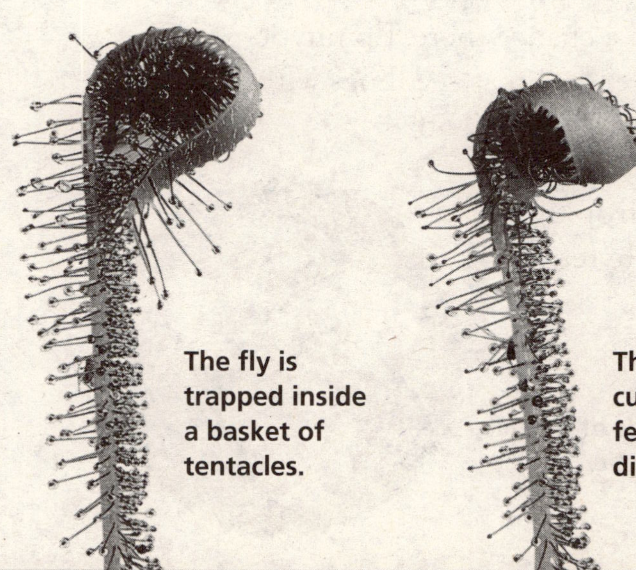

The fly is trapped inside a basket of tentacles.

The plant stays curled up for a few days as it digests the fly.

Epiphytes

Epiphytes are plants that grow on larger plants. They are like passengers going along for a ride! Epiphytes produce their own food through photosynthesis. They collect their own water and nutrients and rarely harm the larger plants they live on. So what's the advantage of being an epiphyte? Position! Most plants begin life as seedlings with their roots in the ground. In woodland forests and rain forests, tall trees block sunlight and absorb most of the water from the ground. Small plants don't have much of a chance there. Epiphytic plants, however, begin as seedlings with their roots on tall plants, off the ground.

Animals drop the seeds of epiphytes in places like tree branches.

Some kinds of orchids are epiphytic.

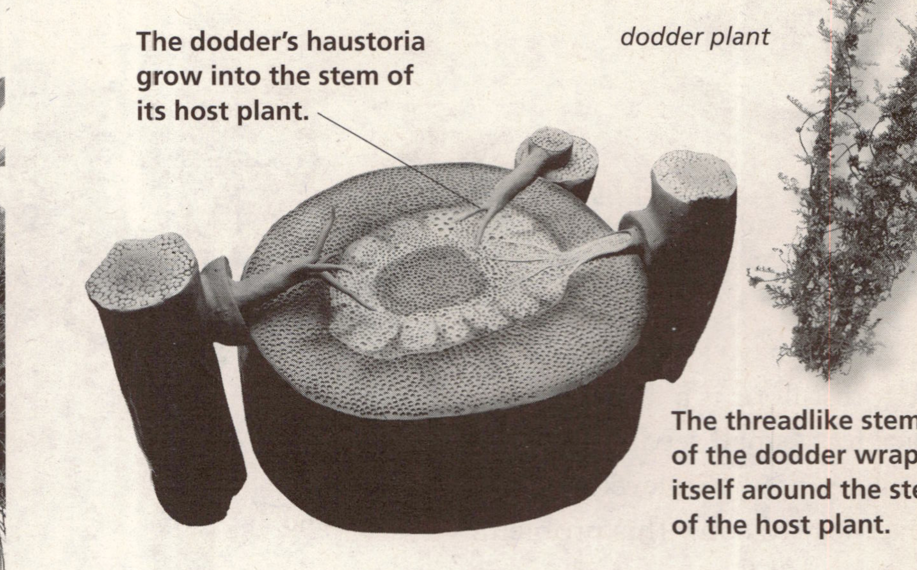

The dodder's haustoria grow into the stem of its host plant.

dodder plant

The threadlike stem of the dodder wraps itself around the stem of the host plant.

However, one of the largest flowers in the world is a parasitic plant. The rafflesia flower lives on the roots of vines that grow in jungles. When the giant sepals of the flower unfold, the flower gives off a terrible odor that smells like rotting meat. The smell attracts flies, which pollinate the flower.

The dodder is another kind of parasitic plant. When a dodder begins to sprout, the young seedling grows roots and immediately sends out stems that search for host plants. When it finds one, it quickly wraps itself around that plant's stem, like tangled string. Then its haustoria grow into the host plant to suck out nutrients. Once this happens, the dodder's own roots die because they are no longer needed.

Parasitic Plants

Parasitic plants are thieves! Instead of making their own food through photosynthesis, they steal their food from other plants. The plants they live on are called host plants. Parasitic plants use suckers to attach themselves to the stems or roots of host plants. The suckers, called haustoria, grow into the host plant and absorb nutrients that the parasitic plant needs. Because parasitic plants do not need sunlight, many of them are hidden and difficult to spot.

Rafflesia flowers weigh about 15 pounds and are about 3 feet in diameter.

Several kinds of epiphytes can live on a single tree branch.

These seeds grow roots in the dirt and debris that collect in the tree bark. The plants get moisture from trapped rainwater and from the air. Since epiphytic plants begin their lives in high places, they don't need to grow long stems to reach the sunlight. They're already there!

Bromeliads

Have you ever seen a pineapple? If so, you've seen a bromeliad. Bromeliad is the name for a very large family of tropical plants.

Many bromeliads are epiphytes. They live on larger plants and collect rainwater that runs off their leaves and bark. This way, they don't have to compete with other plants for the water in the soil.

Bromeliads are often called "air plants" because they can take nutrition and moisture from the air. Bromeliads can also store water better than most plants. Their thick, waxy leaves overlap tightly at the base of the plant. They form a bowl that catches and stores water. Tiny scales on the leaves help the plant absorb water.

The largest kinds of bromeliads can hold several gallons of water. Because of this, they often become miniature ecosystems that provide water and shelter for small animals.

Tree frogs, salamanders, snails, beetles, worms, and crabs often live in these plants. Larger animals know that bromeliads are good places to hunt for food.

An opossum searches for smaller animals that are attracted to the bromeliad.

poison-arrow frog

flatworm

crab

Many bromeliads bury their roots in the plant they live on rather than in soil on the ground. They also provide homes for small water animals.

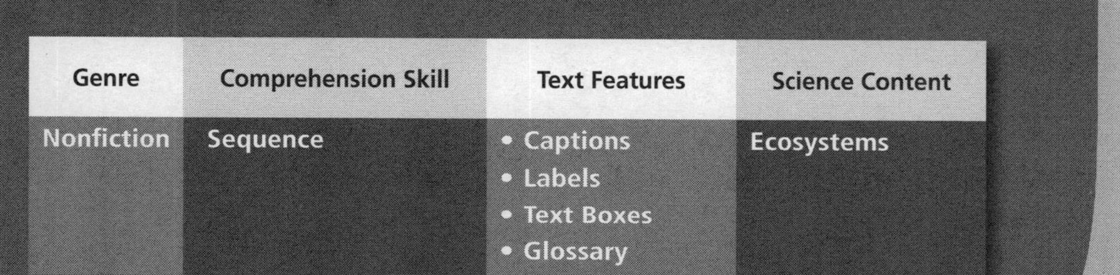

Genre	Comprehension Skill	Text Features	Science Content
Nonfiction	Sequence	• Captions • Labels • Text Boxes • Glossary	Ecosystems

Scott Foresman Science 4.3

PEARSON
Scott Foresman
scottforesman.com

ISBN 0-328-13867-3
9 780328 138678 90000

Science

Life Science

Pond Life

by Barbara Fierman

What did you learn?

1. What happens if one part of a food web disappears?

2. How has the whirligig beetle adapted to pond life?

3. How are newt tadpoles different from frog and toad tadpoles?

4. **Writing** in Science Decomposers are important to a pond ecosystem. Explain what role decomposers play, and why that role is important. Include details from the book to support your answer.

5. **Sequence** Describe how energy can pass from a plant to a newt.

Vocabulary	Extended Vocabulary
carnivores	absorb
community	consumer
decomposers	emerges
ecosystem	enable
herbivores	hibernate
niche	nymph
omnivores	producer
population	school

Picture Credits
Every effort has been made to secure permission and provide appropriate credit for photographic material. The publisher deeply regrets any omission and pledges to correct errors called to its attention in subsequent editions.

Photo locators denoted as follows: Top (T), Center (C), Bottom (B), Left (L), Right (R), Background (Bkgd).

3 Fotosearch; 7 (CL) David Hamman/Animals Animals/Earth Scenes; 9 (TL) David Boag/Alamy Images; 13 Milkins Colin/Oxford Scientific Films; 15 (B) Michael Gadomski/Animals Animals/Earth Scenes; 19 (CL) John A.L Cooke/Animals Animals/Earth Scenes; 20 David Hamman/Animals Animals/Earth Scenes; 21 Derek Middleton/FLPA-Images of Nature; 23 Photolibrary/Oxford Scientific Films.

ISBN: 0-328-13867-3

2 3 4 5 6 7 8 9 10 V004 13 12 11 10 09 08 07 06 05

Glossary

absorb to soak up

consumer an organism that takes in other organisms for food

emerges comes into view; comes out

enable to make someone or something able to do something

hibernate to spend all winter sleeping or resting

nymph the form of certain young insects

producer an organism that makes food for other organisms in an ecosystem

school a group of fish that travels together

Pond Life

by Barbara Fierman

What You Already Know

An ecosystem is all the living and nonliving things in an environment and the ways in which they interact. Tropical rain forests and deserts are examples of ecosystems. Both have many different populations of organisms. The populations of an ecosystem make up a community.

The area in an ecosystem where an organism lives is called a habitat. Everything an organism needs is in its habitat. Each organism has a niche, or role, in its habitat. An organism's niche is what it eats, the ways it gets its food, and the other organisms that use it for food.

A rain forest is a large ecosystem with many plants and animals.

tubifex worms

Many different types of organisms live in ponds all over the world. Some live in a pond community for their whole lives, while others stop by for a visit. You can see how important each pond organism is to the life of every other organism. Pond organisms depend on one another for oxygen, food, and shelter. If one living thing becomes endangered and is removed from the food web, the others organisms are also affected.

Decomposers

When plants and animals die, their remains decay on the pond floor. Decomposers are the pond organisms that eat the remains of dead plants and animals. Bacteria and fungi are tiny, but they are the most important decomposers in the pond ecosystem. They feed on dead matter. Earthworms and tubifex worms break down rotting matter in the soil. As a result, minerals and other nutrients are released into the water. Plants absorb these nutrients through their roots. Then the process of photosynthesis begins again.

earthworms

Energy from the Sun is an important part of an ecosystem. Plants use this energy to make food. This is why we call them producers. Consumers are organisms that don't make their food. They get their food by eating other things. Two types of consumers are herbivores and carnivores. Herbivores consume only plants, while carnivores eat only animals. A third kind of consumer is an omnivore, which eats both plants and animals for energy. But consumers and producers aren't the only members of an ecosystem. Decomposers also have an important niche.

In the following pages you will learn more about pond ecosystems. You will be introduced to some of the producers, consumers, and decomposers that live in them.

Ducks are omnivorous consumers in a pond ecosystem.

Pond Life

Suppose you were walking by a pond on a lazy summer day. Do you notice the bullfrog sunning itself on the leaf of a water lily? Look, a dragonfly swoops through the air to grab a snack. There go the ducklings waddling clumsily as they follow their mother into the water for their first swim. The pond may seem like an animal playground. Actually, a pond is a busy community of plants and animals living and working together.

A pond is a small, fairly shallow body of fresh water. Ponds can be formed when rivers overflow, when rainwater collects, or when beaver dams stop the flow of a river. Other ponds are made by people. Unlike lakes, ponds are still, which means that they are not fed by streams or rivers. As a result, ponds may become very shallow when there is a drought.

Water shrews are actually black and white but appear to be silver when underwater.

Minks are adapted to pond life in several ways. They have webbed feet that help them swim. They will eat just about any pond animal, including larger muskrats.

Water shrews are tiny animals that spend their entire lives in one pond. They hunt for tadpoles, insects, and worms underwater during the day and at night. Beavers make their own ponds. They use branches, sticks, stones, and mud to build a dam. This stops the flow of water from a river or stream.

Life on the Water's Edge

Several different mammals live near the pond and feed on the plants and animals that live there. The muskrat is in many pond communities. Muskrats build lodges on the banks of ponds, using leaves, cattail stems, branches, and mud. A muskrat's lodge is quite complex. It has tunnels, an underwater entrance, and even a different sleeping area for each family member. Muskrats eat mostly plants, such as cattails, but they will also eat small pond animals. The name *muskrat* comes from the musk glands that are located under their tails.

Muskrats are excellent swimmers and can stay underwater for up to fifteen minutes.

In spite of its size, a pond is home to a great variety of plants and animals. The plants range from tiny duckweed in the water to tall reeds and cattails that grow along a pond's edge. The animal community is just as varied, including as many as one thousand different species.

Pond plants provide food, shelter, and oxygen for all of the animals living there.

pond habitat in Florida

Pond Ecosystems

Plants have a very important job in a pond ecosystem. They are the producers. Producers make food for all the creatures living there. Animals are consumers. Examples of consumers that are herbivores and live in pond ecosystems are water fleas and snails. Omnivores, such as turtles, are also consumers that live in ponds. Carnivores make up a third group, including most frogs and some fish. They eat only other animals.

Decomposers are organisms that eat rotting plants or remains of dead animals in the pond. As they do this, important nutrients are released from the dead matter. Plants absorb these nutrients.

Food Web of a Pond Ecosystem

Frogs and toads eat insects.

Small insects eat plants.

Newts eat insects.

mallard duckling

Swallows

The swallow is a small bird with a blue back and a red throat. Its tail resembles streamers in the air. Swallows visit the pond as they migrate south each winter.

Water birds, such as ducks and swans, are suited to life on the water. Their webbed feet and the structure of their legs make them good swimmers. A special type of oil causes water to slide off their wings. Ducklings that hatch along the edge of the pond can swim right into the water. They may stay at the pond all year long. Swans leave the pond in winter and fly to a warmer climate. Canada geese fly south in winter and use the pond as a rest stop on their way. Other bird visitors include kingfishers, hawks, and osprey.

Birds

Many common species of birds are adapted to pond living. In a pond, birds find water to drink, fresh food to eat, and a place to bathe. The grasses and reeds along the edge of the pond provide a perfect spot for birds to make their nests.

Wading birds, such as the heron, will stand in the shallow water for hours at a time, waiting to catch a meal. The heron stands on one foot and then dips its long beak into the water to grab its prey. The heron will eat insects, fish, frogs, turtles, and snakes. While the adult heron doesn't have many enemies, other birds will steal and eat its eggs.

The great blue heron has a wingspan of almost six feet.

Scientists use a diagram called a food web to explain how energy passes from one living thing to another. In a food web, arrows point to the living things that *get* energy. Notice the arrows pointing from plants to small insects and small mammals. When these pond creatures eat plants, they get energy.

You can see that all the living things in the pond depend on each other. When one part of the food web changes, the whole web is affected.

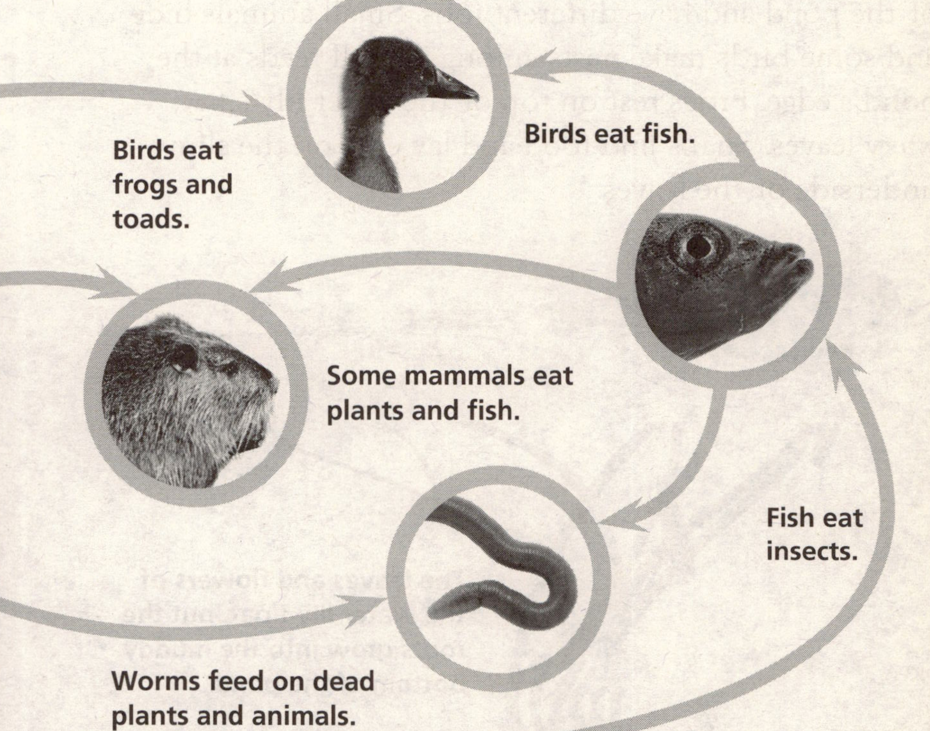

Plant Life

Plants absorb light from the Sun and carbon dioxide from water in a process called photosynthesis. During photosynthesis, plants make food and give off oxygen. Animals breathe oxygen and get energy from the food. Every pond animal gets energy from plants, either by eating them or by eating other animals that eat the plants.

Different kinds of plants grow in different parts of the pond and have different jobs. Small animals hide and some birds make nests among the tall reeds at the pond's edge. Frogs rest on top of the water lily's flat, waxy leaves. Snails find food and lay eggs on the slimy underside of the leaves.

The leaves and flowers of the water lily float, but the roots grow into the muddy bottom of the pond.

Turtles

Turtles are also adapted to pond living. Like that of other reptiles, the body temperature of a turtle is just about the same as the temperature of the air or water where it lives. During the cold winter, turtles burrow deep into the muddy bottom of the pond and hibernate. They can survive underwater for long periods of time. Turtles are omnivores that eat all kinds of plants and animals. They are also scavengers and will eat dead fish and other animals. A snapping turtle like the one in the picture below has a small, fairly soft shell. Since this turtle can't hide in its shell, it uses its sharp beak to protect itself. Even a young turtle will snap at just about anything that moves past it.

Snapping turtle

Newts

Juvenile newt

Like frogs and toads, newts are amphibians. Newts lay their eggs on underwater plant leaves. The eggs hatch into tadpoles. Newt tadpoles differ from frog and toad tadpoles in that they keep their gills even after their legs develop. Newts are carnivores. They will eat shrimp, insects, snails, worms, and tadpoles. Adult newts use their tongues to catch their prey when they are on land. In the water, they use their teeth to grab their victims. Newts are nocturnal animals. They are active at night, but they hide and sleep during the day.

Palmate newt

Algae

Algae are tiny but important organisms. Since all animals eat algae, or eat animals that eat algae, they are considered to be one of the most important producers in the pond.

The Canadian waterweed lives completely underwater, but its leaves can float. The leaves get enough sunlight to produce oxygen for the pond creatures to breathe. Plants such as frogbit and bladderwort just float around the pond. Bladderwort is especially unusual because it is a carnivore. It hangs traps down into the water and catches insects to eat!

Reeds and rushes, such as the branched bur-reed, grow in the shallow water along the edge of the pond.

Insects at Work

Hundreds of different kinds of insects are adapted to life in a pond. Insects lay eggs in the water. Some young insects, such as the mayfly and dragonfly nymphs, stay underwater while they grow. When they are adults, they leave the pond and fly above the water. Other insects, such as the diving beetle, spend their lives in the water. Pond skaters have tiny bunches of hair on the ends of their legs that let them walk on the surface of the water.

The adult dragonfly carries its food as it flies.

Pond skaters glide across the water, hunting for other insects to eat.

Frogs and toads are well adapted to the food in the pond ecosystem. They are not picky eaters. They will eat insects, snails, small animals, and even tadpoles.

Different kinds of frogs and toads may live in a pond. The largest frog found in North America is the bullfrog. It can grow about eight inches long. The American toad is smaller.

American toad

bullfrog

Frogs and Toads

Frogs and toads are amphibians that are well adapted to pond life. Amphibians have features that enable them to live on land and in water. Frogs and toads hatch from eggs into tadpoles. Gradually, the tadpoles develop back legs, lose their tails, and develop front legs. Nostrils and lungs replace gills for breathing. Now they are ready to live on land.

Small tadpoles use their tails to swim.

Adult toads live most of their life on land. They return to the water to lay their eggs. Frogs hibernate in the mud at the bottom of the pond during the winter. During the summer, they rest on the leaves of water lilies, soaking up the sunshine and catching insects.

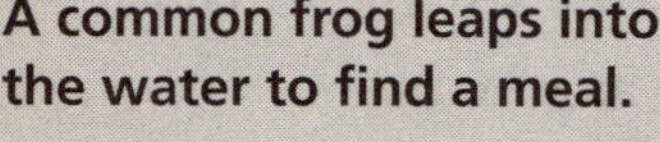

A common frog leaps into the water to find a meal.

The whirligig beetle also lives on the surface of a pond and zooms around in circles. This beetle has special features that have helped it adapt to life on the pond. Its antennae help it find prey. And its eyes are divided into two parts. This enables the beetle to look in different directions at the same time to catch an insect for its meal.

The mayfly nymph eats algae, tiny plants, and animals. The adult mayfly doesn't eat at all. That's not really a problem though, since it lives for less than a day!

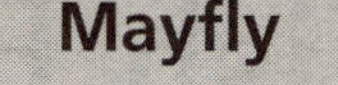

Mayfly

A baby mayfly is called a nymph. The nymph lives and grows underwater for as long as three years. It emerges from the pond as an adult and lives for less than a day.

Unlike the mayfly, the dragonfly will attack and eat other insects and animals. The dragonfly nymph has a pointy tip on its lower lip. It uses this tip to attack its prey. The adult uses its large jaws to grab tadpoles, fish, and other insects. The dragonfly can fly as fast as eighteen miles per hour and grab its prey while it flies!

Fish Friends

Many species of fish are adapted to the freshwater pond habitat. One of the most common is the stickleback. Sticklebacks are an important part of the food web. They will eat baby insects, snails, water fleas, worms, other fish, and fish eggs. They use their jaws to suck in their prey. Then they grab whatever they catch with their sharp teeth. The male stickleback builds a nest where the female fish can lay eggs. The male will guard the eggs until they hatch and then watch over the babies until they are about one week old. Pond creatures such as larger fish, herons, water shrews, and otters make a meal of the stickleback.

The male stickleback can change color. Its throat becomes bright red and its eyes turn bright blue.

Freshwater shrimp

Minnows are tiny fish that travel about in groups called schools. Pike, including pickerel and northern pike, are long, narrow fish with very sharp teeth. They often hide among the stems of underwater plants. They wait for prey, such as fish, frogs, snakes, or ducklings, to swim past, and then they attack. Freshwater shrimp provide food for other pond animals, such as newts.

Science

Genre	Comprehension Skill	Text Features	Science Content
Nonfiction	Cause and Effect	• Labels • Text Boxes • Diagrams • Glossary	Ecosystem Changes

Scott Foresman Science 4.4

scottforesman.com

ISBN 0-328-13870-3
9 780328 138708 90000

Science

Life Science

Parasitic LIFE

by Sam Brelsfoard

What did you learn?

1. How is a parasitic relationship different from a symbiotic relationship?

2. What are some examples of endoparasites?

3. What is a parasitoid?

4. **Writing** in Science Some parasites live outside their hosts. Write to explain how ectoparasites survive outside their host. Include details from the book to support your answer.

5. **Cause and Effect** What effects can parasites have on their hosts?

Vocabulary	**Extended Vocabulary**
competition	ectoparasite
endangered	endoparasite
extinct	flagella
hazardous waste	parasitoid
host	symbiotic
parasite	vector
succession	

Picture Credits
Every effort has been made to secure permission and provide appropriate credit for photographic material. The publisher deeply regrets any omission and pledges to correct errors called to its attention in subsequent editions.

Photo locators denoted as follows: Top (T), Center (C), Bottom (B), Left (L), Right (R), Background (Bkgd).

1 ©The American Museum of Natural History/DK Images; 10 (B) Lester V. Bergman/Corbis; 11 Eye of Science/Photo Researchers, Inc.; 13 (TR, BR) ©The American Museum of Natural History/DK Images; 14 (CR, BR) ©The American Museum of Natural History/DK Images; 15 (TL) ©The American Museum of Natural History/DK Images, (BR) Dr. Dennis Kunkel/Visuals Unlimited; 16 (CR) ©The American Museum of Natural History/DK Images; 17 (BR) Martin Dohrn/Photo Researchers, Inc.; 19 (C, CB, BC) ©The American Museum of Natural History/DK Images; 21 (BC) Alan Barnes/NHPA Limited; 22 (TR) ©The American Museum of Natural History/DK Images.

ISBN: 0-328-13870-3

2 3 4 5 6 7 8 9 10 V004 13 12 11 10 09 08 07 06 05

Glossary

ectoparasite a parasite that lives outside its host

endoparasite a parasite that lives inside its host

flagella long, threadlike structures that help an organism to move

parasitoid an organism that is a parasite for only part of its life

symbiotic a relationship of mutual benefit or dependence

vector an organism, such as a mosquito, that carries disease-causing microorganisms from one host to another

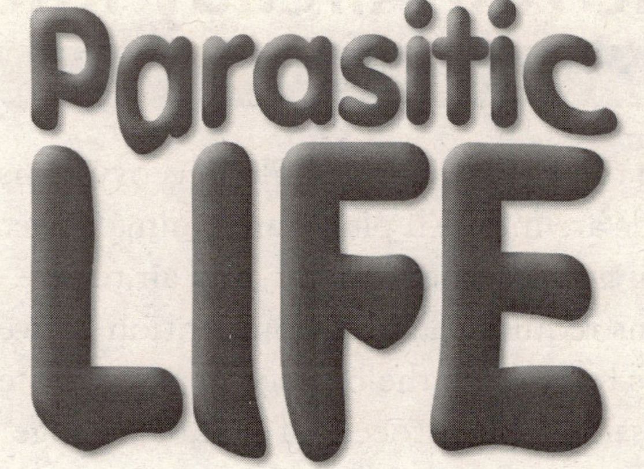

by Sam Brelsfoard

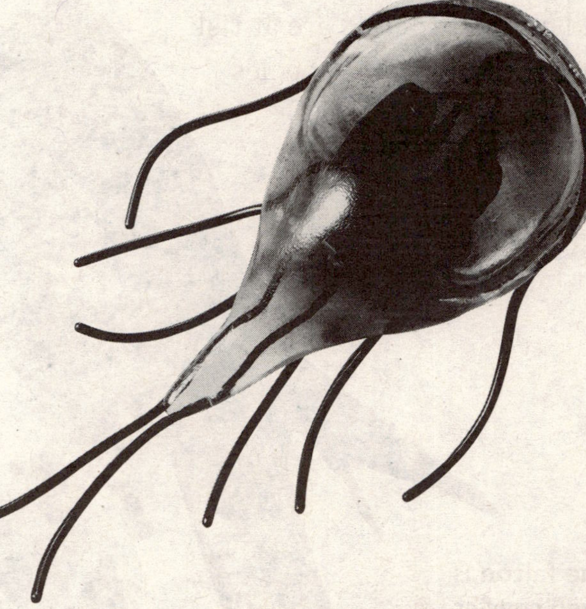

PEARSON Scott Foresman

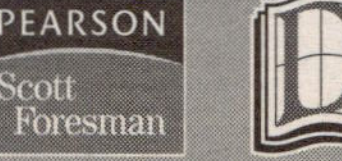

What You Already Know

Living things can survive only in ecosystems where their needs are met. All plants and animals need food, water, living space, shelter, light, and air to live. Healthy ecosystems require balance. Competition between organisms helps keep the balance in an ecosystem.

Succession is the process of gradual change from one community of organisms to another. Many things, including a change in climate, can cause this. Climate changes can also cause a species to become extinct. Endangered species are at risk of becoming extinct. These species must be watched. Fossils give us a great deal of information about extinct animals and how they lived.

The peregrine falcon is an endangered species.

Many Parasites

Parasites exist in all forms of life. Ectoparasites, such as fleas and ticks, live outside of their host, while endoparasites, such as hookworms and flatworms, live inside. Microscopic parasites are the main causes of diseases such as malaria and sleeping sickness. Microscopic parasites can be found in contaminated food or water. Some parasites use vectors to find their hosts. Mosquitoes can be vectors for malaria parasites. A jewel wasp is an example of a parasitoid, an organism that lives only part of its life as a parasite. Brood parasites, such as the cuckoo, use other animals to feed and raise their young for them.

Parasites play a vital role in ecosystems. Even though they can harm their hosts, parasites benefit ecosystems. They help to keep certain populations under control. Without parasites many ecosystems would not have the balance they need to remain healthy.

horse leech

Parasitic Plants And Fungi

Plants and fungi can be parasites too. Mistletoe, ivy, dodder, birch tree fungus, and strangler fig are all parasitic.

Some kinds of fungi cause growths on birch trees. This type of birch tree fungus has been found on Earth since the time of cavemen! Some of these fungal growths can cause the tree to die.

Birch tree fungus

Dodder attaches itself to other plants and penetrates the host's tissue in order to absorb its nutrients.

Threads grow out of dodder and push their way through the host plant's cells.

Dodder is a parasite in the morning-glory family of plants.

Sometimes environmental changes happen very fast because of natural events, such as floods and fires. People can also harm the environment. Dumping hazardous waste into an ecosystem can harm plant and animal life. People should be careful of how they treat Earth.

Some of the organisms in ecosystems are parasites and hosts. The relationship between parasite and host can have important effects on environments. Parasites are important to some ecosystems because they help balance the population of plants and animals.

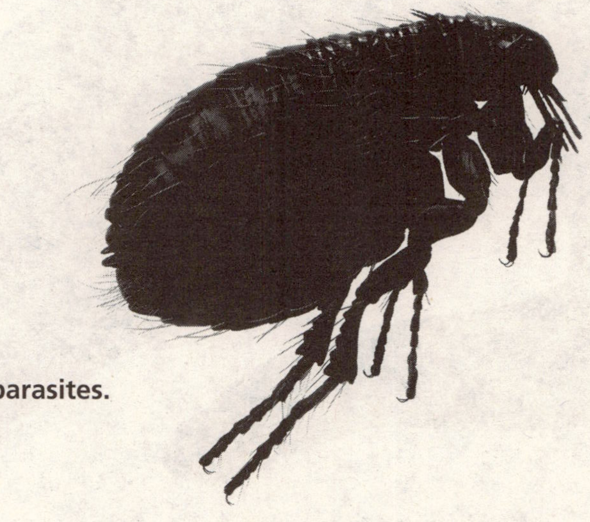

Fleas are parasites.

Introduction

A parasite is an organism that lives in or on a host organism. It often harms the host. A parasite's goals are to survive and to reproduce. Parasites can be found almost everywhere.

There are many different kinds of parasites. They can live on the inside or outside of the host. Most parasites are harmful. But in some cases, such as leeches, parasites have been found to have helpful medical uses.

Leech

Ichneumon (ik-NOO-muhn) wasps are parasites that use different hosts at different stages in their lives. As larvae, the insects feed on the larvae and pupae of butterflies and moths. When mature, the wasps feed on the body fluids of larger hosts.

An ichneumon wasp laying eggs in a sawfly grub.

Cuckoos exhibit similar behavior to parasitoids. Cuckoos are brood parasites. They leave their eggs in other birds' nests to be raised by the other birds. Cowbirds are also brood parasites.

A cuckoo lays its eggs in another bird's nest.

cuckoo egg

Parasitoids

Parasitoids (PAH-ruh-si-toids) are organisms that are parasitic for only one part of their life cycle. Often, parasitoids begin their lives as larvae on or in a host, living on the nutrients from the host. When the parasitoids mature, they leave their host and lead a nonparasitic life.

The jewel wasp is a parasitoid that is a parasite in the larval stage. Before an adult jewel wasp lays her egg, she attacks and paralyzes a cockroach. She then lays her egg on the cockroach and buries both in a hole. When the larva hatches, it feeds on the cockroach. The shell of the cockroach protects it until it develops into a fully formed wasp.

A jewel wasp attacks a cockroach.

Parasitic relationships are different from symbiotic relationships in an important way. In a symbiotic relationship, both organisms benefit. In a parasitic relationship, only the parasite benefits.

Parasites?

The oxpecker and the buffalo have a symbiotic relationship. The oxpecker eats ticks, fleas, and insects that are on the buffalo. This, in turn, keeps the buffalo clean.

Oxpecker and buffalo

Vampire bats have parasitic relationships with other creatures. They drink the blood of other animals. These bats often drink blood without disturbing the other creatures.

Vampire bat

Ectoparasites

An ectoparasite is a parasite that lives on the outside of a host. Ticks, fleas, lice, and mites are ectoparasites. These kinds of parasites typically feed on the blood or skin of their host. Most ectoparasites have adapted to life outside their host in a variety of ways. Usually their legs are extremely strong. Their short bodies lie flat and tightly grip the skin of their host so they do not fall off.

An ectoparasite such as a flea spends nearly its entire life on its host. It feeds on its host, and then it lays its eggs. The eggs hatch and mature, and the cycle starts again.

A flea is an ectoparasite.

Sometimes symptoms of malaria can occur within ten days of being bitten. Other times, people do not realize they are sick for as long as four weeks after they were bitten. Symptoms of malaria include headache, muscle aches, tiredness, fever, and chills. If an infected person does not get treated right away, malaria can lead to kidney failure, seizures, mental confusion, and coma. Sometimes malaria is fatal. Mosquitoes that carry malaria tend to live in Africa, Asia, and Central and South America.

The Malaria Parasite

The malaria parasite attacks the red blood cells of its host. The parasites mature within the blood cells. Once mature, they burst out and attack other red blood cells, making their host sick in the process.

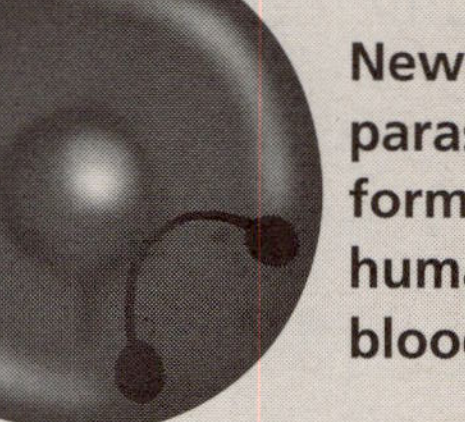

50

Mosquitoes And Malaria

mosquitoes

Mosquitoes are also vectors for parasites. A mosquito draws blood from a host by injecting its saliva. The saliva prevents the blood from clotting. The mosquito can also inject microscopic parasites, or sporozoites (spor-uh-ZOH-eyets), into the host. The parasites can penetrate the cells of the liver, where they multiply before returning to the bloodstream to infect blood cells. The toxins from the parasite make the host ill. The malaria parasite is one of the parasites that mosquitoes can carry.

capillary

Mouthparts stab skin and suck blood.

When a mosquito sucks blood from a host, it can inject parasites.

One ectoparasite sucks the sap of hemlock trees. This parasite is called the hemlock woolly adelgid. The adelgid drinking the sap of a tree is similar to a flea drinking the blood of an animal.

The Life Cycle of a Flea

The first stage of a flea's life cycle often begins on a host.

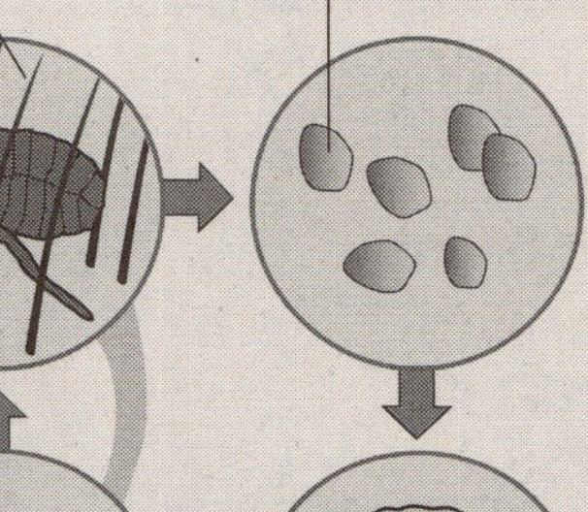

The itch mite is an ectoparasite that lives in the skin of its host. It can cause a disease called scabies. Itch mites are different from most ectoparasites. They lay their eggs inside the host. They do this by first burrowing under the skin, then laying their eggs.

Spider mites are also ectoparasites. They spin webs on the underside of the leaves of plants and trees. These mites live on the plants' nutrient-rich juices. The mites will reproduce and live on a plant until the plant has no nutrients left.

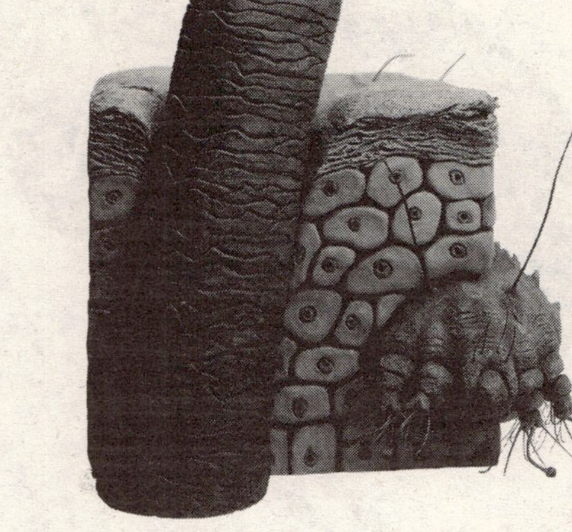
Itch mites burrow under skin.

skin

hair

itch mites

trypanosoma parasites

Assassin bugs, also known as kissing bugs, feed only on the blood of mammals. Assassin bugs come out at night and pierce their hosts' eyelids, ears, or lips in order to feed. These bugs sometimes carry the trypanosoma (tri-pan-uh-SOH-muh) parasite, which causes Chagas' disease. Chagas' disease is an illness that causes a mild fever. Sometimes Chagas' disease develops into far more serious problems.

The assassin bug's bite can transmit the parasite that causes Chagas' disease.

Parasite Carriers

Some parasites find their hosts with the help of insects and other creatures. The parasites travel inside insects, letting the insects take them to their hosts. When insects are used this way, they are called vectors.

Tsetse (TSEE-tsee) are flies that can be vectors of a parasite that causes sleeping sickness. Tsetse are found only in certain parts of Africa, and they usually feed on humans only by accident. Still, they are a way for parasites to find their hosts.

This tsetse is swollen with blood from feeding.

Ticks are another example of ectoparasites. They feed on the blood of birds, reptiles, and mammals. A tick has mouth parts that are like beaks. These parts help it feed. A tick will wait on a blade of grass. When a potential host approaches, the tick grabs on and attaches itself to any part of the skin it can.

Leeches, even though they are parasites, have been found to be useful tools in medicine. A leech's saliva contains a chemical that stops blood from clotting. A leech can help in surgery by removing pooling blood and helping to prevent a wound from clotting too quickly.

Many parasites are known to be harmful to their host's health, though. Itch mites, spider mites, and ticks are examples of harmful parasites. A colony of spider mites can turn a perfectly healthy plant into nothing more than a twig.

After burrowing, itch mites lay their eggs under the surface of their host's skin.

Endoparasites

An endoparasite is a parasite that lives inside the body of its host. Flatworms, such as flukes and tapeworms, are common endoparasites. Roundworms, such as pinworms and hookworms, are also endoparasites. Many endoparasites spend their entire lives inside their host.

Hookworms are a kind of roundworm. They hatch from eggs laid in the soil. When a barefoot person or an animal walks on the soil, hookworms can break through the skin. After about a week, the hookworms travel to their host's small intestine. Hookworms can cause serious illness in their host.

roundworm

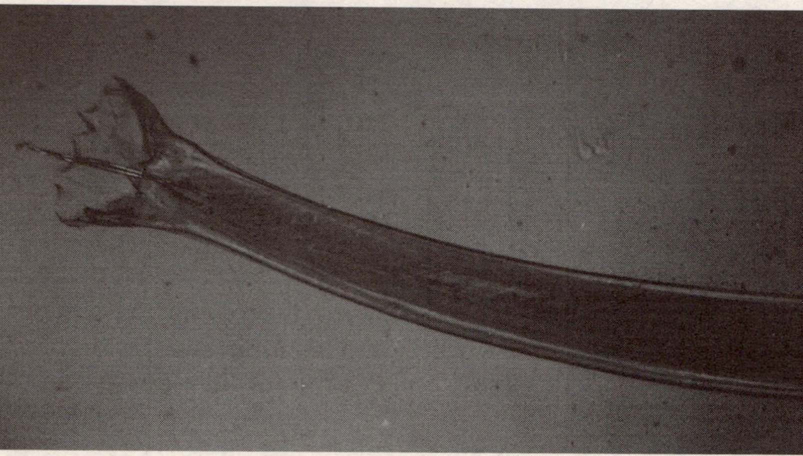

male hookworm

The entamoeba histolytica (en-tuh-MEE-buh his-toh-LI-ti-kuh) protozoa are microscopic parasites similar to the giardia lamblia. These parasites can survive outside their hosts in water and soil. Humans become infected by consuming contaminated food or water. The entamoeba protozoa start in the small intestine. Then they mature and move to the large intestine, where they burrow into the lining. Once they are in the large intestine, they reproduce by division.

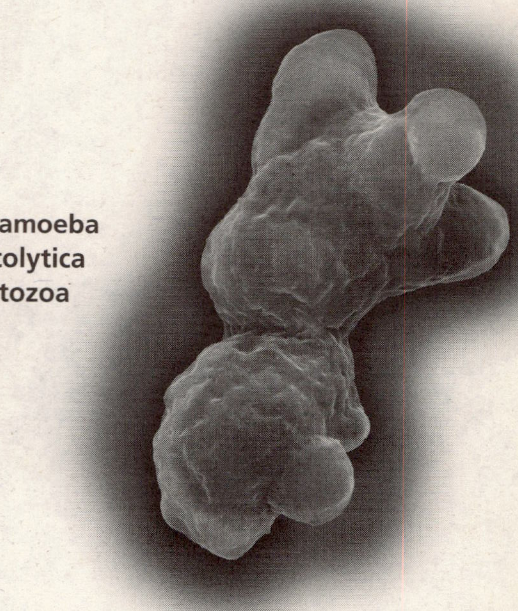

entamoeba histolytica protozoa

Microscopic Parasites

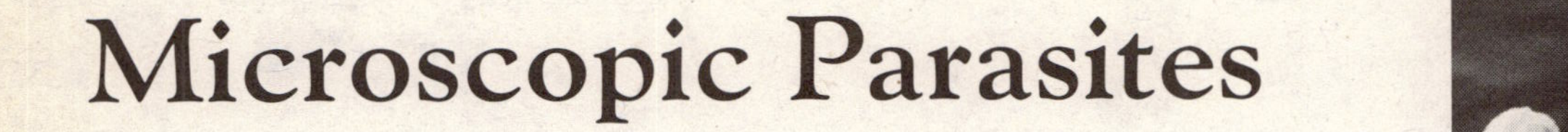

Microscopic parasites are too small to be seen by the naked eye. They are often found in contaminated water and uncooked food. The giardia lamblia protozoa (jee-AR-dee-uh LAM-blee-uh proh-tuh-ZOH-uh), which can cause intestinal disease, are often found in contaminated drinking water. When people and animals drink water that has giardia lamblia in it, the parasites enter their intestines. The parasites have a protective outer shell that allows them to live outside of their hosts for long periods of time. This means they don't have to stay in one host. The giardia lamblia parasites have long, threadlike structures called flagella (fluh-JEL-uh) that help them swim.

flagella

Giardia lamblia is protected by its outer shell. Its flagella help it move with ease.

Trichinella roundworms live in the intestines of some mammals. The host has eaten raw or undercooked meat that contains trichinella larvae.

Tapeworms are parasites that can live in the intestines of animals. Often a host is infected by eating raw or undercooked meat that contains the young form of a tapeworm. A tapeworm attaches itself to the host's intestines by using the curved spines on the top of its head. Once it is attached to the host, it grows a long tail. Some tapeworms are able to reproduce on their own. They have male and female reproductive organs. Tapeworms are usually between one-half inch and one and one-half inches long. However, some can grow longer than fifteen feet.

This body segment contains male and female reproductive organs.

A segmented tapeworm can reproduce on its own.

curved spines

sucker

tapeworm head

The bilharzia (bil-HAHR-zee-uh) fluke is a parasitic flukeworm that causes the disease bilharzia. The worm starts its life as a larva inside snails that live in ponds. People often pick up the parasite while swimming in water that has the infected snails. The mature worms are usually less than half an inch long. They live on the host's red blood cells and dissolved nutrients, such as sugars and amino acids.

bilharzia fluke

Science

Science

Genre	Comprehension Skill	Text Features	Science Content
Nonfiction	Draw Conclusions	• Captions • Text Boxes • Call Outs • Glossary	Body Systems

Scott Foresman Science 4.5

ISBN 0-328-13873-8

scottforesman.com

Life Science

Fighting Infections

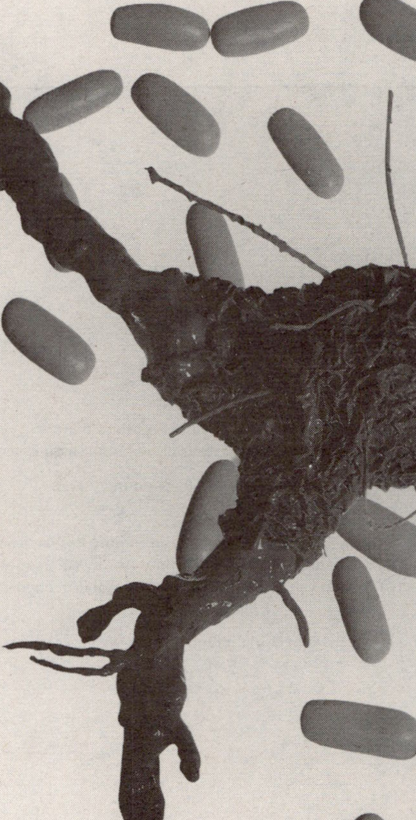

by Steve Miller

What did you learn?

1. What is your body's first defense against pathogens?
2. How do white blood cells fight infections?
3. How do vaccines protect you from infections?
4. **Writing** in Science *E. coli* is one kind of bacteria that causes food poisoning. Describe how *E. coli* attacks the body. Include details from the book to support your answer.
5. **Draw Conclusions** Why do you think vaccines are given to children when they are young?

Vocabulary	Extended Vocabulary
immune system	antibody
infectious disease	antigen
involuntary muscles	lymphocyte
neuron	lysozyme
pathogens	noninfectious disease
vaccine	phagocyte
voluntary muscles	tonsillitis

Picture Credits
Every effort has been made to secure permission and provide appropriate credit for photographic material. The publisher deeply regrets any omission and pledges to correct errors called to its attention in subsequent editions.

Photo locators denoted as follows: Top (T), Center (C), Bottom (B), Left (L), Right (R), Background (Bkgd).

2 (BL) Kent Wood/Photo Researchers, Inc.; 3 Ryabchikova-Voisin/Photo Researchers, Inc.;
7 (TL, B, CR, CL) American Museum of Natural History/DK Images; 11 (CR) NIH/Science Source/Photo Researchers, Inc;
12 (B) American Museum of Natural History/DK Images; 13 (T) American Museum of Natural History/DK Images;
16 (B) American Museum of Natural History/DK Images; 17 (T) American Museum of Natural History/DK Images;
18 American Museum of Natural History/DK Images.

ISBN: 0-328-13873-8

2 3 4 5 6 7 8 9 10 V004 13 12 11 10 09 08 07 06 05

Glossary

antibody a chemical, produced by B cells, that identifies or attacks pathogens

antigen a substance on cells that tells the immune system if the cell comes from inside or outside the body

lymphocyte a white blood cell that fights infection

lysozyme a substance produced by sweat glands, tear ducts, and mucous membranes that destroys the cell walls of harmful bacteria

noninfectious disease a disease that cannot be passed from one person to another

phagocyte a white blood cell that surrounds and digests harmful organisms

tonsillitis an infection of the tonsils that causes a sore throat and a fever

Fighting Infections

by Steve Miller

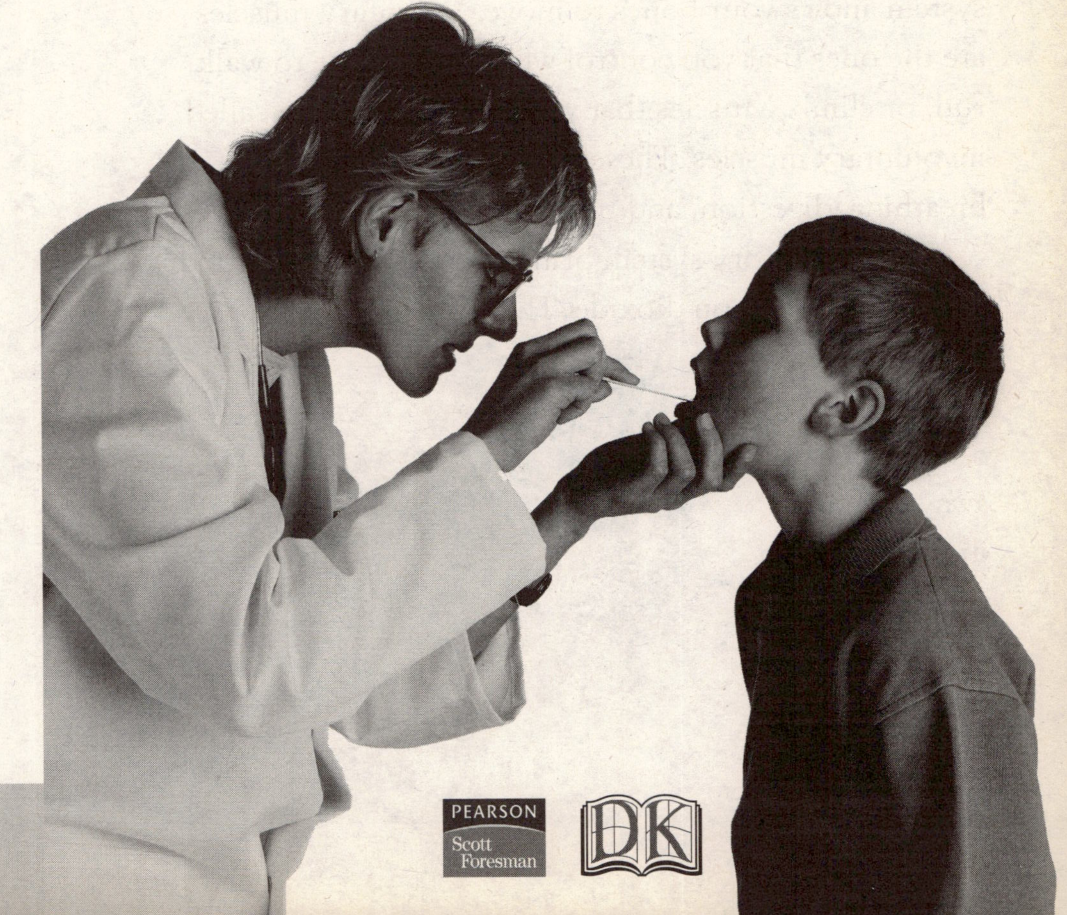

PEARSON Scott Foresman DK

What You Already Know

Your body is made of many kinds of cells that do different jobs. Cells make up tissues. Tissues of different kinds work together as organs. Organs include your heart, your lungs, your bones, and even your skin. A group of organs work together as an organ system.

The shape of your body comes from the skeletal system, which is made of 206 bones. The muscular system allows your bones to move. Voluntary muscles are the ones that you control when you decide to walk, run, or climb. Muscles that you can't control are called involuntary muscles. These are the muscles used for breathing, digestion, and blood flow.

The respiratory system brings oxygen into your body and removes carbon dioxide. The circulatory system brings oxygen and nutrients to your cells and takes away carbon dioxide and other waste.

This is a virus under magnification.

You can also help other people stay healthy if you are careful when you are sick. Always cover your mouth when you cough or sneeze. This helps keep germs from passing to other people.

Some bacteria multiply very quickly, so the immune system might need help fighting them. Your doctor may be able to help you feel better by prescribing medicine. Antibiotics are medicines that kill bacteria in the body. If the doctor prescribes antibiotics, you must take all of the medicine, even if you feel better. Doing your part to stay healthy helps the immune system to do its job.

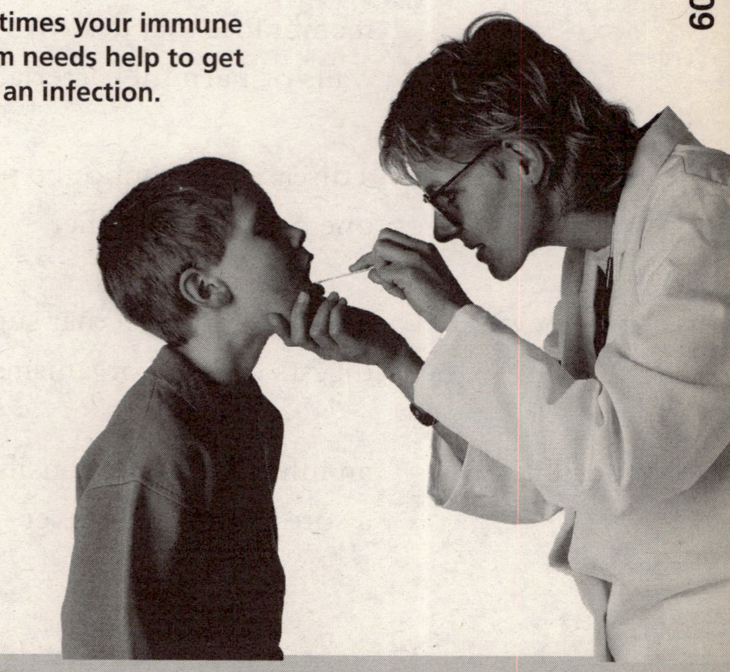

Sometimes your immune system needs help to get rid of an infection.

Staying Healthy

The human body has an amazing system to fight infections. Your immune system is always on guard against infections. It works all the time, sending out white blood cells to destroy pathogens before they can make you sick. You can help the system work by taking care of your health. Eating healthful foods and getting enough rest gives the immune system the things it needs. You can also help by avoiding pathogens. When you get sick, you need lots of rest so that your body can fight the infection.

Eating healthful food will help your immune system fight infections.

The digestive system breaks food down into nutrients that your cells need. The nervous system controls the other organs and systems. Its two main parts are the brain and the spinal cord. Nerves are groups of neurons that carry messages between the brain and other organs.

Organisms such as bacteria and viruses that cause disease are called pathogens. When they get inside your body, they can destroy cells or change the way the cells work. The immune system protects your body from these pathogens.

A disease that can be transferred from one organism to another by pathogens is called an infectious disease. One kind of infectious disease is the common cold. A vaccine is a medicine that helps your immune system fight pathogens. The vaccine helps the immune system identify the disease quickly. The immune system is then able to fight the disease faster.

Your immune system may face many kinds of pathogens and diseases. Let's find out about some of these invaders and how your body fights against them.

Diseases

You can see that the girl in the photo does not feel well. She is wrapped in a blanket to fight a chill. The thermometer in her mouth is checking for a fever. If you have ever had a bad cold, you know these symptoms.

Sometimes parts of the body have a disease. When this happens, these parts cannot perform their normal functions. Some diseases are inherited. Some are caused by exposure to toxic chemicals. Still other kinds of diseases are caused by organisms that invade your body.

Many illnesses, such as cancer or heart disease, are noninfectious diseases. You cannot get sick just from being close to someone with a noninfectious disease.

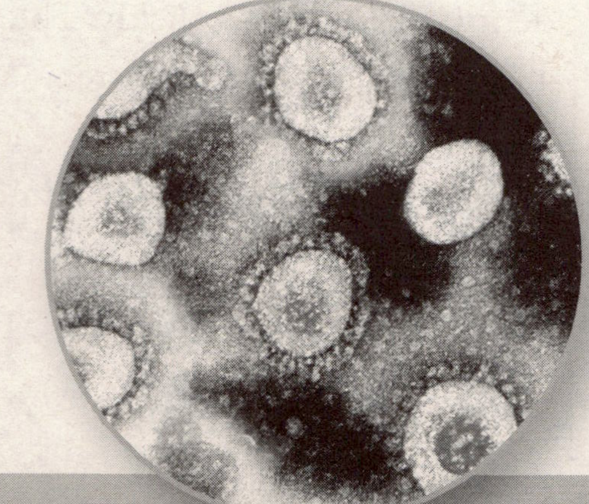

This is a cold virus under magnification.

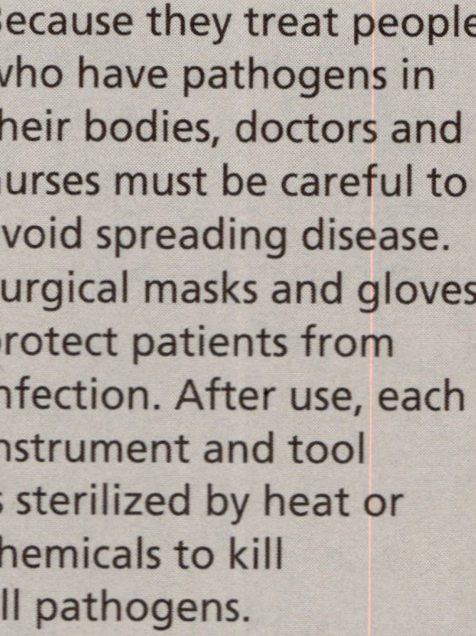

Hospital Hygiene

Because they treat people who have pathogens in their bodies, doctors and nurses must be careful to avoid spreading disease. Surgical masks and gloves protect patients from infection. After use, each instrument and tool is sterilized by heat or chemicals to kill all pathogens.

In order to make you sick, the pathogens need to get into your body. A cut or scrape is a way for germs to get past your skin. You can help your skin protect you by cleaning cuts and scrapes right away. Keeping the cut covered with a bandage protects the wound while it heals.

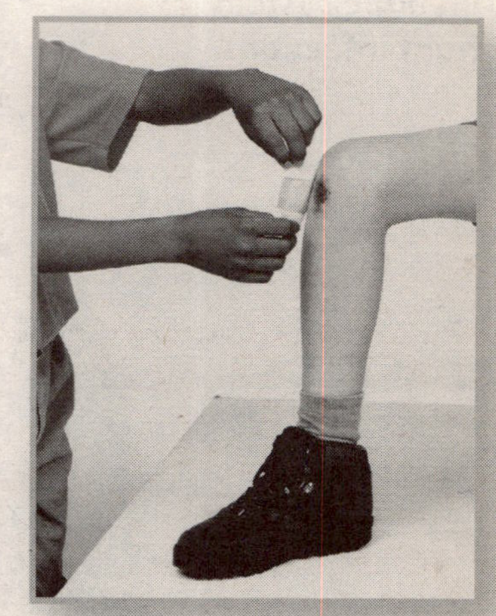

Covering cuts and scrapes helps keep infections from occurring at skin openings.

Avoiding Infection

You can avoid infections by keeping your body healthy and by avoiding germs. One of the best things you can do is wash your hands often. Many pathogens enter your body when you touch your eyes, nose, or mouth. Wash your hands with soap before you eat, after you use the bathroom, and whenever you touch something used by a person who is sick. You can also protect yourself by keeping your home and body clean, so that bacteria don't have a place to grow.

You can protect yourself from food infections by using care in your kitchen. Wash fresh fruits and vegetables before eating them. Always be sure that meats and eggs are completely cooked, because heat kills bacteria. Wash all surfaces that have touched raw meat right away.

Researchers have found that washing hands with soap is the most effective way to keep pathogens out of your body.

Infectious diseases, such as colds, the flu, and chicken pox, can be passed from one person to another. These illnesses are caused by microorganisms that invade your body. When you are around someone who has an infectious disease, the organisms that he or she has can travel to your body. The human body has a strong defense system to protect itself from these disease-causing organisms.

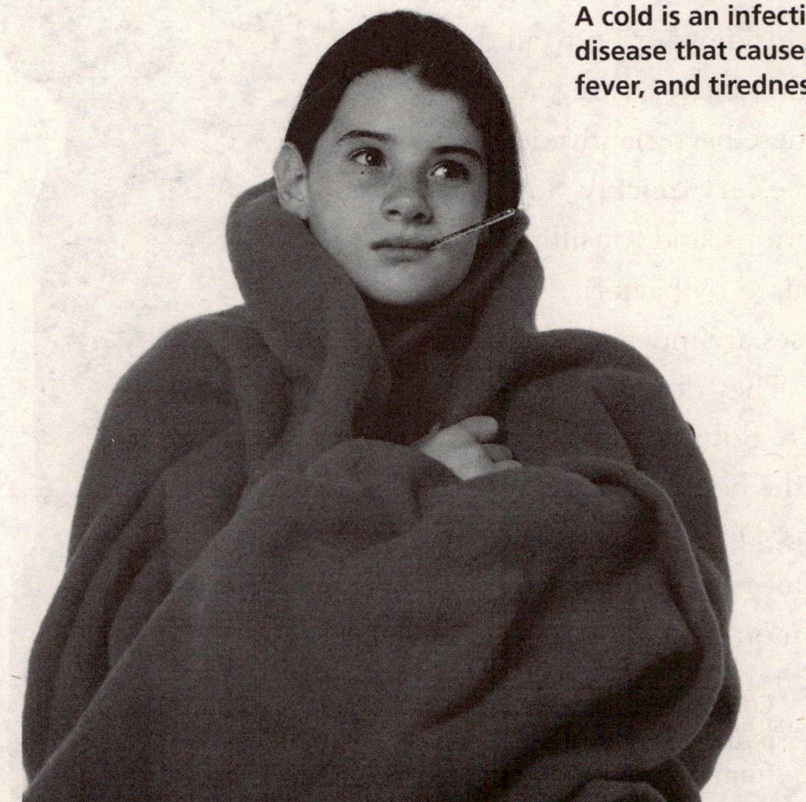

A cold is an infectious disease that causes chills, fever, and tiredness.

Bacteria and Viruses

Pathogens are organisms that cause disease. Many common pathogens are too small to see. They include bacteria and viruses. When these pathogens get inside a body, they can destroy cells or change the way cells work.

Bacteria are one-celled organisms. They are very small—as many as one thousand bacteria could form a line across the head of a pin. Most bacteria are harmless and live inside your body all the time. Other bacteria are pathogens. When these bacteria invade, they reproduce very quickly. Sore throats, ear infections, and tonsillitis are often caused by bacteria.

Viruses are much smaller than bacteria. They don't have cells of their own. Some viruses enter the cells of the body and take over their functions. Diseases caused by viruses include measles, chicken pox, and the common cold.

Coughs and sneezes can send pathogens through the air, from one person to another.

E. coli bacteria that are common in meats that are not completely cooked and on the surface of raw vegetables and fruits cause one infection. Chemicals on the surface of these *E. coli* damage the lining of the intestines.

Another common illness caused by food is salmonella poisoning. Salmonella bacteria live in eggs and raw meat and sometimes on unwashed fruit.

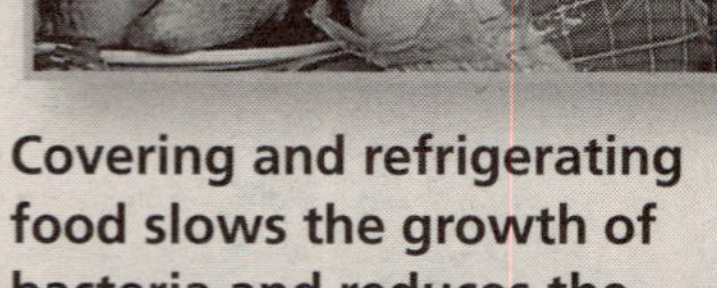

Covering and refrigerating food slows the growth of bacteria and reduces the chance of food poisoning.

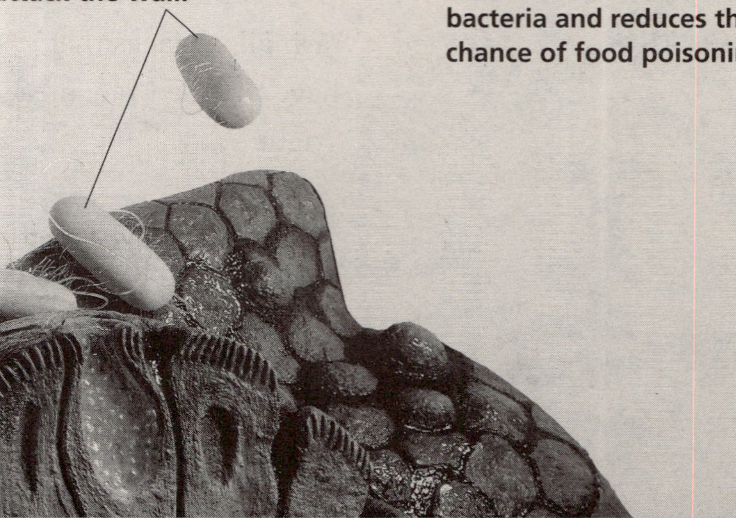

Bacteria release harmful toxins that attack the wall.

Food Poisoning

Food is a common way for bacteria and viruses to get past your body's defenses. Most of the time, strong acids and other chemicals in your stomach kill any harmful bacteria in your food. Sometimes, however, harmful bacteria pass through the stomach and multiply rapidly in the intestines. Millions of people in the United States get sick each year by eating contaminated food. Although most cases are mild, food poisoning sometimes causes serious health problems.

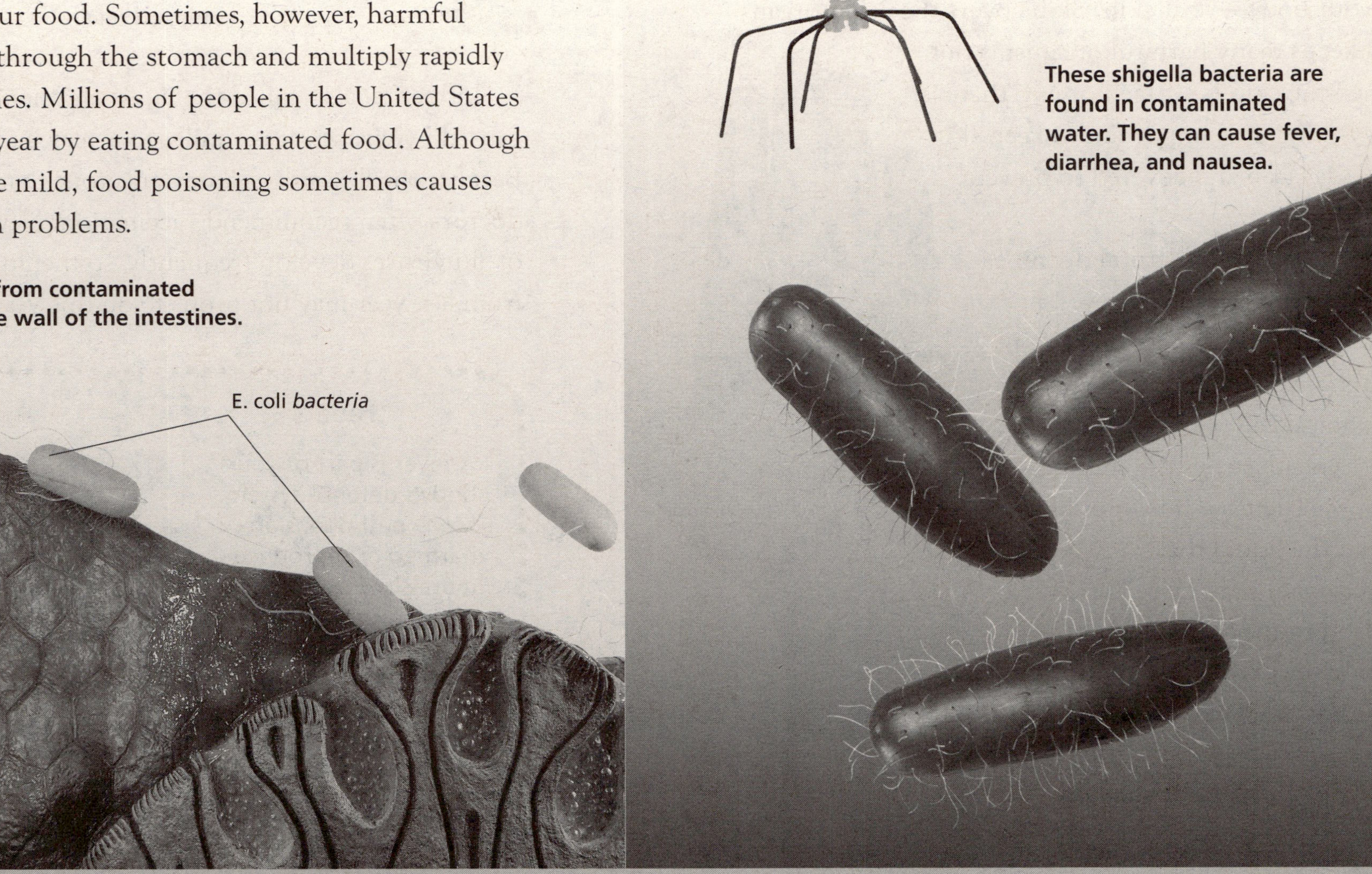

E. coli **bacteria from contaminated food stick to the wall of the intestines.**

This is a model of one kind of virus. Viruses have very small, simple structures compared to cells.

These shigella bacteria are found in contaminated water. They can cause fever, diarrhea, and nausea.

Outer Defenses

Your body can protect itself from pathogens. The best way to stay healthy is to keep pathogens out of your body in the first place. This is the job of the largest organ of your body—your skin. Skin covers the other organs and keeps many harmful organisms out. When the skin is scraped or cut, there is an opening. It is important to keep skin wounds clean and covered to prevent infections.

Your body has natural openings in the skin, such as your eyes, nose, and mouth. To protect them from bacteria, your body produces a chemical called lysozyme. Lysozyme destroys the cell walls of some bacteria. It is found in sweat, the liquid that your body uses to cool your skin. Lysozyme is also produced in mucous membranes, which are the soft tissues inside your mouth and

The first protection against pathogens is the skin.

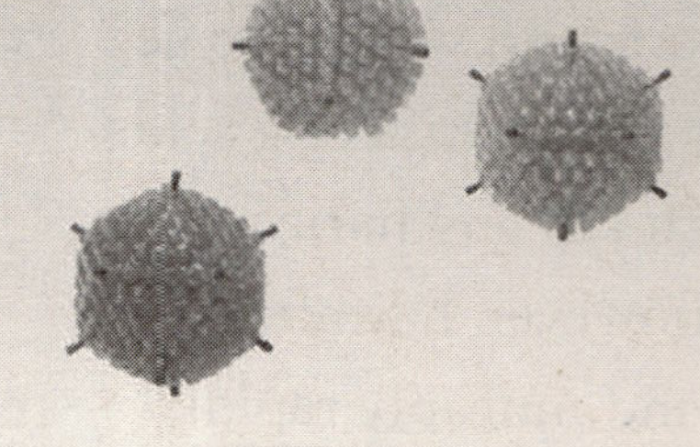

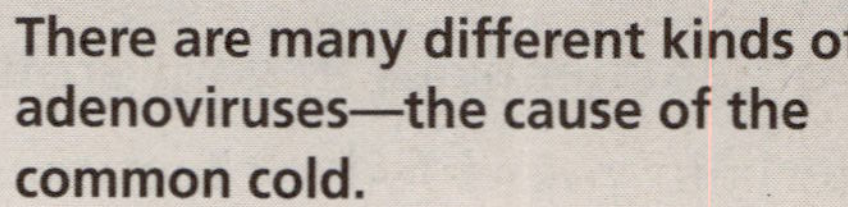

There are many different kinds of adenoviruses—the cause of the common cold.

Influenza, also called the flu, is another disease caused by viruses. It is similar to a very bad cold. Because the flu can be more dangerous than a cold, doctors often recommend vaccination. New kinds of flu viruses develop frequently, so the flu vaccine from last year may not protect you this year.

Fevers

A fever is part of your body's defense system. Many pathogens are harmed or reproduce more slowly at higher temperatures. The fever gives the immune system time to make more white blood cells to fight these pathogens.

Coughs and Colds

Some illnesses are very common. One common disease is a sore throat caused by bacteria. One symptom of this bacterial infection is white or yellow spots on the back of the throat. Streptococcus (strep-tuh-KAH-kuhs) bacteria are often the cause, so you may hear the disease called strep throat. Your doctor might give you antibiotics to help you fight this infection.

The most common of all illnesses is a cold. Colds are caused by viruses. Everyone knows what happens when cold viruses get into the body—coughing, sneezing, runny nose, and generally not feeling well. There is no vaccination to prevent colds because there are so many different viruses that cause them.

These streptococcus bacteria can cause a painful infection in your throat.

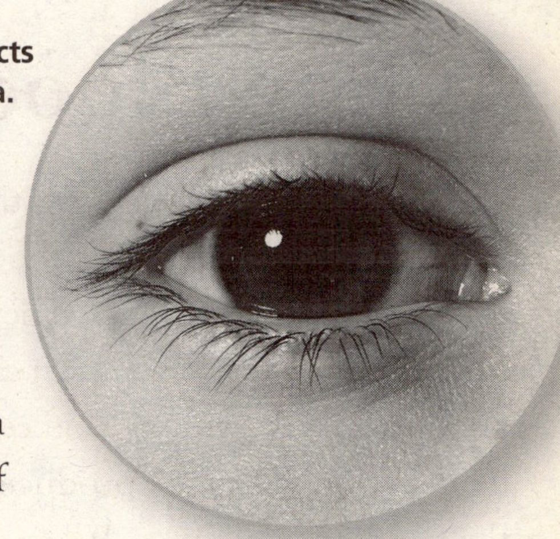

The fluid produced by tear ducts has chemicals that kill bacteria.

Tear ducts make the fluid that keeps your eyes from becoming too dry. Tear ducts add lysozyme to the fluid to kill bacteria that land on the surface of your eye.

Vitamin A is needed for your body to produce lysozyme. Without vitamin A, eyes are more likely to be affected by bacterial diseases.

Tonsils

Tonsils are found at the back of your throat. They can produce substances that help fight respiratory disease, but they can also become infected. If your tonsils have an infection, you have tonsillitis. Some symptoms of tonsillitis are a sore throat, difficulty swallowing, and a fever.

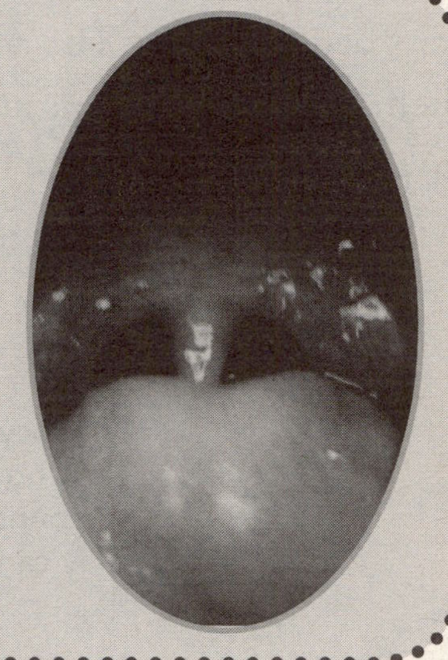

White Blood Cells

When pathogens get into the body, the immune system fights them. White blood cells are part of the immune system's defense. They are part of the blood, so they flow to nearly every part of the body. Phagocytes are one kind of white blood cell. They rush to the site of infection. They are produced in marrow, which is the tissue inside bones. When a phagocyte finds a bacterium or other pathogen, it surrounds the enemy and digests it. Some phagocytes are able to squeeze through very small gaps between cells. This allows them to get into organs and attack invaders throughout the body.

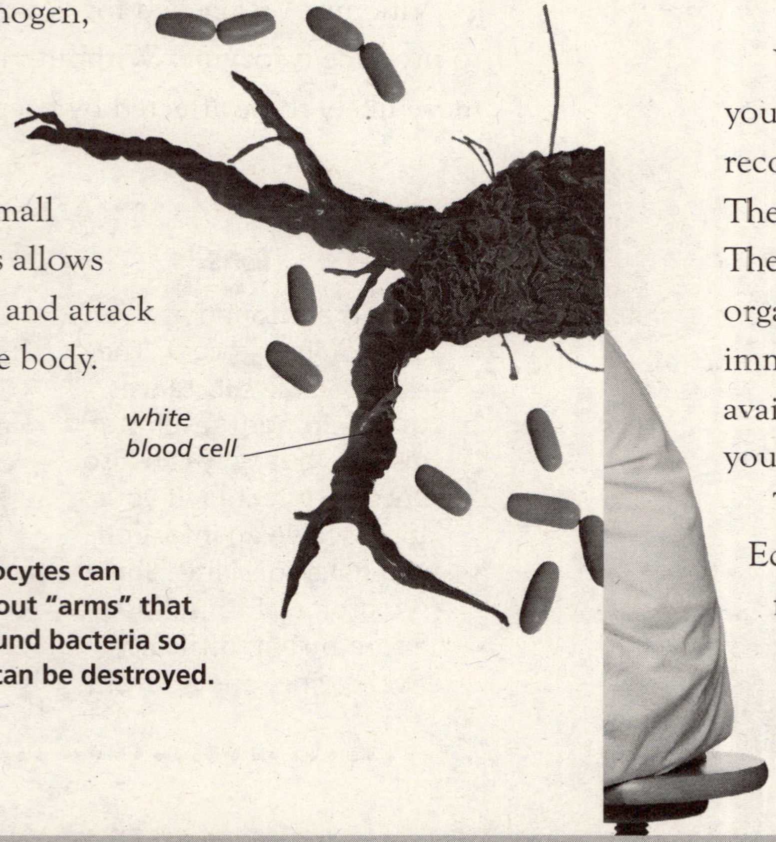

white blood cell

Phagocytes can send out "arms" that surround bacteria so they can be destroyed.

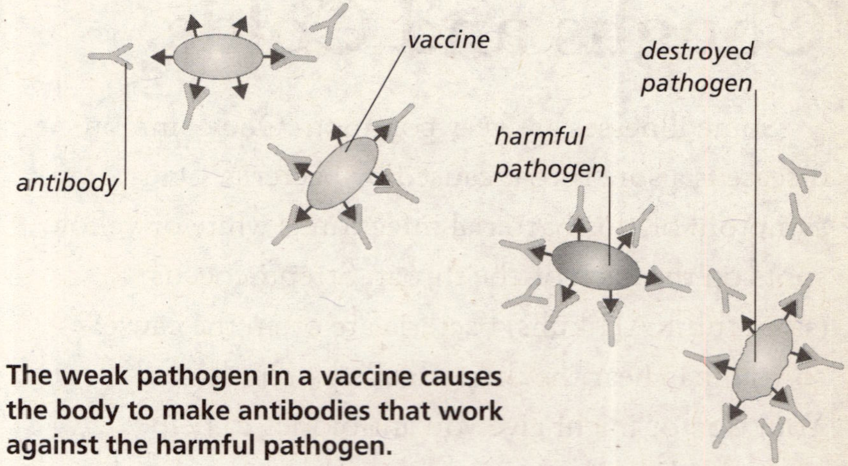

vaccine

antibody

harmful pathogen

destroyed pathogen

The weak pathogen in a vaccine causes the body to make antibodies that work against the harmful pathogen.

Vaccines are usually given to children when they are young. When you are injected with a vaccine, your body recognizes that it is something that does not belong. The immune system makes antibodies to remove it. The immune system can remember disease-causing organisms. If you are exposed to the disease later, your immune system recognizes it right away. Antibodies are available quickly. The bacteria or virus is removed as if you had already had the disease.

The first vaccine was produced by an English doctor, Edward Jenner, in 1796. He did many experiments to find out how smallpox could be prevented. Smallpox was a fatal disease in the 1700s. Jenner's experiments led to the first vaccine against smallpox.

Vaccinations

Lymphocytes use only antigens to identify an organism as harmful or safe. Your body defeats many kinds of bacteria by forming antibodies. Some bacteria, however, are too strong for your body to defeat on its own. Doctors inject a vaccine into your body to help fight some infections. A vaccine is made from a dead or weak form of a pathogen.

Why do people get sick if they have phagocytes to find and destroy pathogens? Some kinds of bacteria have coatings that can trick the white blood cells for a while. The coating on the outside of the cell makes the pathogen appear to be harmless. This trick allows the invader to reproduce and spread to many parts of the body before it is detected.

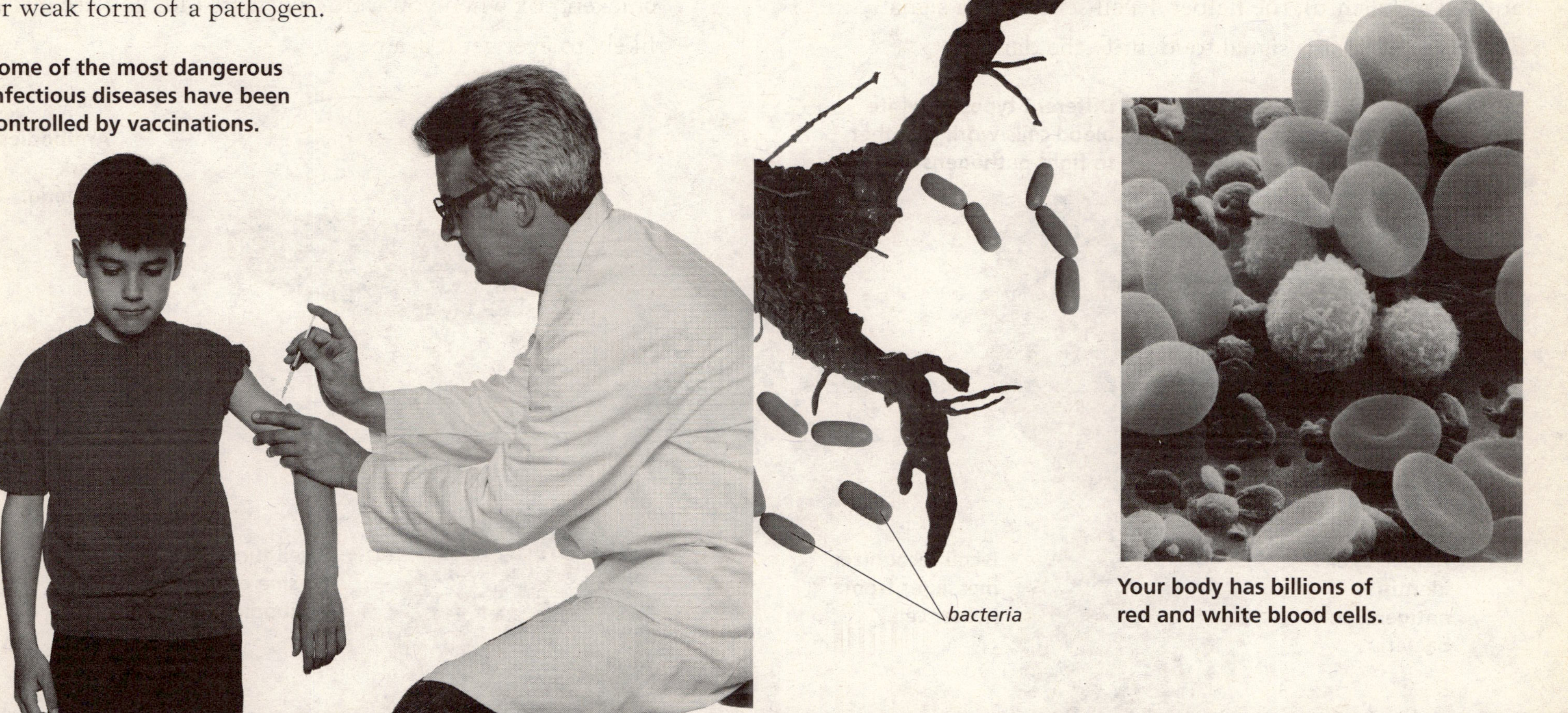

Some of the most dangerous infectious diseases have been controlled by vaccinations.

Your body has billions of red and white blood cells.

Antibodies

Antigens are molecules covering the surface of a cell. They give the cell a unique set of characteristics. White blood cells can recognize antigens. White blood cells called lymphocytes fight infections. T cells and B cells are two kinds of lymphocytes. T cells determine what antigen is on a cell. If the immune system recognizes the antigen as harmful, the helper T cell sends out a signal. The B cell uses this signal to identify the danger.

The B cell turns into a plasma cell. It then makes another chemical, called an antibody, which attaches to the antigen. The antibody then attacks the pathogen. There are many different antibodies. Each one marks and protects the body from a specific pathogen.

Because the immune system remembers antigens, it can respond faster the second time it encounters an infection. Some diseases occur only once. If you had chicken pox when you were two years old, you are not likely to ever get it again.

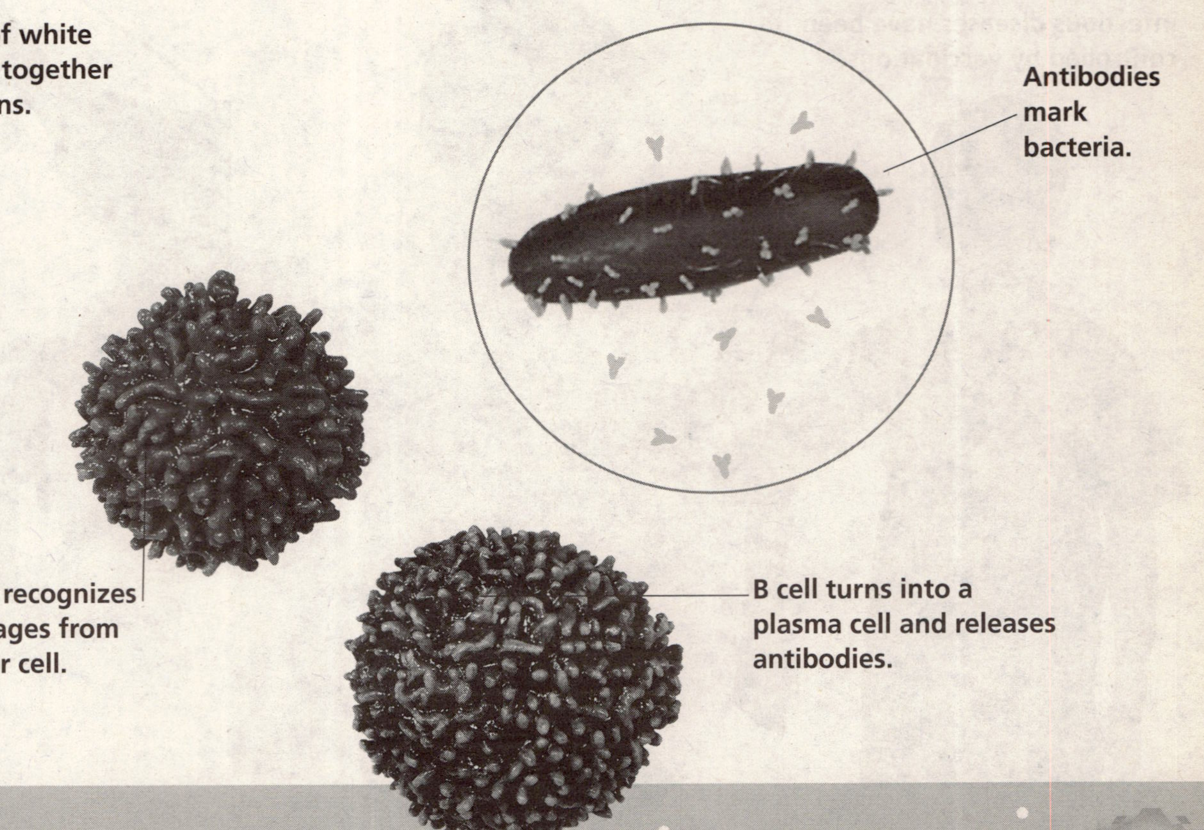

Different types of white blood cells work together to fight pathogens.

Earth Science

Weather AND Currents

by Steve Miller

Science

Genre	Comprehension Skill	Text Features	Science Content
Nonfiction	Cause and Effect	• Captions • Diagrams • Maps • Glossary	Weather and Water Cycle

Scott Foresman Science 4.6

scottforesman.com

ISBN 0-328-13876-2
90000
9 780328 138760

What did you learn?

1. How does a climate in an area near the North Pole differ from a climate in an area near the equator?

2. How do warm surface currents affect weather near the coast?

3. What is the effect of El Niño along the western coast of the Americas?

4. **Writing** in Science The temperatures of places on the same latitude can be different. Write to describe how ocean currents affect temperature. Include details from the book to support your answer.

5. **Cause and Effect** What weather conditions cause El Niño? What effect does El Niño have?

Vocabulary	Extended Vocabulary
anemometer	Coriolis effect
barometer	doldrums
condensation	El Niño
evaporation	ENSO
front	gyre
humidity	La Niña
meteorologist	surface current
precipitation	trade winds
wind vane	

Picture Credits
Every effort has been made to secure permission and provide appropriate credit for photographic material. The publisher deeply regrets any omission and pledges to correct errors called to its attention in subsequent editions.

Photo locators denoted as follows: Top (T), Center (C), Bottom (B), Left (L), Right (R), Background (Bkgd).

2 Digital Vision; 3 Getty Images; 6 (T) Tom Van Sant/Corbis; 8 David Muench/Corbis; 10 (CL) Michio Hoshino/Minden Pictures; 13 Will & Deni McIntyre/Photo Researchers, Inc.; 16 (B) National Maritime Museum, London/DK Images; 18 Jet Propulsion Laboratory/NASA Image Exchange; 20 Michey Welsh/Montgomery Adviser/Sygma/Corbis; 21 Nguyen Dong/UNEP/Peter Arnold, Inc.; 22 Frans Lanting/Minden Pictures.

Scott Foresman/Dorling Kindersley would also like to thank: 14 NASA/DK Images;17 (TR) NASA/DK Images.

ISBN: 0-328-13876-2

2 3 4 5 6 7 8 9 10 V004 13 12 11 10 09 08 07 06 05

Glossary

Coriolis effect a force, due to the rotation of the Earth, that causes large northward or southward movements to curve

doldrums a region near the equator with very calm winds

El Niño a warm surface current that flows from the western Pacific toward South America every three to eight years

ENSO the El Niño–Southern Oscillation event that combines the effect of unusual trade winds and El Niño

gyre a circular flow of surface currents in the ocean

La Niña a strong cold current that flows westward after an El Niño

surface current a "river" of water that flows in the upper part of the ocean

trade winds the winds north and south of the equator that generally blow from the northeast in the Northern Hemisphere and from the southeast in the Southern Hemisphere

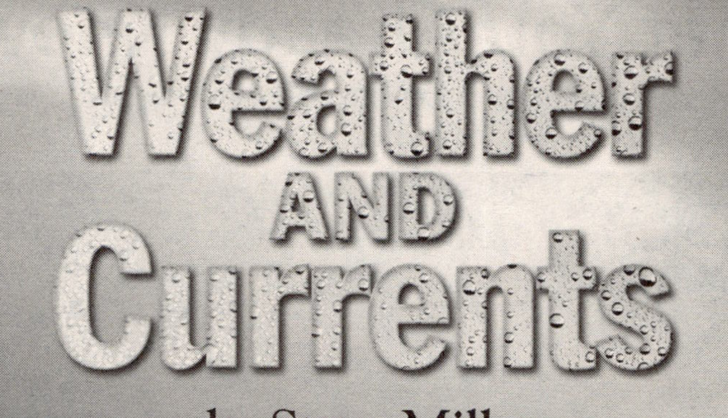

Weather AND Currents

by Steve Miller

PEARSON Scott Foresman

What You Already Know

There are many kinds of weather on Earth, ranging from hot to cold and wet to dry. The weather at a particular place is affected by flowing water and air. The effects of energy from the Sun, wind, and oceans help determine the weather.

Water enters the atmosphere by evaporating from lakes, rivers, and especially the oceans. Condensation occurs when the water vapor in the atmosphere becomes liquid. Then it forms clouds or fog. These are collections of tiny water droplets or ice crystals. As the droplets or crystals grow, they combine with each other. When they are heavy enough, they fall to Earth as precipitation. Precipitation occurs in several forms of liquid or solid water, including rain, snow, and sleet.

Meteorologists use that information to improve weather forecasts. The tools that they use include large ships full of measuring instruments and satellites far above the atmosphere. Some projects use floats that are carried around the ocean by the currents. They send radio signals back to the laboratory to tell their location and to report on the weather. A better understanding of ocean currents means a better understanding of weather.

74

Oceans and the Weather

The atmosphere and the oceans work together to move energy from the Sun around Earth's surface. Surface currents act like huge rivers in the ocean. As they move water from one place to another, they also move heat. Part of the difference in climate from one place to another comes from that heat transfer.

Many scientists study the ocean currents. Oceanographers want to understand the complicated way that the oceans and the atmosphere work together.

An air mass is a portion of the atmosphere in which the conditions are uniform. This means that both the humidity, which is the amount of water in the atmosphere, and the temperature are about the same throughout the air mass. When two air masses collide, the boundary between them is known as a front. Fronts are areas of unstable weather where conditions are changing.

Meteorologists are scientists who study the weather—how it occurs and how to predict future weather. They use several kinds of tools to study weather. A wind vane indicates the direction of the wind, and an anemometer measures its speed. A barometer is a tool used to measure air pressure. Changes in air pressure often indicate a front.

There are different kinds of weather all over the world. Let's look at some of the things that cause weather patterns.

Clouds form over an ocean.

Hot and Cold

You know that weather conditions vary from one place to another. Compare the climates of northern Alaska and Mexico. The main reason they differ is the way that sunlight reaches them. You can see in the picture of the globe that the light from the Sun shines more directly on Earth near the equator than it does at the North and South Poles. More direct sunlight means that more solar energy reaches the land and water. More solar energy becomes more heat and causes a warmer climate.

The amount of solar energy at the equator is greater than at the poles.

Near the North Pole, ice covers the Earth much of the time.

The warm currents carry moisture away from Asia, causing droughts such as this one in Vietnam.

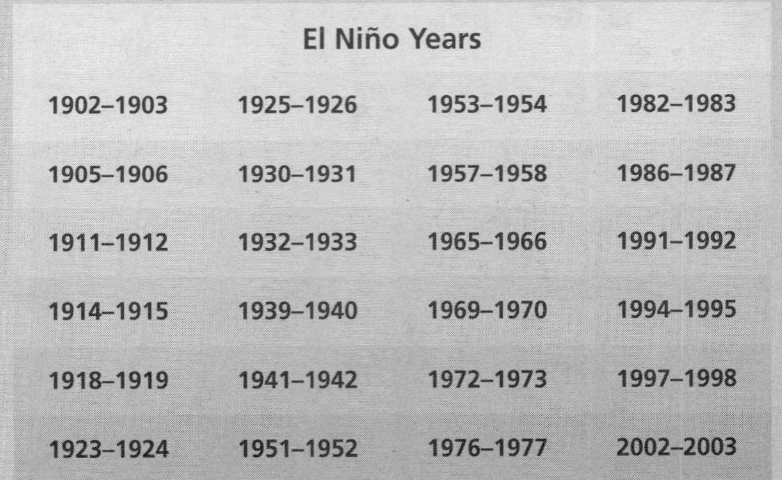

El Niño Years

1902–1903	1925–1926	1953–1954	1982–1983
1905–1906	1930–1931	1957–1958	1986–1987
1911–1912	1932–1933	1965–1966	1991–1992
1914–1915	1939–1940	1969–1970	1994–1995
1918–1919	1941–1942	1972–1973	1997–1998
1923–1924	1951–1952	1976–1977	2002–2003

El Niño Devastation

ENSO events cause changes in weather patterns, not just in the Pacific but in other places very far away. As the warm water of El Niño arrives in the eastern Pacific Ocean, it brings moisture and increased evaporation to the American coasts. From Chile to California, massive rainfall causes floods and landslides. In the southeastern United States, warm air from ENSO hits cold polar air masses. The clashing air masses cause large thunderstorms and tornadoes.

El Niño brings rain and floods to Alabama.

At the same time, the movement of warm water away from the western Pacific brings changes to the weather there. In Southeast Asia, southwest Africa, and New Guinea, the normal rains do not come. Because of the dry conditions, farm crops fail and wildlife habitats are destroyed.

After El Niño, the usual current sometimes recovers quickly. The result is a larger-than-normal flow of cool water toward the west. It brings cool temperatures to the eastern part of the Pacific Ocean's tropical areas. This is called La Niña. The effects of La Niña are the opposite of El Niño.

Less solar energy explains why a polar climate, such as the Arctic coast of Alaska, is cold. The average high temperature in summer in Barrow, Alaska, is only 45°F. Winter nights are especially cold at –20°F. The temperature falls below freezing about 320 days every year in Barrow.

Areas near the equator have much higher temperatures. In Acapulco, Mexico, the average high temperature is about 90°F in the summer. Even the winter nights stay warm, with a low of about 70°F. Freezing temperatures have never been recorded in Acapulco.

Warm days and nights help plants grow in equatorial climates.

Earth is sometimes called the "Blue Planet" because of its oceans.

Oceans

The view of the Earth on the left shows one of its most obvious features—the ocean. About seven-tenths of Earth's surface is sea water. Light passing through the water interacts with it. The top layer of water absorbs most of the light and changes it into another form of energy—heat. So the water just a short distance below the surface of the ocean is always dark.

In fact, the top ten feet of the ocean surface holds as much heat energy as the entire atmosphere. Even if the water feels cold when you go swimming, it is storing heat energy. This energy means that the oceans play a major role in climate and weather all around the world.

The water of the oceans stores most of the solar energy of Earth.

Normal Conditions: The current carries warm surface waters toward the western Pacific.

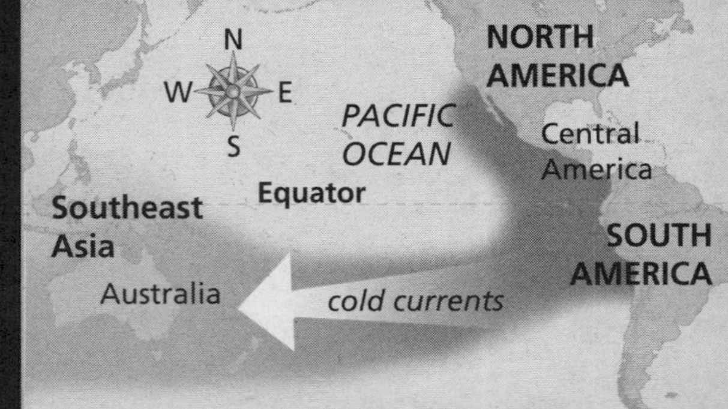

El Niño Years: When the winds weaken, the warm water flows eastward.

N
W
E
S
NORTH AMERICA
PACIFIC OCEAN
Central America
Equator
Southeast Asia
warm currents
SOUTH AMERICA
Australia

For some reason, every few years, the wind patterns change. The trade winds become weaker, or they even reverse direction in a change called the Southern Oscillation. The direction of the ocean current also changes. The warm water that has been pushed to the west begins to flow eastward. The reversal of the equatorial current is called El Niño. This change in the flow of energy, known as the El Niño–Southern Oscillation (ENSO) event, usually begins in December. This is the beginning of summer in the Southern Hemisphere. El Niño can last for months or even years.

Changing Patterns

In the Pacific Ocean, the trade winds drive a current known as the South Pacific Equatorial Current. Normally the winds push the surface waters of the South Pacific westward. Cold water comes from deep in the ocean near the coast of South America. The current carries this water across the Pacific, as shown in the top map on the next page.

Because of this current, places on the eastern side of the Pacific, such as western Peru, are relatively dry.

The current pushes the warmer waters near Australia farther west, causing rainy weather in New Guinea and Indonesia.

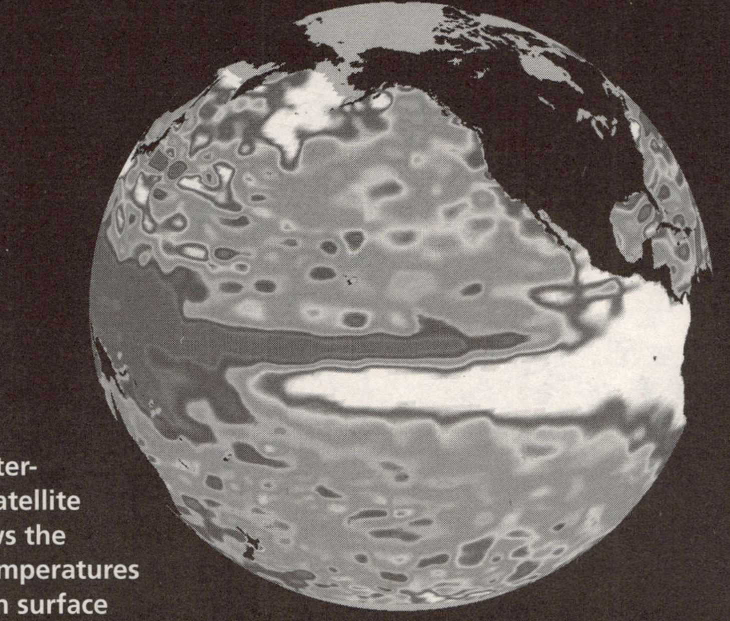

This computer-enhanced satellite image shows the different temperatures of the ocean surface during El Niño.

2. Water falls back to Earth as rain, snow, sleet, or hail.

1. Water evaporates from Earth's surface.

3. Water flows and seeps back into the rivers and seas.

Water moves between Earth and the atmosphere in an endless cycle that makes life possible on land.

Water evaporating from the oceans drives the global water cycle. Some of the water vapor that makes up the clouds over the ocean is carried inland by wind. As water vapor cools in the atmosphere, it falls to Earth as rain and other kinds of precipitation. The water then flows through streams and rivers to return to the ocean. This is the source of all the water you need to drink and grow food.

Coastal Differences

If you have ever traveled between an inland area and the coast, you know that the weather can be very different. Sometimes the coast is cooler than inland areas, and sometimes it is warmer. Coastal regions also tend to be breezy or windy most of the time.

If you stand in the waves as they reach the shore, you can feel some of the ocean's energy.

Jet Streams

High in Earth's atmosphere, rivers of air travel very rapidly. Airplanes flying at high altitudes can get an extra push from a jet stream.

Trade winds were named by sailors who used them to sail trading ships across the ocean. Along the equator, where the trade winds meet, there are very calm regions known as the doldrums. When ships relied on the wind, they could become stranded in these areas. Often sailors had to wait for weeks for the wind in the doldrums to start blowing again.

Wind Patterns

If you watch a small pond or a puddle on a windy day, you can see that wind causes water to flow. Currents in the ocean are very large, so it takes a lot of wind to get them moving. The map of Earth shows the patterns of how winds blow through the atmosphere.

North and south of the equator, winds blow most of the time. These are the trade winds, which carry large amounts of air from the northeast in the Northern Hemisphere and from the southeast in the Southern Hemisphere.

jet stream

Trading ships, like this clipper ship, relied for centuries on the wind for power.

Ocean waters warm more slowly than nearby land areas. During the day, as the land heats, warm air rises. Cool air over the water moves in to replace it. This causes cool ocean breezes. The temperature does not rise as much by the ocean as it does inland. At night, the effect reverses. The land holds less energy, so it cools faster than the water. The cooling air flows toward the water, and the breezes blow away from the land.

In the morning warm air rises over the land.

In the evening warm air rises over the water.

The same kind of thing happens on a longer time scale. During the summer months, the oceans absorb heat, which they release slowly in the winter. Throughout the year, coastal regions have smaller temperature changes than places farther inland. In San Francisco, average temperatures range from a high of about 70°F in the summer to a low of about 45°F in winter. An inland city such as Sacramento experiences a wider range of temperatures. Even though Sacramento is only about 100 miles from San Francisco, temperatures range from 90°F in the summer to 38°F in the winter. The difference is due to the cool waters of the Pacific Ocean.

Ocean Currents

Take one look at their long fur coats and you know what kind of climate polar bears like—very cold. In fact, polar bears are so well insulated that they get too hot if they run very far. James Bay in northern Canada is the perfect polar bear habitat. In winter, ice forms over the water. The polar bears go hunting for food in the cozy –25°F weather.

You can see on the globe that the latitude of London, England is about the same as that of James Bay in Canada. In London, polar bears would have a hard time surviving on their own.

52° North

Polar bears walk across the frozen James Bay.

As Earth revolves, the motion causes a force that deflects north-south movements.

Another factor affects surface currents and other large movements on Earth. As Earth rotates on its axis, a force causes things that are moving northward or southward to turn. This force is called the Coriolis effect. It causes the currents to curve to the right in the Northern Hemisphere and to the left in the Southern Hemisphere.

As the Gulf Stream flows from the Gulf of Mexico, it travels northward and then curves right, toward the east. Water that flows southward, such as a large current along the west coast of Africa, turns westward due to the Coriolis effect.

Look at the map of currents on page 12. You can see several places where the forces combine causing the water to move in a circular pattern. These circular flows are known as gyres. Gyres flow clockwise in the Northern Hemisphere and counterclockwise in the Southern Hemisphere.

Pushing the Water

One of the driving forces for the Gulf Stream is actually moving air—the winds. The wind generally blows from southwest to northeast above the Gulf Stream flowing in the Atlantic Ocean. Although the wind does not always move in exactly the same direction, it is constant enough to cause a lot of water to flow toward the northeast.

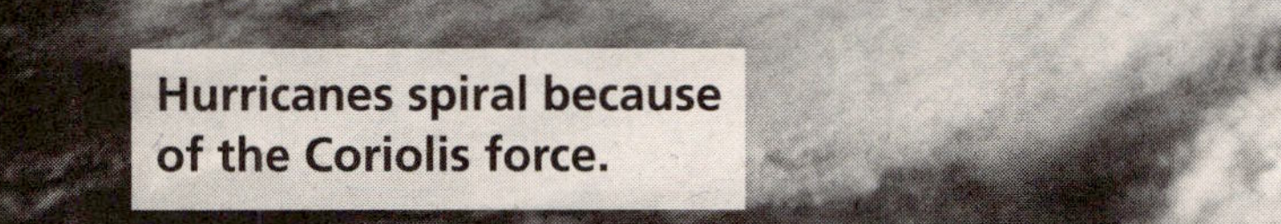

Hurricanes spiral because of the Coriolis force.

The climate of London is mild—never very hot, never very cold.

James Bay and London—same latitude, same amount of solar energy, different temperatures

The ocean water near England does not freeze into a layer of ice. The average winter lows in London are just below the freezing point of fresh water. The lowest temperature ever recorded is 10°F—much warmer than winter temperatures in polar bear country.

Why is London so much warmer than James Bay? The ocean carries heat to England. Streams of water, called currents, flow through the oceans like huge rivers. One of these currents, the Gulf Stream, warms London with water from the warm Gulf of Mexico.

Rivers in the Ocean

The Gulf Stream is just one of many surface currents. Surface currents flow through the upper part of the ocean and carry water great distances. The map below shows the paths followed by water in some of the large currents. Notice that there are two kinds of currents—warm and cold. The Gulf Stream is a warm current. Many of the warm currents begin near the equator, and many of the cold currents begin near the North and South Poles.

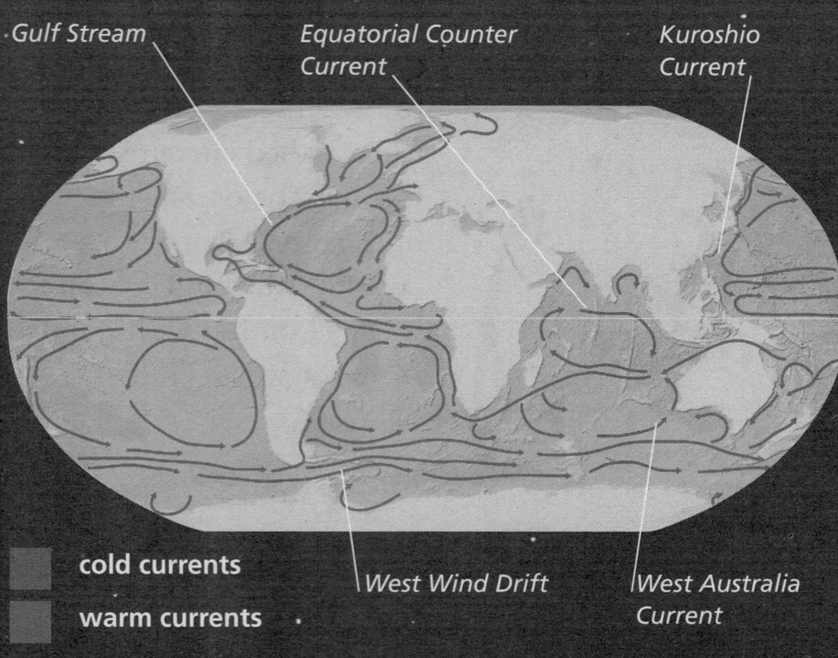

Surface currents generally carry warm water from the equator and cold water from the Poles.

The waves at the beach were caused by wind far away.

Warm currents carry heat that keeps the climate warm in nearby land areas. Usually, warm currents bring more rain as well because more evaporation occurs above warmer water. This means more clouds form and more rain falls. Coastal areas near a cold current often have shorter growing seasons than other areas nearby. This is because the cool water lowers the temperature along the coast.

What causes the water in the ocean to move? Long ago, people thought the Gulf Stream was caused by water flowing from the Mississippi River into the Gulf of Mexico. However, the Gulf Stream carries almost three thousand times as much water as that huge river. There must be another explanation.

84

Science

Genre	Comprehension Skill	Text Features	Science Content
Nonfiction	Main Idea and Details	• Captions • Labels • Diagrams • Glossary	Severe Storms

Scott Foresman Science 4.7

scottforesman.com

ISBN 0-328-13879-7
9 780328 138791 90000

Science

Earth Science

Hurricanes

by Peggy Bresnick Kendler

What did you learn?

1. Why are hurricanes such dangerous weather events?

2. List two factors that must be present in order for a hurricane to form.

3. Explain how a storm surge happens.

4. **Writing** in Science Scientists and meteorologists have ways to monitor storms such as hurricanes. Write to describe some of the ways they do this. Use details from the book to support your answer.

5. **Main Idea and Details** Hurricanes are severe storms. What details from the book support this idea?

Vocabulary	Extended Vocabulary
hurricane	atmospheric pressure
storm surge	cyclones
tornado	landfall
tropical depression	lull
tropical storm	torrential
vortex	typhoons
	wall clouds

Picture Credits
Every effort has been made to secure permission and provide appropriate credit for photographic material. The publisher deeply regrets any omission and pledges to correct errors called to its attention in subsequent editions.

Photo locators denoted as follows: Top (T), Center (C), Bottom (B), Left (L), Right (R), Background (Bkgd).

Opener: The Science Museum/©DK Images;1 ©Bettmann/Corbis; 4 (B, BR) Getty Images; 5 (BR) The Cinema Museum/Ronald Grant Archive; 6 (TL) ©Bettmann/Corbis, (BL) The Science Museum/©DK Images, (T) Schenectady Museum/Hall of Electrical History Foundation/Corbis, (CR) Brand X Pictures; 8 (TL) ©Bettmann/Corbis, (B) Science Museum, London/DK Images; 9 (TR) ©Alfred Pasieka/Photo Researchers, Inc.; 10 (TL) ©Bettmann/Corbis; 11 (CR) Reuters/Corbis; 12 (TL) ©Bettmann/Corbis, (B) Science Source/Photo Researchers, Inc.; 14 (TL) Hulton-Deutsch Collection/Corbis.

ISBN: 0-328-13879-7

2 3 4 5 6 7 8 9 10 V004 13 12 11 10 09 08 07 06 05

Glossary

atmospheric pressure the pressure caused by the weight of the atmosphere

cyclones hurricanes that form in the Indian Ocean

landfall the act of a hurricane reaching land

lull a brief calm

torrential flowing rapidly

typhoons hurricanes that form in the western Pacific Ocean

wall clouds the storm clouds that surround a hurricane's eye

by Peggy Bresnick Kendler

What You Already Know

A hurricane is a dangerous storm with very strong winds. A hurricane is made up of many groups of thunderstorms that are wrapped around its center.

Tropical storms form from heat and water vapor from the ocean. Warm, moist air rises, causing a tropical disturbance. The clouds in a tropical disturbance can become thunderstorms. The storms' winds increase and begin to swirl, causing a tropical depression. Winds blow faster and form a tropical storm. When winds reach a speed of 119 kilometers per hour, the tropical storm becomes a hurricane. The center of a hurricane is called the eye. Winds are calm in the eye.

A hurricane can knock down trees or change the shape of a coastline. A slow-moving hurricane can produce many inches of rain in one place. This can cause dangerous mudslides and floods. A hurricane's winds can push large waves of ocean water onto the shore. This rise in sea level is called a storm surge.

Computer models can predict a hurricane's strength, direction, and speed. Satellites can send data on storms and hurricanes to meteorologists. Many scientists work together to forecast storms.

A weather-research plane flies into the eye of a hurricane to gather information and monitor the storm.

Devices on the weather-research planes measure air pressure, humidity, temperature, and wind direction and speed. This gives scientists a good idea of the structure and intensity of the storm.

Hurricanes are very powerful storms. They can cause great damage when they reach land. Their strong winds and heavy rains can destroy anything in their path. Scientists study hurricanes so they can learn as much as possible about these dangerous storms.

Monitoring Storms

Predicting and tracking hurricanes are important jobs of weather forecasters and meteorologists. They alert people to the growing storm. People in areas where the hurricane might strike have time to prepare for the storm.

Weather forecasters use images from satellites to help them follow a hurricane's development over the ocean. The images help them track a hurricane's progress and its path. This way, the forecasters can have a good idea where the storm will make landfall.

The National Oceanic and Atmospheric Administration, known as NOAA, sends specially equipped planes to fly right into the center of hurricanes. The planes carry meteorological equipment that gathers data inside the storms. The data are fed into computer models that help forecasters make accurate predictions during a hurricane. Data also help researchers better understand what goes on inside storms and hurricanes. This information helps meteorologists to be better hurricane forecasters.

Meteorologists study satellite images to help them understand and predict hurricanes.

A funnel cloud is a rapidly spinning column of air that drops down out of a thunderstorm. It is called a tornado when it touches the ground. A tornado forms from a spinning area inside a thunderstorm. A vortex is an area where air or liquid spins in circles. A tornado is a vortex that forms in a thunderstorm.

Tornadoes form and move quickly. They are difficult to forecast. Their strong winds can cause a great deal of damage.

Hurricanes and tornadoes are both strong storms. Tornadoes have faster winds than hurricanes have. Hurricanes are bigger than tornadoes, and they last longer. Keep reading to learn more about hurricanes.

What are hurricanes?

Hurricanes are very large tropical storms that form over warm water. Hurricanes, typhoons, and cyclones are all different names for the same type of storm. In the western Pacific Ocean, hurricanes are called typhoons. In the Indian Ocean, they are called cyclones. In the Atlantic Ocean, they are called hurricanes.

satellite image of a hurricane

Hurricanes have winds that have reached a constant speed of at least 119 kilometers per hour. These winds blow in a spiral pattern around a calm center area called the eye.

The strong winds of a hurricane can knock over trees.

Besides flooding coastal areas, storm surges can do plenty of damage to property. Rapid rises in sea level can damage or destroy portions of bridges. Storm surges also can lift large boats, wrecking them as they wash up on the shore or even onto roads. Storm surges can also be very dangerous for animals and people who get caught in the rushing water.

Waves pounded the island of Bermuda as a hurricane struck in 2003.

Storm Surge

A hurricane can cause storm surges. A storm surge occurs when the hurricane pushes ocean water onto the shore. During a hurricane, ocean water is pulled up into the eye. This makes enormous waves that gain even more power from the strong hurricane winds. The result is a wall of seawater that crashes onto land.

Some of the worst damage from a hurricane is caused by storm surges. They are especially dangerous in areas where the coast is at almost the same level as the ocean. During a storm surge, ocean water pours onto land with tremendous force, flooding streets and buildings. Buildings on hills are not as likely to flood, but they are sometimes damaged by mudslides that result from the heavy rain.

Storm surges form when ocean water is pulled into the hurricane's eye.

When Hurricane Frances struck Florida in 2004, some boats were washed inland.

The eye of a hurricane is usually between twenty and one hundred kilometers wide. The storm can bring heavy rains, powerful winds, and storm surges. A single hurricane can spend more than two weeks over open water.

Hurricane season in the Atlantic Ocean north of the equator lasts from June 1 through November 30. During these months, the water in the Atlantic Ocean is warmest. Most hurricanes happen in August and September.

Storm Names

All tropical storms are given male or female names. The names help meteorologists identify and track storms—especially when more than one happens at the same time.

How Hurricanes Form

Hurricanes start as small thunderstorms over warm, tropical oceans. They begin over a warm layer of water at the top of the sea. This layer has a surface temperature of at least 26.5° Celsius, or 80° Fahrenheit. The warm seawater is absorbed by the air. This moist, warm air affects the atmospheric pressure. Atmospheric pressure is the pressure caused by the weight of air.

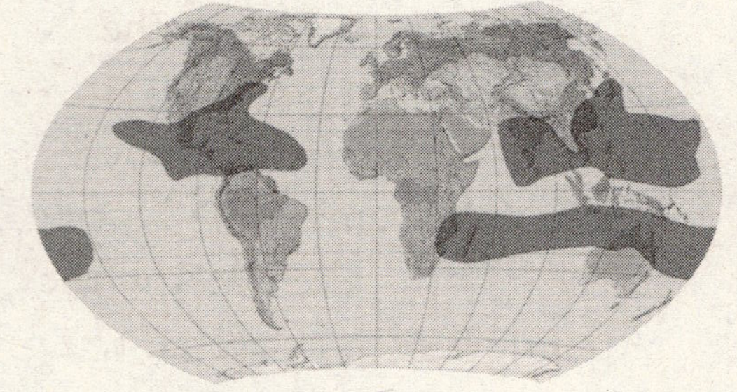

The map shows the places where severe storms are most likely.

Hurricane Mitch 1998

October 22, 1998: A storm begins to form over the Atlantic Ocean.

October 25, 1998: As the storm develops into a hurricane, the eye becomes visible.

As the hurricane's eye passes over an area, the winds slow and the sky might clear. There is a lull, or a brief calm, in the storm. When the lull passes, the intense winds and heavy rains resume. This is because the most powerful winds of the storm surround the hurricane's eye.

Hurricanes weaken as they move over land. They need energy from the warm sea air to stay powerful.

This destruction was caused by Hurricane Frances, which battered Florida in 2004.

Storm Damage

When a hurricane strikes land, we say it has made landfall. As the hurricane moves over land, powerful winds and heavy rains can remain over an area for several hours. Its raging winds can reach a speed of more than 250 kilometers per hour. The winds and rains can do tremendous damage. Hurricane winds can rip trees out of the ground, tear the roofs off buildings, and shatter windows. The torrential rains can cause heavy flooding.

Most hurricanes in North America happen when different water currents meet. When these currents come together, they produce a group of thunderstorms called a tropical disturbance. The disturbance grows as warm, moist air moves upward. As the air rises, it cools and the water in it condenses and releases heat. This causes lower atmospheric pressure, which pulls even more air into the system.

As the wind moves faster, the tropical disturbance becomes a tropical depression. As air moves into it, the system begins to spin around. When the storm's winds grow to 62 kilometers per hour or greater, it becomes a tropical storm, and it is given a name. If the storm keeps growing and its wind speeds reach 119 kilometers per hour, it is a hurricane.

October 26, 1998: Hurricane Mitch becomes larger and more powerful.

October 28, 1998: After it reaches land, Hurricane Mitch loses strength.

Inside a Hurricane

At Earth's surface, the air pressure in a hurricane is low. When the air moves from areas of high pressure to areas of low pressure, strong winds develop. The warm, moist air from the ocean moves to areas of low pressure. There the air rises and forms bands of rain. These rain bands can produce more than five centimeters of rain per hour.

The powerful winds of a hurricane swirl around the eye of the storm. A hurricane's eye is calm. Within the eye, there are few winds or clouds.

hurricane structure

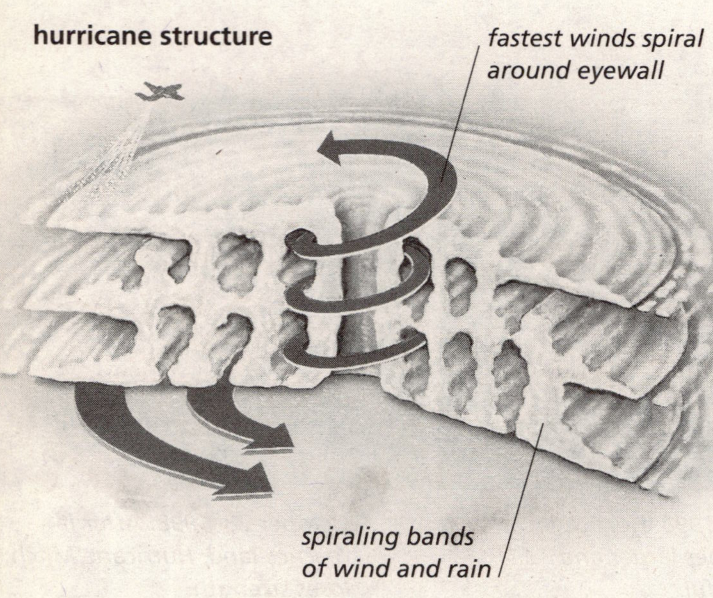

Storm clouds called wall clouds surround the eye to form the eyewall. A hurricane's strongest winds and heaviest rains happen within wall clouds that spin around the eye. In the eyewall, warm air spirals upward, causing the most powerful winds of the storm.

Science

Genre	Comprehension Skill	Text Features	Science Content
Nonfiction	Summarize	• Captions • Labels • Text Boxes • Glossary	Rocks and Minerals

Scott Foresman Science 4.8

ISBN 0-328-13882-7
9 780328 138821 90000

scottforesman.com

Science

Earth Science

FOSSIL DETECTIVES

by Joyce A. Churchill

What did you learn?

1. How is a fossil formed?

2. What is Mary Anning famous for discovering?

3. What led to the feud between Othniel Charles Marsh and Edward Drinker Cope?

4. **Writing** in Science The people in this book enjoyed the study of fossils. Explain on your own paper why you think someone would want to become a paleontologist. Include details from the book to support your answer.

5. **Summarize** Write a brief summary of the life and work of Barnum Brown.

Vocabulary	Extended Vocabulary
igneous rock	anatomy
luster	Cretaceous
metamorphic rock	extinct
mineral	Jurassic
sediment	paleontology
sedimentary rock	protruding
	quarry

Picture Credits
Every effort has been made to secure permission and provide appropriate credit for photographic material. The publisher deeply regrets any omission and pledges to correct errors called to its attention in subsequent editions.

Photo locators denoted as follows: Top (T), Center (C), Bottom (B), Left (L), Right (R), Background (Bkgd).

4 Richard T. Nowitz/Corbis; 6 (CR) ©The Natural History Museum, London; 8 (TR) Photo Researchers, Inc.; 12 (T, B) Bettmann/Corbis; 14 (TR) ©The Natural History Museum, London.

Scott Foresman/Dorling Kindersley would also like to thank: 9 (BR) Natural History Museum, London/DK Images; 15 (TR) Natural History Museum, London/DK Images.

ISBN: 0-328-13882-7

2 3 4 5 6 7 8 9 10 V004 13 12 11 10 09 08 07 06 05

Glossary

anatomy the science of the parts of living things

Cretaceous a period of time at the end of the Mesozoic era that ended 66.4 million years ago

extinct no longer existing

Jurassic a period of time in the middle of the Mesozoic era when dinosaurs lived

paleontology the science of studying fossils

protruding sticking out from its surroundings

quarry a place where stone is dug, cut, or blasted out

FOSSIL DETECTIVES

by Joyce A. Churchill

What You Already Know

You can learn a great deal about Earth, and the plants and animals that live on it, from rocks. Rocks can form both above and below the surface of Earth. They form in many layers. By studying the different layers, scientists can figure out Earth's past and present.

Minerals, which are natural, nonliving crystals, combine to form rocks. Scientists can identify rock-forming minerals through their properties. Color and luster are properties of minerals that relate to the way light reflects from the surface of rocks. A mineral's hardness is measured by how easily it can be scratched. The color of the powder that the mineral leaves behind after being scratched is another property called streak.

Three kinds of rock have been found on Earth: igneous, metamorphic, and sedimentary. All three kinds can change from one to another over time. This process is called the rock cycle.

igneous rock

metamorphic rock

sedimentary rock

Horner explains that hunting for dinosaur fossils is not a simple or exact science. It is not just collecting and organizing fossil bones. You have to look carefully at the clues you collect. Then you need to consider many possibilities about how these animals lived.

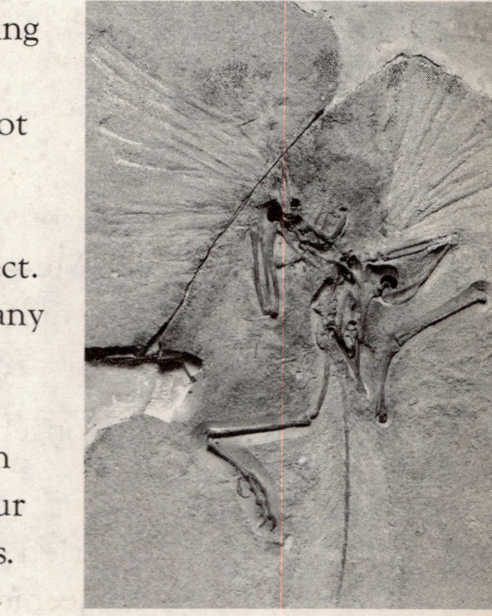

The Archaeopteryx was both a bird and a reptile.

98

Men and women have been hunting and collecting dinosaur fossils for more than 200 years. Yet they still don't know the complete history of dinosaurs. They know that these giants once lived on each of the Earth's continents. They know what some of them looked like and how they lived. But they don't know exactly why they suddenly became extinct.

Some scientists say we have only found and collected a small number of the fossilized remains of dinosaurs. We don't know the full story yet. We have to keep digging. There is still much work for fossil detectives to do.

John R. Horner

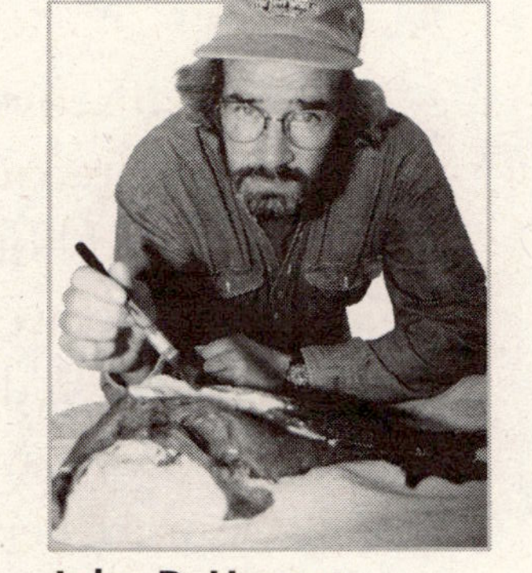

John R. Horner

John R. Horner had trouble in school as a boy because of a learning disability. Yet he has collected and cataloged fossils since he was seven years old.

In 1978, he found the first nest of baby dinosaurs in Montana. He named this new dinosaur the Maiasaura. The babies were about the size of a crow.

The next year he found the remains of a herd of more than ten thousand Maiasaurs. He also has found eggs and more nesting grounds. Horner's discoveries show that some dinosaurs were cared for by their parents, instead of having to fend for themselves as soon as they hatched.

model of a Maiasaura nest

Igneous rocks form from molten (melted) or partly molten rock deep below Earth's surface. Rock is melted by the intense heat that causes volcanic eruptions. Dead plant and animal matter combines with bits of rock to form soil, which settles on the bottoms of lakes, rivers, and oceans. This is called sediment. This material can be moved by water, ice, wind, or gravity to form layers. These layers press together and become sedimentary rock. Metamorphic rock can form from any kind of rock as a result of heat and pressure deep below Earth's surface.

Fossils in sedimentary rock give scientists clues to what lived on Earth hundreds of millions of years ago. Fossils are the bones, teeth, leaves, or any evidence of a living thing from long ago. Scientists must be good detectives to find and figure out the clues.

fossil of a dinosaur footprint

Layers of Clues

Do you like to spend hours solving riddles, playing games, and fitting together puzzles? Then you might want to become a paleontologist. You would be a scientist who studies fossils to discover what Earth was like long ago. You would be a fossil detective!

Paleontologists search for the answers to many questions. What creatures lived on Earth? What did they eat? Were these creatures mammals? Were they reptiles? Were they birds? Why did they disappear? The list of questions goes on and on.

Over the past 200 years, fossil detectives have answered some of these questions. Giant birds and reptiles that we now call dinosaurs lived from 65 million to over 200 million years ago. Scientists know that these strange creatures lived on each of Earth's continents.

A paleontologist searches for fossils.

Brown discovered his first *T rex* in 1902. He then discovered an even better skeleton in 1908. He assembled both in the Museum of Natural History. Years later, the first skeleton Brown discovered was moved to the Carnegie Museum in Pittsburgh, Pennsylvania.

The fossils revealed that the *T rex* had a huge jaw that helped it devour nearly any food it wanted. It was between fifteen and twenty feet tall and almost forty feet long. It weighed between five and seven tons.

Barnum Brown also discovered the duck-billed Corythosaurus from the Cretaceous period. He found its skeleton in the Red Deer River in Alberta, Canada.

Tyrannosaurus rex

Reconstructing Fossils

Putting together the skeleton of a giant, extinct reptile such as the Allosaurus is a challenging job. You must know anatomy and the bone structure of similar animals in order to put each part in the right place.

reconstructing an Allosaurus skeleton

Barnum Brown

Barnum Brown

Barnum Brown was named after P. T. Barnum, the nineteenth-century American showman and circus founder. He began picking up the fossils of extinct animals as a boy in Kansas. He collected fossils for more than sixty-six years as a paleontologist.

Brown loved working in the field collecting fossils. He searched for dinosaur remains in the United States, Canada, South America, India, and Ethiopia.

Brown discovered the skeletal remains of *Tyrannosaurus rex*. The *T rex* was displayed in the American Museum of Natural History in New York City, where Brown was the curator for many years.

Barnum Brown supervised the assembly of many dinosaur skeletons.

fossilized fish

Scientists have developed a geologic time scale to study fossils in the layers and layers of sedimentary rock. They agree that dinosaurs first appeared, lived, and then disappeared during the Mesozoic era on their scale. This is the middle period in the history of Earth.

Using pieces of skeletons and other fossils as clues, scientists have figured out what some dinosaurs looked like and how they lived. But before they can figure all that out, they first have to find the pieces and put them together!

How a Fossil Is Formed

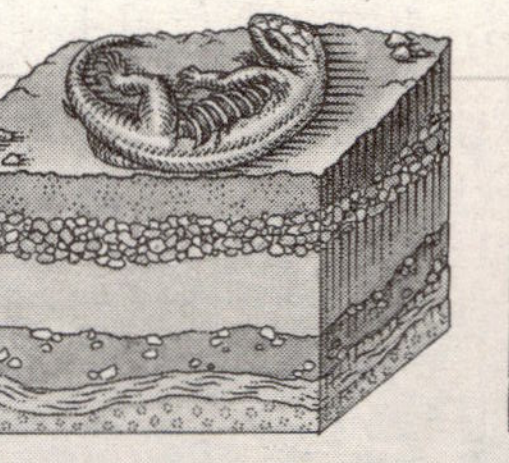

Fossils are the remains of plants and animals that once lived. When a dinosaur died, its body was slowly covered by layers of sedimentary rock.

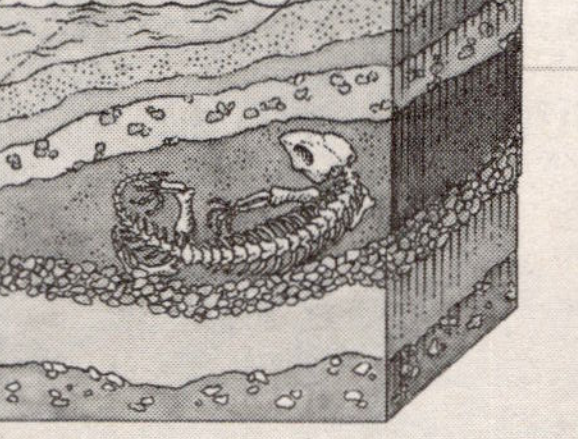

The hard parts of the animal, such as the bones, are preserved in the layers. Eggs, skin, and even footprints of dinosaurs harden as they slowly become fossils.

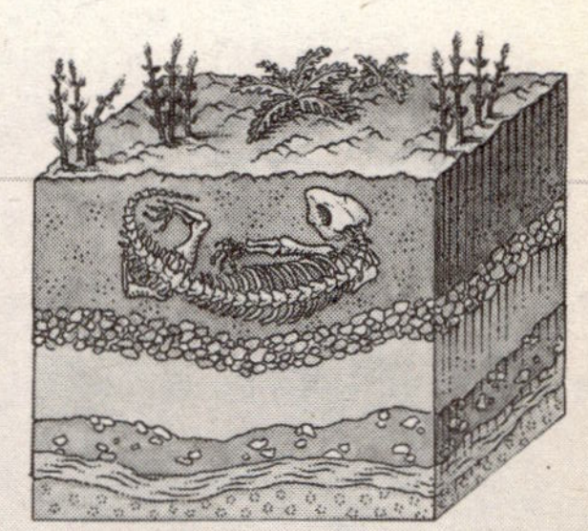

After millions of years of erosion and weathering, the bones appear at the surface. They poke through the soil, where they are discovered.

Paleontology Pioneers

Before the 1800s, a few large fossil bones were found sticking out of the ground. No one knew what they were from. Once scientists identified the fossils as the remains of dinosaurs, they became fascinated with these mysterious creatures.

Mary Anning

Mary Anning

You might not think of a young, uneducated girl as being an important dinosaur fossil collector, but Mary Anning was one. Anning, born in 1799, and her brother collected fossils with their father. After his death, they continued scouring the cliffs near their home in Lyme Regis in southern England. They sold the fossils they found to help support the family.

Anning and her brother looking for fossils

Werner Janensch

Werner Janensch

The huge Brachiosaurus, or "arm lizard," was a giant land animal from the late Jurassic period. Werner Janensch, a German paleontologist, first collected its bones during an expedition to East Africa, in what is now the country of Tanzania, from 1909 to 1913.

Janensch shipped tons of bones back to the Natural History Museum of Berlin. He and other scientists unpacked the bones and assembled them piece by piece into a giant skeleton. Their work was like putting together a jigsaw puzzle that is as tall as a four-story building!

Janensch and workers with a Brachiosaurus bone

Extracting Fossils

Fossils have to be chipped out of rocks with great care. The more carefully preserved the fossil is, the more scientists can learn from it.

removing a fossil

Edward Drinker Cope

Edward Drinker Cope

Edward Drinker Cope was a hard-working paleontologist who looked for dinosaur remains. He explored in the western United States between 1870 and 1890.

Some of the biggest dinosaur graveyards are in the western United States. The bones of giant animals such as the Diplodocus, Stegosaurus, and Triceratops have been found there.

In the science of paleontology, if you find a new dinosaur species, you have the honor of naming it. After Othniel Charles Marsh insulted Cope, they became enemies. They competed in the West to find, document, and name new species. This was called the Bone War.

Cope used dynamite to blast his way through to hidden bones.

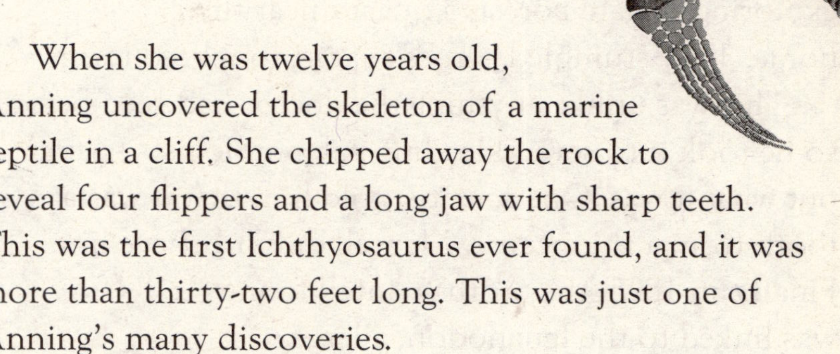

Plesiosaurus fossil

When she was twelve years old, Anning uncovered the skeleton of a marine reptile in a cliff. She chipped away the rock to reveal four flippers and a long jaw with sharp teeth. This was the first Ichthyosaurus ever found, and it was more than thirty-two feet long. This was just one of Anning's many discoveries.

The leading scientists of the time did not want to give Anning credit for her findings. Finally, after Anning's many years of hard work, they recognized the importance of her discoveries.

Tools for Fossil Hunting
Uncovering a skeleton embedded in rock takes time and patience. The hammer and chisel remove fossils from a rock. The pick chips away dirt from a bone. The brush dusts away any remaining dirt.

Gideon Mantell

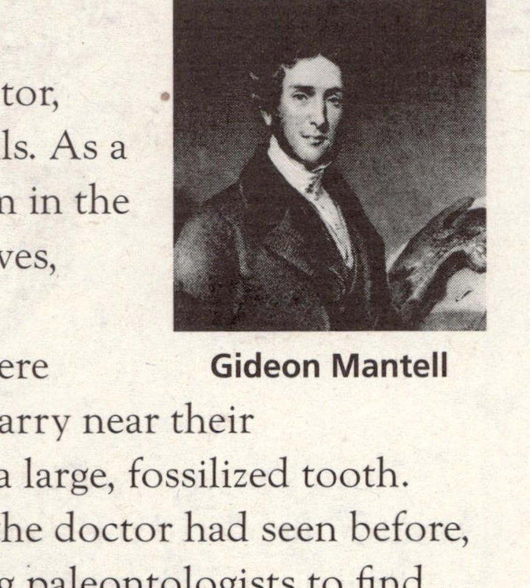

Gideon Mantell

Gideon Mantell was a doctor, but he loved hunting for fossils. As a young boy he hunted for them in the quarries near his home in Lewes, Sussex, England.

In 1822, he and his wife were exploring Tilgate Forest, a quarry near their home. They stumbled across a large, fossilized tooth.

This was unlike anything the doctor had seen before, so he took it to several leading paleontologists to find out what it was. One scientist told him that it was a tooth from a rhinoceros. Mantell didn't believe him. Finally, in 1825, the tooth Mantell found was linked to the Iguanodon, a large, plant-eating dinosaur.

Mantell lecturing on his discoveries

fossilized Iguanodon tooth

Othniel Charles Marsh

Othniel Charles Marsh

Othniel Charles Marsh was a respected vertebrate paleontologist in the 1800s. Marsh was an "armchair paleontologist," who collected fossils as a hobby. He didn't like to go into the field to collect the fossils. Marsh preferred to quietly sort and catalog fossils at the Peabody Museum at Yale University, where he worked.

Marsh discussing his fossil finds

His friend Edward Drinker Cope, a younger paleontologist, had proudly assembled the skeleton of the Elasmosaurus, a giant dinosaur. So Marsh went to look at the skeleton. He quickly pointed out to Cope where the body parts were mixed up. This started a bitter feud between the two men that lasted more than twenty years.

Keeping Records

Keeping accurate records of where bones are found is important. Paleontologists can match the location of fossils in sedimentary rock with the times that animals lived on the Earth.

Genre	Comprehension Skill	Text Features	Science Content
Nonfiction	Compare and Contrast	• Labels • Call Outs • Maps • Glossary	Earth's Surface

Scott Foresman Science 4.9

scottforesman.com

ISBN 0-328-13885-1
9 780328 138852 90000

Science

Earth Science

Ice!

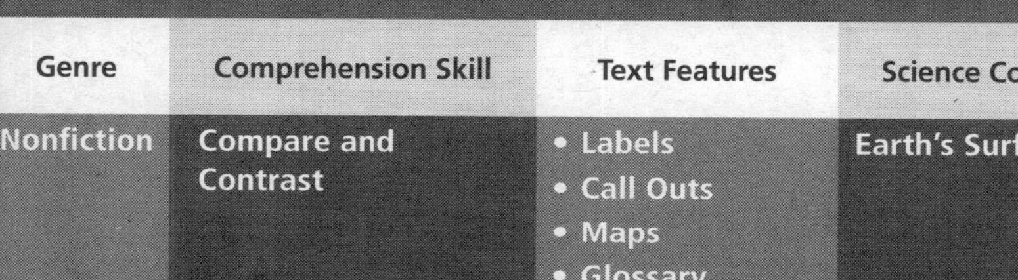

by Anne Cambal

What did you learn?

1. What effect does melting ice have on Earth's surface?
2. What places on Earth are included in the area known as the Arctic?
3. Where can glaciers be found?
4. **Writing** in Science Icy weather can take many forms. Describe some of these forms. Include details from the book to support your answer.
5. **Compare and Contrast** How are ice shelves and icebergs similar? How are they different?

Vocabulary	Extended Vocabulary
deposition	cryosphere
earthquake	fjords
erosion	hexagonal
fault	ice shelf
landform	pellet
landslide	permafrost
volcano	topsoil
weathering	

Picture Credits
Every effort has been made to secure permission and provide appropriate credit for photographic material. The publisher deeply regrets any omission and pledges to correct errors called to its attention in subsequent editions.

Photo locators denoted as follows: Top (T), Center (C), Bottom (B), Left (L), Right (R), Background (Bkgd).

2 William W. Bacon III/Photo Researchers, Inc.; 7 Gavin Hellier/Alamy Images; 8 Norbert Wu/Minden Pictures; 10 Tui De Roy/Minden Pictures; 11 (T) Digital Stock; 12 (C) Per Breiehagen/Getty Images; 14 (TL) David Boag/Alamy Images.

ISBN: 0-328-13885-1

2 3 4 5 6 7 8 9 10 V004 13 12 11 10 09 08 07 06 05

Glossary

cryosphere the part of Earth's surface where ice and snow are found year-round

fjords long, narrow bodies of water between steep slopes

hexagonal having six sides

ice shelf a thick, permanent sheet of ice that is attached to land

pellet a little ball

permafrost a layer of permanently frozen soil

topsoil the upper part of the soil

by Anne Cambal

PEARSON Scott Foresman

What You Already Know

The outer layer of Earth is made of rock. It is called the crust. The Earth's crust can have many different shapes. It also has many landforms, such as plains, valleys, and canyons. Landforms are broken down into smaller pieces through weathering. Physical weathering changes only the size of rocks. In chemical weathering, there is a change in the material that makes up rocks.

Erosion is the process by which pieces of Earth's surface are moved from one place to another. Erosion can be caused by water, ice, gravity, and wind. Deposition is when pieces of rocks are left in a new place. This can happen slowly or quickly. Erosion can be controlled. Plants grown on hills help hold topsoil in place, which stops erosion.

Gravity pulls loose material from a high place to a low place. In a landslide, many rocks and pieces of soil move downhill quickly. An avalanche happens when a great deal of snow and ice move down a mountain quickly.

Fun with Ice

Ice is more than just a product of cold weather. You can use ice to cool a warm drink. You can even make art from a piece of ice! In icy or snowy weather, you can go ice skating, skiing, and sledding.

Ice is one of Earth's features. It can be as huge in scale and wonder as the glaciers at the poles or as small as frost on a cold morning. Either way, ice is an important part of life on Earth.

This swan sculpture is made of ice.

Frost can form on trees and leaves when it is cold.

Frost is often found on cold mornings. Water from the air can form on cooler objects and freeze. These crystals of ice can be so thick that they look like snow.

There are three kinds of these icy coatings. Hoarfrost is frozen dew that creates a crystal-like, white covering on whatever it touches. Rime is a thicker coating of ice that can take the shape of spikes or feathers. Fern frost is frozen dew that forms fernlike patterns on glass.

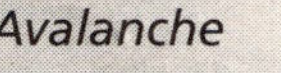

Avalanche

Far below the ground churns magma, which is very hot rock that has partly melted into a liquid. When gas forces the magma upward, it breaks through the Earth's crust and erupts, forming a volcano. Volcanoes that have erupted in recorded history are active, while those that have not are dormant.

The layer below Earth's crust is the upper mantle. The crust and upper mantle are divided into plates. A fault is a crack in rocks where Earth's crust can move. Rocks may get stuck at a fault, but the plates continue to move. This puts pressure on the rocks, forcing them to break. The plates then move suddenly and cause the crust to shake. This shaking is an earthquake. Volcanoes and earthquakes cause quick changes to Earth's surface.

Ice also changes Earth's surface. It can be found in many places and take many shapes. Let's look at the different shapes ice can have.

Ice on Earth

Two of the coldest places on Earth are the North and South Poles. The freezing, icy section around the North Pole is called the Arctic. This very large area includes the Arctic Ocean and parts of North America, Asia, and Europe. Greenland, the world's largest island, is also part of the Arctic, as are many other islands. The South Pole is in Antarctica, the coldest and windiest continent on Earth.

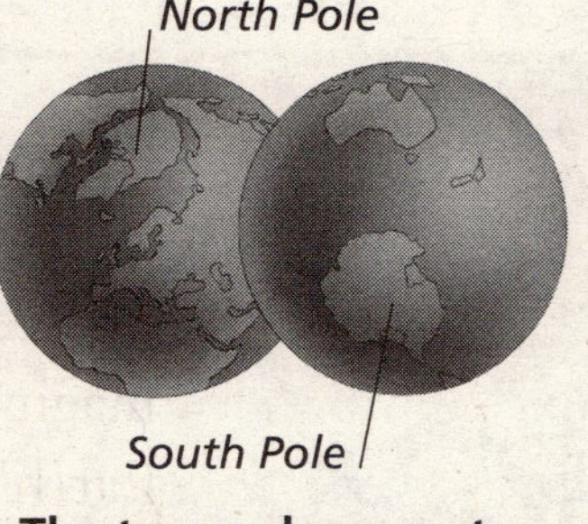

The two poles are at the top and bottom of Earth.

The Arctic and Antarctic regions are part of the cryosphere. The cryosphere refers to the parts of Earth where water is found year-round as ice or snow. This includes areas with glaciers, sea ice, freshwater ice, and frozen ground, which is called permafrost.

People can live in the Arctic, but it is very cold.

As pieces of ice fall and rise in a cloud, water sticks to them and freezes. Strong winds may carry the ice up and down many times. The layers of ice form hail. When hailstones get heavy, they fall to the ground. They can be as small as peas or larger than golf balls.

When rain hits objects that are colder than 32°F, it freezes. This icy glaze is freezing rain. Freezing rain can be dangerous and costly. Tree limbs may break from the weight of the ice. Icicles form on houses. When the ice on a house melts, it may seep into cracks and cause leaks.

Icicles form in cold weather.

Icy Weather

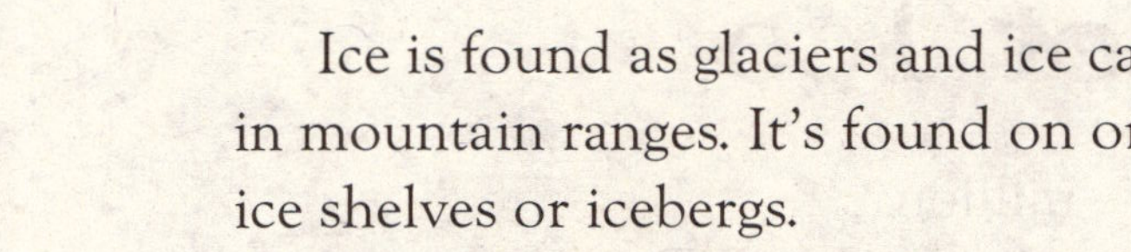

No two snowflakes are alike.

Icy weather is a feature of many regions on Earth. Snow, sleet, hail, freezing rain, and frost all cause icy conditions. How do these forms of ice differ? Why do they occur?

Snowflakes form when tiny ice crystals in clouds stick to one another. Snowflakes are hexagonal. These six-sided wonders can be fancy or plain, and each one is unique.

When rain falls through colder air near the ground and freezes, it forms sleet. Sleet looks and feels like small pellets of ice.

Ice is found as glaciers and ice caps at high altitudes in mountain ranges. It's found on or below the seas as ice shelves or icebergs.

Due to its freezing conditions, the cryosphere includes some of the most remote places on Earth. Scientific research has been conducted in these regions for many years, but it can be dangerous. Fortunately, with satellite technology, scientists can electronically measure and monitor conditions and changes in these regions. They no longer must be exposed to potentially dangerous weather.

Ice covers mountains in the cryosphere all year long.

An Age of Ice

Approximately one million years ago, glaciers covered mountains on all of Earth's continents. At that time some glaciers were several thousand feet thick. This time is known as the beginning of the Great Ice Age.

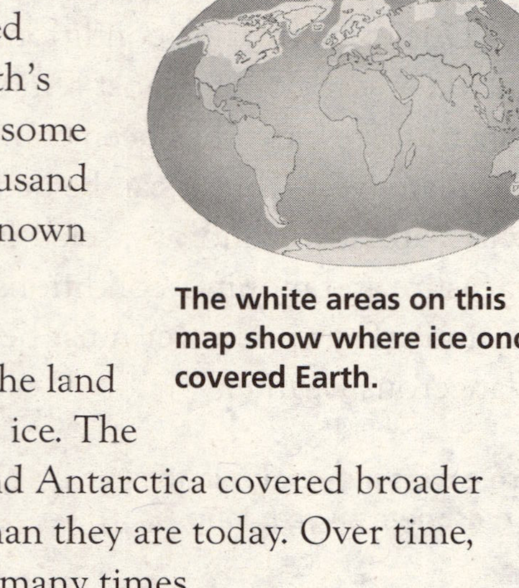
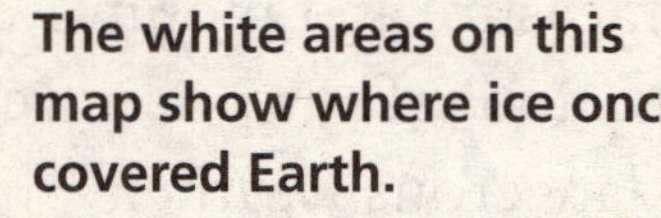

The white areas on this map show where ice once covered Earth.

Nearly one-third of the land on Earth was covered by ice. The ice caps of Greenland and Antarctica covered broader areas and were thicker than they are today. Over time, the ice melted and froze many times.

This process was repeated until about ten thousand years ago, when rising temperatures caused much of the ice on Earth to melt. As vast areas of ice disappeared, so did some types of animals. The woolly mammoth and the saber-toothed tiger were well adapted to the colder climates. Both have been extinct since the end of the Ice Age.

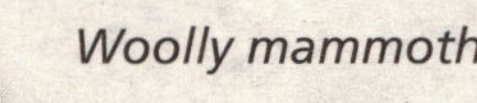

Woolly mammoth

Icebergs

Most of an iceberg is below the surface of the water.

Icebergs are giant, floating pieces of ice that have broken away from an ice shelf. Some icebergs may look white. Older, denser ice often looks blue.

Icebergs are made of fresh water. A thin layer of dust or salt water may be on the iceberg's surface. But the water in the middle of an iceberg is relatively pure.

Icebergs can change in size. Waves hitting an iceberg's sides can cause it to melt. Changes in temperature can also cause melting. This melting may cause pieces of the iceberg to break off.

The part of the iceberg that is visible above water is only the tip. As much as nine-tenths of an iceberg is under water, which makes icebergs dangerous for ships passing near them.

Melting causes the size of an iceberg to change.

Ice Shelves

Another body of ice found in the coldest regions of Earth is an ice shelf. Ice shelves are thick sheets of ice. They are extensions of ice sheets. Because they consist of floating ice that's still attached to land, ice shelves help slow the melting of the glacier and its movement due to gravity. When parts of ice shelves break free from land, they become icebergs.

This ice shelf extends far into the ocean.

Since the end of the Ice Age, the world's climates have warmed. This reduced the ice cover to what it is today—about one-tenth of the land surface on Earth. The warming made glaciers melt and ice sheets move. These frozen masses carried rocks, sand, clay, and minerals with them and deposited the materials in new areas. Sometimes they formed hills. Other times they flattened hills into plains. They also fractured mountainsides, leaving rock so smooth that it looked polished. They helped carve long, winding ocean inlets called fjords (FYORDZ). A fjord is a narrow body of deep water between steep slopes.

Fjords are typical of the geography of Norway.

Glaciers

Glaciers did not disappear completely when the Ice Age ended. They are still common in the polar regions of Earth. In this harsh climate, snow builds up over time and turns to ice. From year to year, the ice builds up and becomes a glacier. A glacier can contain ice, snow, water, rocks, and other materials. A glacier may have many cycles of melting and freezing, yet still increase in overall size.

A huge mass of ice that covers millions of acres of land is called an ice sheet. An ice sheet is a glacier that occupies space on land. The thickness and weight of ice sheets can be so great that the land under them sinks. Antarctica's ice sheet is nearly three miles thick! It covers five million square miles of land. If all of its ice gradually melted, Antarctica would slowly rise.

Gravity brought this valley glacier to its position between these mountains.

Glaciers are not just found at the poles. They can be found in nearly every freezing area on Earth, including the United States. Most U.S. glaciers are in Alaska. The Bering Glacier is more than 125 miles, or 204 kilometers, long.

Valley glaciers start near the tops of mountains. Gravity pulls them down the sides of the mountains, leaving them in the U-shaped valley below. Valley glaciers tend to be very long.

Antarctic ice sheet

Science

Science

Genre	Comprehension Skill	Text Features	Science Content
Nonfiction	Cause and Effect	• Captions • Text Boxes • Call Outs • Glossary	Natural Resources

Scott Foresman Science 4.10

PEARSON Scott Foresman

scottforesman.com

ISBN 0-328-13888-6

9 780328 138883 90000

Earth Science

Wind Power

by C. A. Barnhart

Vocabulary

conservation
fossil fuels
humus
ore
petroleum
recycling
solar cells
solar energy

Extended Vocabulary

efficiency
gearwheel
power plants
prevailing winds
rig
turbine
wind farm

Picture Credits
Every effort has been made to secure permission and provide appropriate credit for photographic material. The publisher deeply regrets any omission and pledges to correct errors called to its attention in subsequent editions.

Photo locators denoted as follows: Top (T), Center (C), Bottom (B), Left (L), Right (R), Background (Bkgd).

Opener: Jorgen Schytte/Peter Arnold, Inc.; 7 Reuters/Corbis; 9 Science Museum, London/DK Images; 11 (T) Science Museum, London/DK Images; 14 Jorgen Schytte/Peter Arnold, Inc.

ISBN: 0-328-13888-6

2 3 4 5 6 7 8 9 10 V004 13 12 11 10 09 08 07 06 05

What did you learn?

1. How can wind be used to produce electricity?
2. What causes wind?
3. What were windmills used for long ago?
4. **Writing** in Science Triangular sails catch the wind better than square sails do. Write to explain why triangular sails are more efficient. Use examples from the book to support your answer.
5. **Cause and Effect** What are some of the effects of burning fossil fuels for power?

Glossary

efficiency production of something with little waste of time or effort

gearwheel a wheel with grooves that fit into another gear

power plants stations that generate power, often by burning fossil fuels

prevailing winds winds that are most common, especially in terms of reliability, force, or direction

rig to fit a boat or ship with equipment, such as a sail, mast, and ropes

turbine a machine that has a rotating wheel with paddles attached to it that spin as the wheel turns

wind farm a cluster of wind turbines built near each other to generate electricity

Wind Power

by C. A. Barnhart

What You Already Know

People, animals, and plants all need natural resources to live. Some natural resources are replaced all the time. Although renewable natural resources are in abundant supply, they must be well cared for. Soil is one important renewable resource. Soil is renewed through weathering, erosion, and deposition. Soil contains humus. Humus is made from decaying plant and animal matter. Clay, silt, and sand are kinds of soil that have different properties. Good farming can replace nutrients in soil. Many things can be made from soil.

Solar energy is another renewable resource. Electricity can be produced from solar energy by collecting the Sun's energy with solar cells. Electricity can also be produced by using energy from moving water.

Plowing the remains of plants into the field returns nutrients to the soil.

Some people object to wind turbines claiming they are noisy. However, most of the turbines are no noisier than leaves rustling in a breeze. Another reason people may object is that they feel that wind turbines are not very nice-looking. But perhaps the benefits of using them, such as less air pollution, will make them seem more attractive.

All countries of the world need more electricity. At the same time, pollution is becoming more of a problem. Use of the world's winds to generate electricity makes wind farms an increasingly appealing way to get the electricity we need without harming the environment.

The turbines that generate electricity are designed to increase the amount of power made by the rotating blades. By increasing their power, turbines are able to produce greater amounts of electricity.

A wind farm must be located where there are steady winds. Some wind farms can produce enough electricity for a small town. Some farmers have put up a few wind turbines to produce just enough electricity to meet their own needs. Some large electric companies have begun to build very large wind farms.

Another location for wind farms is in the ocean, along a coastline. The winds are steadier over the water. They can produce electricity more efficiently.

Offshore wind farms are built in coastal waters, where they take advantage of steady winds.

Other resources that we rely upon, including fossil fuels such as natural gas, coal, and petroleum, are not easily or quickly replaced. An ore is a mineral-rich rock found in Earth's crust. Many nonrenewable mineral resources are found in ores. All natural resources are important and must be used wisely. Production of energy is a major use of fossil fuel. Electricity and gasoline keep our factories operating, our houses warm, and our transportation moving.

wind farm

There are several ways to practice conservation of our natural resources and still produce the power we need. One way is by recycling. Recycling reduces the amount of nonrenewable resources we use. Some paper and plastics are recyclable. Another way is to increase the use of renewable resources to produce power.

Wind is another natural source of renewable energy. People have used the power of the wind for centuries. Today, we are using it more and more. Read on to find out about wind power.

The Power of Wind

In order to learn how wind can be used as a source of power, first you must understand what wind is. Wind is caused by differences in temperature in Earth's atmosphere. Air flows constantly over Earth. Pockets of air rise from Earth's surface as they become warmer and their molecules become less dense. Cool air, which has more densely packed molecules, rushes in to take the place of the warm air. This movement of cold, heavy air falling and warm, lighter air rising is called wind.

Wind can have a powerful effect on landforms, or features of Earth's surface. Wind can cause erosion, changing the shape of rock formations.

Blowing wind changes the shapes of rocks by erosion.

Fossil Fuels

Smoke rising from a power plant that burns fossil fuels spreads through the air and pollutes the environment.

Wind for Electricity

Most electricity in the United States is produced in power plants that burn fossil fuels or use nuclear power or water power. There is a limited supply of fossil fuels. When fossil fuels are burned, pollutants are released into the environment. Nuclear waste from nuclear power plants is difficult and expensive to dispose of.

One solution to these problems is to produce electricity by using the wind. It is an abundant, renewable resource, which makes it an appealing source of power. Wind is also appealing because it doesn't cause pollution.

Electricity produced by wind is generated in a wind turbine. This is a kind of modern windmill designed especially to make electricity. The wind turbine has three huge blades at the top of a tall tower. These blades are turned by the wind. Similar to the Dutch and American windmills, the blades are attached to a horizontal pole. The pole turns a wheel directly behind the blades. The turbine generates electricity that is then sent over power wires. Groups of wind turbines built in one place are called wind farms.

A wind farm such as this one contains many wind turbines.

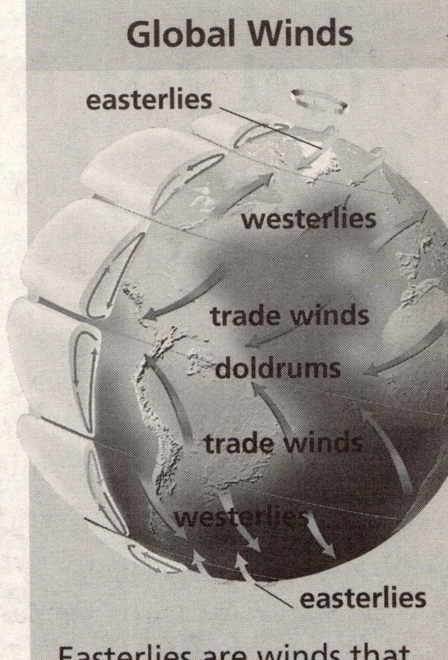

A toy pinwheel demonstrates how wind power turns a wheel.

Global Winds

easterlies
westerlies
trade winds
doldrums
trade winds
westerlies
easterlies

Easterlies are winds that blow from east to west. Westerlies are winds that blow from west to east. Trade winds are found above and below the equator and blow almost constantly. Few winds blow in the doldrums.

Earth's prevailing winds form at the equator where the air is hot and rises high into the atmosphere. Little wind results. On each side of the equator, however, a band of brisk winds blows toward it. These winds are drawn toward the equator by the heated air moving upward. Winds farther north and farther south are also affected by the hot air from the equator when they meet cold air from the North and South Poles.

Although you can't see wind, it is a very powerful force. The spinning motion of this toy pinwheel is physical evidence of the wind's effect.

Wind for Movement

Until the 1900s, the main power for ships was the wind. Today, sailing ships are used mostly for education and sport.

A sailboat today is not very different from ships of ancient times. All are moved by the wind. All have sails controlled by ropes.

A newer and portable sailboat is the sailboard. It is a surfboard with a sail. The rider sails or windsurfs while standing up and steers by pulling in and letting out the sail. Sailboards tip easily.

Sailboats and sailboards used for sport have triangular sails to catch the wind.

Windmills

A windmill such as this was used to grind grain. This model shows the gearwheel, which changed the direction of power from horizontal to vertical. The grindstone was used for grinding the grain.

This vertical pole worked the pump that was located at the bottom of the windmill. Later windmills had wheels that could be turned in any direction to face the wind. This marked a great improvement in their efficiency. These new windmills could use the wind no matter which way it was blowing.

These windmills in La Mancha, Spain, were used for grinding grain.

It is thought that the first windmills were built in what is now Iran, about fourteen hundred years ago. These early windmills had a wheel with sails that turned as they caught the wind. The wheel was fastened to the top of a pole. The wheel turned this pole. These early windmills were used mostly to grind grain.

Since the wheel of this early windmill was fastened to the top of the pole, the wind had to blow directly on the sails from a particular direction. This meant the windmills were quite inefficient.

By about 1100, windmills appeared in Europe, especially in what is now the Netherlands. There they were used mostly to pump water away from land that was often flooded by the sea. In these Dutch windmills, the wheel or sails were attached to a horizontal pole. People used gears and pulleys to transfer the power from the horizontal pole to a vertical pole.

The ancient Egyptians were probably the first people to use the wind to move boats. They are credited with developing cloth sails around 3300 B.C. The first sails were square. Square sails worked well when the wind came from behind the boat. The wind would then fill the sail and move the boat forward. If the wind came from the wrong direction, however, the only way to move a boat with a square sail was by rowing.

Clipper ships have many sails that can catch the wind.

About two thousand years ago, ships traveling on the Mediterranean Sea began using triangular sails. The sail was fixed to a pole called a mast. Ropes were used to move the sail from one side to another. The sail could catch the wind from any direction. Later, ships were rigged with a combination of square and triangular sails. Many sails meant more power and speed from the wind. Ships could be larger. A clipper ship is an example of a ship with such rigging.

Gliders, hang gliders, and balloons move through the air and return to Earth's surface using only wind power. Gliders fly along wind currents after being towed into the air by a plane or after catching the wind on a hillside or cliff. Hang gliders catch the wind in the same way. Weather balloons are carried by winds to make weather observations. A kite catches the wind in its sails and soars through the air. All these ways of flying use the wind not only to go higher, farther, and faster, but also to steer and to land.

glider

A kite is released into the air. You can guide it with a string while the wind carries it.

Wind for Machines

People have used wind power to operate machines for centuries. Wind is turned into power for machines in a way similar to the way a paper pinwheel works. A wheel catches the wind and turns, changing the power of the wind into a power that works machinery.

In the United States, windmills were used on farms in the 1800s to pump water from wells deep underground. These windmills had a wheel that could turn in any direction to face the wind. The wheel was guided by a vane at the other end of a horizontal pole. This horizontal pole transferred power to a vertical pole. This power operated a pump underground.

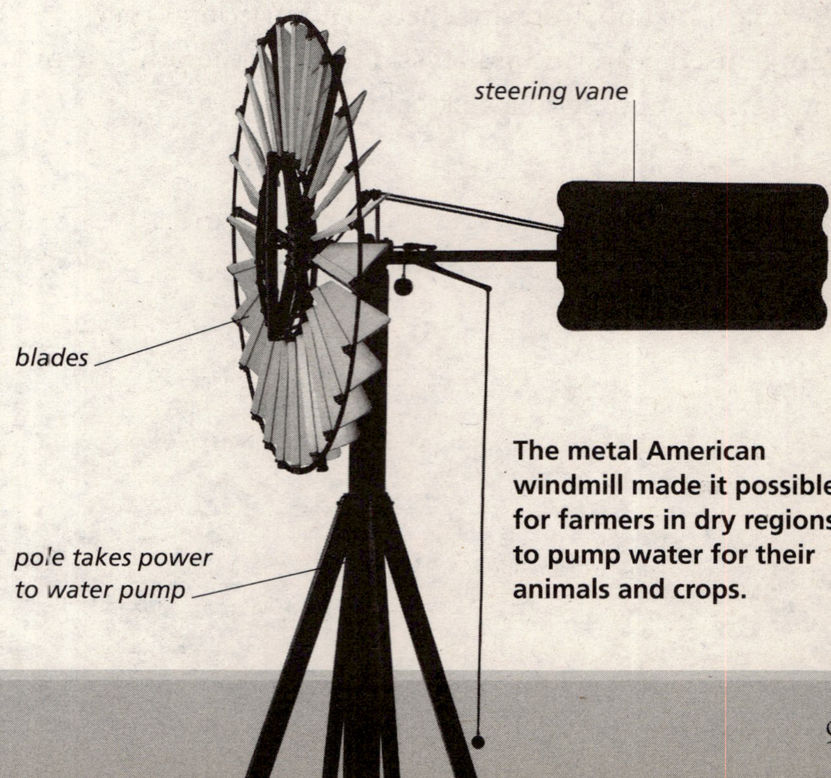

The metal American windmill made it possible for farmers in dry regions to pump water for their animals and crops.

Genre	Comprehension Skill	Text Features	Science Content
Nonfiction	Compare and Contrast	• Captions • Diagrams • Text Boxes • Glossary	Matter

Scott Foresman Science 4.11

scottforesman.com

ISBN 0-328-13891-6
9 780328 138913 90000

Science

Science

Physical Science

Lighter Than Air

by Johanna Lee

Vocabulary

chemical change
density
mixture
physical change
solubility
solute
solution
solvent

Extended Vocabulary

ballonets
buoyancy
dirigible
displace
helium
hover
hydrogen

Picture Credits
Every effort has been made to secure permission and provide appropriate credit for photographic material. The publisher deeply regrets any omission and pledges to correct errors called to its attention in subsequent editions.

Photo locators denoted as follows: Top (T), Center (C), Bottom (B), Left (L), Right (R), Background (Bkgd).

Opener: Michael Howell/Index Stock Imagery; 5 Michael Howell/Index Stock Imagery; 7 ©Science Museum/DK Images; 14 Bob Kramer/Index Stock Imagery; 19 Topham/The Image Works, Inc.; 22 Reuters/Corbis; 23 Balloon Program Office/NASA.

ISBN: 0-328-13891-6

2 3 4 5 6 7 8 9 10 V004 13 12 11 10 09 08 07 06 05

What did you learn?

1. How did the Montgolfier brothers make the first hot-air balloon?

2. How does a hot-air balloon rise?

3. Why was the *Hindenburg* famous?

4. **Writing** in Science The dirigible was invented after the hot-air balloon. Explain how the dirigible improved upon the hot-air balloon. Support your answer with details from the book.

5. **Compare and Contrast** What do hot-air balloons and zeppelins have in common? What are some of their differences?

Glossary

ballonets the airbags that line the inside of an airship

buoyancy the force that allows an object to float

dirigible an airship that can be steered

displace push away and take the place of

helium a gas that is less dense than air and does not burn

hover float in the air

hydrogen a gas that is less dense than air and can burn

Lighter Than Air

by Johanna Lee

What You Already Know

Matter is anything that has mass and takes up space. There are many ways to identify properties of matter, such as by using your senses or by performing simple tests. The three most familiar states, or phases, of matter are solid, liquid, and gas. The state of matter is determined by the movement and arrangement of its particles.

Matter has properties that can be measured. Scientists use metric units when they measure and compare matter. Mass is the amount of matter in an object. Mass can be measured with a pan balance. Volume is the amount of space that matter takes up. Volume can be measured with a graduated cylinder or unit cubes. Density is the amount of mass in a certain volume of matter.

The cork has the least density of any substance in the container.

Scientists use balloons for research and to forecast the weather. The National Aeronautics and Space Administration, or NASA, sends about 25 scientific balloons into space each year. Although smaller than most hot-air balloons, NASA's balloons carry several tons of equipment and soar 25 miles into the atmosphere. The instruments on the balloons help NASA learn more about the Earth's atmosphere and record data on the stars and planets. The National Oceanic and Atmospheric Administration, or NOAA, also gathers information using hot-air balloons.

More than 200 years after balloons were first invented, people continue to experiment to find more and better uses for balloons and airships.

NASA scientists are developing the Ultra Long Duration Balloon, a balloon that can stay in flight for a very long period of time.

Modern Uses

Several different industries use modern airships and hot-air balloons. Companies use blimps to advertise the brand names of their products. Blimps carry cameras to film sporting events.

Modern hot-air balloons are much like the first ones invented. However, there are some important differences. The new balloons are made of lighter but stronger materials, such as nylon. Nylon melts at a very high temperature. That means it is unlikely to catch fire or become damaged by the balloon's propane burners, which provide the heat to lift the balloon.

Balloons can travel greater distances than in the past. In 1999, two men flew a hot-air balloon around the world without stopping or refueling. Then, in 2002, a man flew around the world solo in a hot-air balloon!

This airship displays a message to the athletes in the 2000 Sydney Olympics.

Matter can be combined to form mixtures. A mixture is a combination of two or more substances that can be easily separated. The substances have the same properties when they are mixed as they had before they were mixed. A solution is a kind of mixture in which one or more substances are dissolved into another. The substance that is dissolved is the solute. The substance that dissolves the other substance is the solvent. Solubility is the ability of one substance to dissolve into another.

When you make a mixture, you are making a kind of physical change. A physical change is a change in the size, shape, or state of matter. A chemical change occurs when the particles of a substance change to form a new substance.

In this book, you will learn about the changes in the volume and density of air that allow hot-air balloons to rise and fly through the sky.

Introduction

Have you ever seen a brightly colored hot-air balloon float above the treetops? Maybe you wondered how the balloon was able to stay in the air without wings or an engine. The explanation is simple. The air inside the balloon is less dense than the air outside the balloon, and this allows it to rise.

Hot-air balloons consist of three basic parts: a basket, a heater, and the balloon itself. The pilot and passengers ride in the basket that hangs under the balloon. A heater is mounted above the basket and below a small opening in the balloon.

A flame from the heater warms the air inside the balloon. When air is heated, a physical change takes place. The air expands, which makes it lighter than the cooler air outside the balloon. Lighter air rises, so the balloon rises too.

People all over the world enjoy the sport of ballooning.

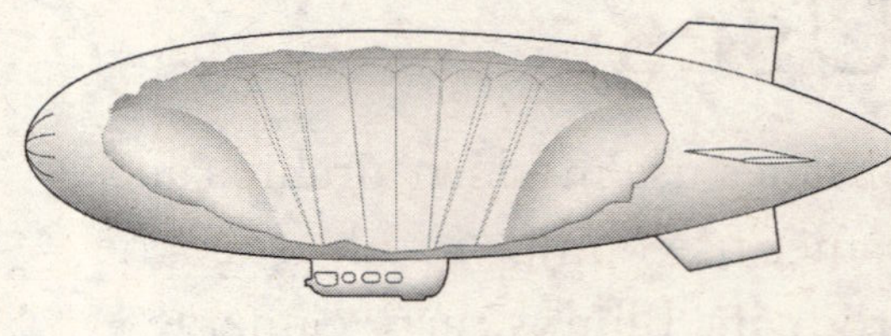

Ballonets, or airbags, line the inside of the airship. They allow the helium to expand safely as the airship climbs in the air.

Another important difference is that the airships of today use helium instead of hydrogen. Helium has a few disadvantages when compared to hydrogen. Although it is much less dense than air, it is denser than hydrogen. This makes it less efficient. Helium is less abundant than hydrogen, so it is also more expensive.

But helium's biggest advantage is that it is safer than hydrogen. Helium will not catch fire. Because of this, laws now require all airships that carry passengers to use helium. Several special systems located within an airship's gondola monitor the pressure of the helium inside of the envelope, or main body, of the airship.

The body of a modern airship is called an envelope.

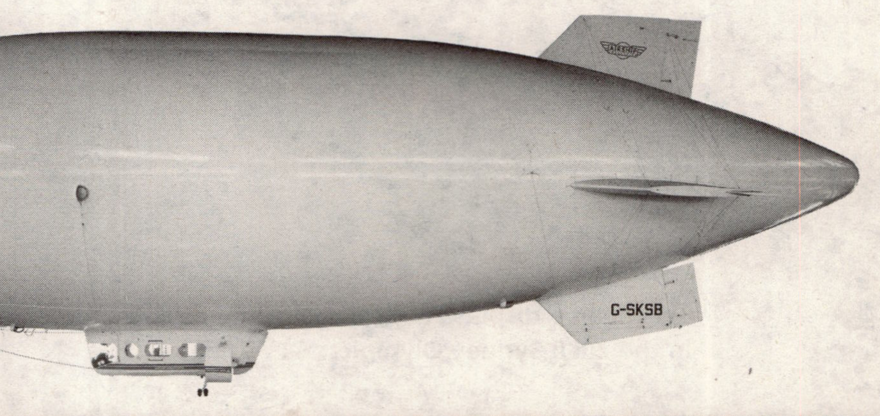

Giants of the Air

Many years have passed since the *Hindenburg* disaster. Airships are being built again. Modern airships still have engines so that pilots can steer them in any direction.

However, the new airships are different from the earlier ones in several ways. Their engines are much lighter and more powerful. New materials, such as Kevlar fibers, are used to construct modern airships. The inside of a modern airship's gondola—the cabin in which the pilots and passengers sit—has the kind of communications, control, and guidance systems found in other modern commercial aircraft.

Modern airships, often called blimps, are also much smaller than the airships of the past. Blimps are only about one-fourth the size of the *Hindenburg.* Early airships had frames, but modern blimps do not.

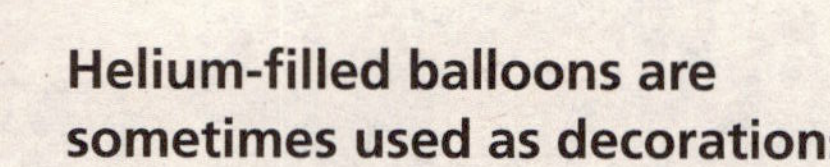

Helium-filled balloons are sometimes used as decorations.

Other balloons contain gases such as hydrogen or helium. Hydrogen and helium have extremely low densities. How low? Approximately 100 elements occur naturally on Earth. Of them, hydrogen and helium are the least dense.

Earth's atmosphere is composed mainly of nitrogen, with lesser amounts of oxygen and argon. Compared to most other elements, these three gases have low densities. However, they are much denser than hydrogen and helium. Because hydrogen and helium are less dense than the gases that make up our atmosphere, balloons containing them can float.

Balloon Pioneers

More than 200 years ago, people became curious about flight. Two of these people were Joseph Michel and Jacques Étienne Montgolfier, brothers who lived in France. They conducted experiments with paper bags filled with hot air. Their experiments led to the invention of the first hot-air balloon.

Their balloon was a silk bag that was lined with paper. In June, the brothers sent a balloon without passengers into the air. On September 19, 1783, they were ready to attempt the first hot-air balloon flight with passengers. A crowd that included King Louis XVI and Queen Marie Antoinette assembled at Versailles, France, to watch as a sheep, a rooster, and a duck were loaded into the basket below the balloon.

The Montgolfier brothers incorrectly thought that smoke caused the bags to rise.

People were so horrified when they learned about the *Hindenburg* disaster that the popularity of airship travel came to an end.

Explosive Beginnings

Zeppelins contained hydrogen gas. The advantage of using hydrogen was that it is less dense than air. The disadvantage was that it is highly flammable, which means that it can catch fire easily. In fact, an explosion of a zeppelin resulted in the end of airship travel.

The most famous zeppelin was the *Hindenburg*. It was more than 800 feet long. After its first flight in 1936, the *Hindenburg* made many flights back and forth across the Atlantic Ocean from Germany to America. Unfortunately, on May 6, 1937, the *Hindenburg* burst into flames just as it was about to dock in New Jersey. Although there were survivors, 36 people died in the explosion.

The *Hindenburg* was many times as large as a jumbo jet.

Pilâtre de Rozier and the Marquis d'Arlandes were the passengers in the Montgolfier balloon.

Ropes were used to keep the balloon from flying away too soon. When the ropes were released, the balloon lifted about 1,500 ft into the air. Several minutes later, the balloon and its passengers landed safely.

Encouraged by the flight's success, the Montgolfiers moved on to the next challenge—a balloon flight with human passengers. In October, 1783, they sent a man eighty feet into the air in a balloon that was tethered to the ground. Then on November 21, 1783, in Paris, two men lifted off in the brothers' balloon. This time, the men would fly free.

The men had to keep a fire burning in order to keep the balloon aloft. After a flight of about 25 minutes, the balloon landed a few miles from Paris, with the men aboard unharmed.

Moving Molecules

The Montgolfiers believed they had discovered a new gas. Naming it "Montgolfier gas," they thought it was less dense than air, and therefore made their balloons fly. But they were wrong. Unlike modern hot-air balloons, the gas inside their balloons contained neither hydrogen nor helium. In fact, it was no different from the gases that make up the air outside.

The real reason the Montgolfiers' balloon flew was that it used heated air. Air is a gas. The molecules in a gas are spread far apart, and they move around on their own. When air is heated, its molecules move faster. The molecules spread even farther apart. As a result, the molecules of hot air take up more space, or volume, than the molecules of cooler air. This means the density of the air has decreased.

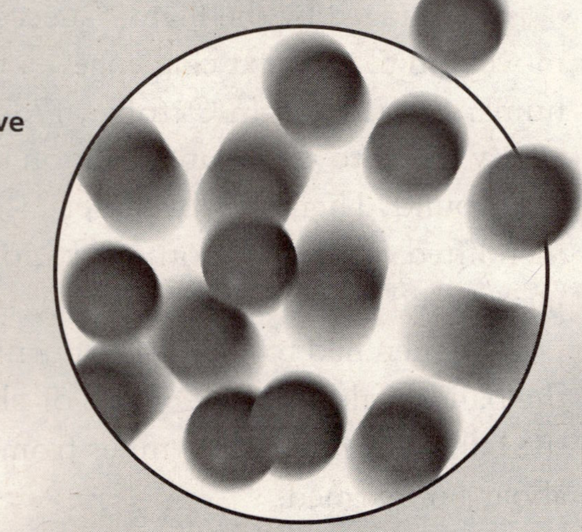

Gas molecules move on their own, but they move faster when heated.

Zeppelins were used as bombers in World War I.

Zeppelin and his team used gas engines to turn the propellers on their airships. Gas engines were lighter than the steam engines used by Giffard. These airships were called zeppelins, after their inventor.

One well-known zeppelin was the *Graf Zeppelin*. This airship was 775 feet long and could fly as fast as 80 miles per hour. The airship flew around the world in less than 22 days.

Airships differed from hot-air balloons in several ways. First of all, airships were much larger, in order to carry passengers and cargo. Also, they were filled with hydrogen rather than hot air. Finally, airships were much more luxurious than hot-air balloons.

Giffard's airship

Airships

In 1852, a determined inventor named Henri Giffard built a long, thin, balloon-like vehicle that could be steered. His vehicle was fitted with a steam engine and a propeller. A device called a rudder was used to steer it. Giffard's vehicle was called a dirigible, from a Latin word meaning "to direct." It was the first airship.

Several years later, a German count named Ferdinand von Zeppelin designed airships that were more efficient than the early ones.

During the 1920s and 1930s, airship travel was luxurious.

poster of an airship

The experiment shown here demonstrates how hot air rises. A bottle with a balloon stretched over its top is placed into a container of water. The water is heated until it becomes warmer than the air inside the bottle. The heat from the water transfers to the air inside the bottle.

The heat forces the air's molecules to move faster and farther apart. In order to do so, they need more space. Where can they find it? The water prevents them from sinking. The bottle blocks them from spreading out. The only way they can escape is by moving up through the bottle's opening. So the warmer air rises and expands into the balloon. This is what happens when the air in a hot-air balloon is heated.

Warm water causes the balloon to expand. What do you predict would happen if the bottle were placed into a container of cold water?

Density

The density of an object is the quotient of its mass divided by its volume. If objects have the same volume but different mass, the density of the objects is also different. For example, the three balls pictured below have the same volume. However, the mass of the balls is different. The hardwood ball has the greatest mass, so it has the greatest density.

The density of an object determines whether or not it will float in water or in air. If the density of an object is greater than the density of water, the object will sink. If the density is less, the object will float.

The human body is about two-thirds water. Overall our bodies are slightly less dense than water. Because of that, we float in water, but just barely.

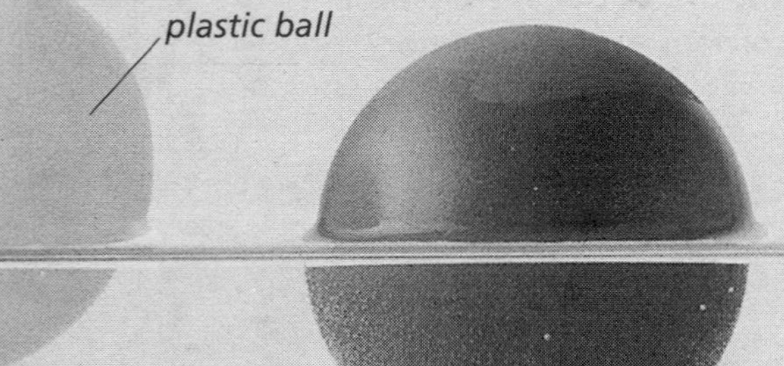

These balls are the same size and shape. However, since their masses are different, their densities are also different.

Up, Up, and Away

After the Montgolfier brothers invented the hot-air balloon, ballooning quickly became a popular sport. Colorful balloons of different shapes and sizes could be seen floating in the sky.

The early balloonists faced several challenges. They had to fill the bags of their balloons with hot air while they were still on the ground or carry open fires while they floated. Since hot-air balloons depend on the wind, balloonists had to move in the direction the wind blew. Without a push from the wind, the balloon would just hover in the air. Balloonists became annoyed with not being able to control the direction of their balloons. They tried to figure out ways to move and steer their balloons.

The Rise and Fall of a Balloon

The balloon is filled with hot air. This allows it to rise. When the air inside cools, the balloon comes back to the ground. The air is let out until the next flight.

Fire is used to heat the air in balloons. Unfortunately, fires can cause accidents.

The picture below of a peeled lemon and an unpeeled lemon shows objects with different densities. The peeled lemon sinks because its density is greater than the density of the water. The unpeeled lemon is less dense than the water because lemon rind is full of air bubbles. So the unpeeled lemon floats.

When you blow into a balloon, you fill it with air from your lungs. That air is warmer than the surrounding air. Its molecules are traveling at a faster speed and spread out farther, making the air less dense. So the balloon floats in the air. But the balloon contains tiny leaks, which allow the warm air inside to escape. Eventually, the air in the balloon will reach the same density and temperature as the surrounding air.

The unpeeled lemon floats, while the peeled lemon sinks.

Buoyancy

Buoyancy is the force that allows a ship to float in water or a balloon to float in air. The density of an object determines its buoyancy. An object is buoyant if its density is less than that of the water or air. That means that an object that is denser than water will sink. An object that is less dense than water will float.

A scientist in ancient Greece, Archimedes, discovered the law of buoyancy. According to Archimedes, when you place an object into water, the object will displace some of the water. In other words, the object will push the water aside and force it to move somewhere else.

An object that is buoyant in water will have the same volume as the volume of the water it displaces. For this to happen, the object must have a density equal to or less than that of water.

A balloon is buoyant when the air inside it is less dense than the air in the atmosphere. Heating the air inside the balloon decreases its density, making it even more buoyant.

The law of buoyancy explains how this ship can float in water.

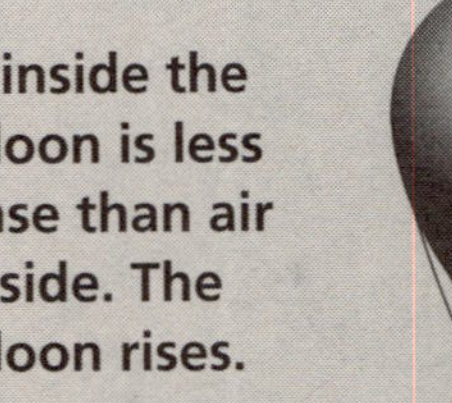

Air inside the balloon is less dense than air outside. The balloon rises.

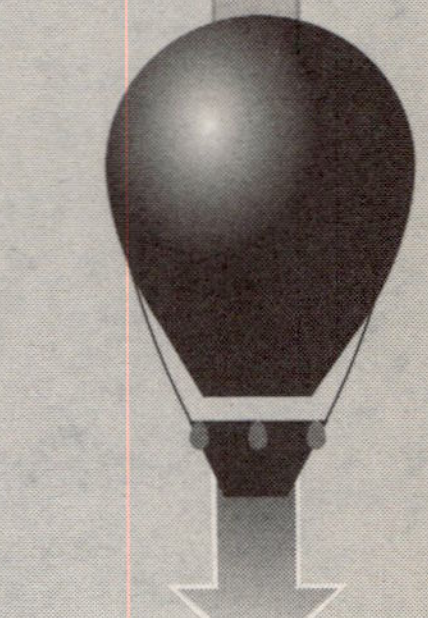

Air inside and outside the balloon are equally dense. The balloon stays at the same altitude.

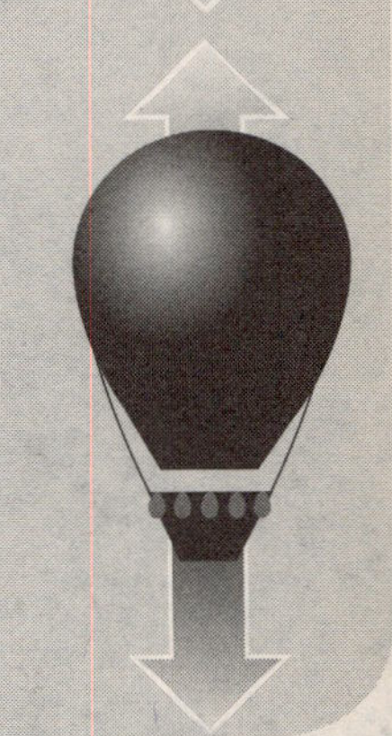

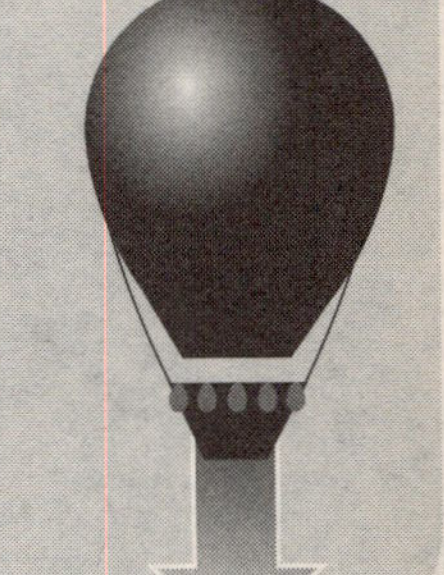

Air inside the balloon is denser than air outside. The balloon sinks.

Science

Genre	Comprehension Skill	Text Features	Science Content
Nonfiction	Cause and Effect	• Captions • Labels • Text Boxes • Glossary	Heat

Scott Foresman Science 4.12

scottforesman.com

ISBN 0-328-13894-0

9 780328 138944 90000

Science

Physical Science

How Hot?

by Anne Cambal

What did you learn?

1. Why does an iceberg have more heat than a cup of coffee?

2. Give examples of when someone might measure temperature using the Fahrenheit scale and using the Kelvin scale.

3. Put these substances in order based on how well they conduct heat: wood, glass, silver. List the best conductor first.

4. **Writing** in Science Eagles use convection currents to glide through the sky. Write to explain how they use these currents. Use examples from the book to support your answer.

5. **Cause and Effect** What causes a metal wok to feel hot when it is placed over a flame?

Vocabulary	Extended Vocabulary
conduction	geothermal
conductor	infrared
convection current	Kelvin
insulator	molecules
radiation	probe
thermal energy	thermal columns
	thermographic

Picture Credits
Every effort has been made to secure permission and provide appropriate credit for photographic material. The publisher deeply regrets any omission and pledges to correct errors called to its attention in subsequent editions.

Photo locators denoted as follows: Top (T), Center (C), Bottom (B), Left (L), Right (R), Background (Bkgd).

Opener: ©Dr. Arthur Tucker/Photo Researchers, Inc.; 8 ©Dr. Arthur Tucker/Photo Researchers, Inc.; 9 ©Bob Krist/Corbis; 13 (T) Digital Stock; 15 ©Anglo-Australian Observatory/DK Images.

ISBN: 0-328-13894-0

2 3 4 5 6 7 8 9 10 V004 13 12 11 10 09 08 07 06 05

Glossary

geothermal	relating to Earth's interior heat
infrared	energy similar to light
Kelvin	a scale used by scientists to measure temperature
molecules	moving particles that make up matter
probe	a small instrument used to explore a wound or an opening
thermal columns	columns of rising hot air
thermographic	used for the purpose of detecting heat

How Hot?

by Anne Cambal

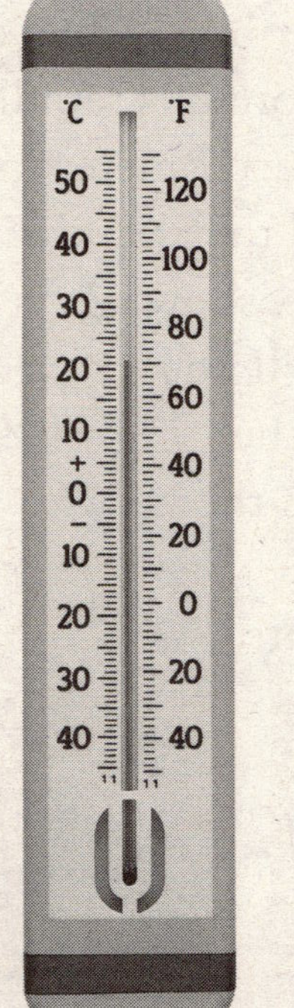

What You Already Know

All matter is made up of tiny particles. In all forms of matter—solid, liquid, and gas—particles move because they have energy.

Particles move faster as matter heats up, and they slow down as matter cools. Thermal energy is the energy made by the movement of the particles in the matter. We feel the movement of thermal energy as heat.

A thermometer is an instrument for measuring temperature. It has a thin glass tube attached to a bulb that holds colored alcohol. When a thermometer touches matter that contains rapidly moving particles, the particles in the thermometer move rapidly as well. This causes the liquid to expand and move up the tube, showing a higher temperature. If the particles slow down, the liquid contracts. Then the thermometer shows a decrease in temperature.

Thermometers can measure body temperature.

Ultimate Temperatures

Suppose you are traveling though our solar system. What kinds of temperatures do you think you would find? The temperature on the surface of the Sun is about 5,500°C (9,900°F)! The Sun affects weather not only on Earth but also in space.

The temperature on the planets varies quite a bit. Mercury reaches about 400°C (755°F) when it is closest to the Sun. When it is farthest from the Sun, it cools to –175°C (–280°F). When the Moon faces the Sun, it may reach a temperature of 101°C (215°F). When the Moon rotates away from the Sun, its temperature can be as low as –153°C (–243°F). Clouds of carbon dioxide gases in its atmosphere help the surface of Venus stay very warm—about 464°C (867°F). The temperature on Mars ranges from –83°C (–118°F) before dawn to –33°C (–28° F) in the afternoon.

Temperature is important to living matter. On Earth, people have learned to adapt to a range of temperatures, but within certain limits. Many plants and animals cannot survive if the temperature of their environment changes much. It is everyone's job to protect Earth for all who live here.

The temperatures in space vary tremendously due to the effects of the Sun.

Metal saucepans are good conductors of heat.

Conduction is the transfer of heat energy when one thing touches another. Many metals are good conductors. A conductor allows heat to move easily through it. But substances such as wood, marble, and plastic are insulators. An insulator limits the amount of heat that passes through it.

A fluid is a substance that flows but has no definite shape. Fluids such as air or water move by convection. A convection current is a pattern of flowing heat energy. It forms when heated fluid expands. Cooler fluid sinks below warmer fluid. The warm fluid is forced up, and the pattern starts again.

Radiation is energy sent out in waves. Objects exchanging heat through radiation do not need to touch. Radiation can move energy over great distances.

These processes explain how heat is transferred. In the next sections, explore different ways of measuring temperature and learn about the temperature extremes on Earth and in space.

Heat and Temperature

Heat and *temperature* are words that are often used as if they mean the same thing. However, they are not the same. In order to know how hot something is, you need to know its temperature.

All objects are made up of moving particles called molecules. Temperature is a measure of the average speed that the molecules are moving. Heat, on the other hand, is a measure of the total energy of all the molecules in the object. These scientific definitions are probably different from how you usually think of the words *heat* and *temperature*.

penguins on an iceberg in Antarctica

When volcanoes erupt, they can shoot hot lava high into the air.

In volcanic eruptions, red-hot lava bursts from deep inside Earth to the outermost surface. This molten, or melted, rock can be as hot as 1,200°C (2,200°F).

Geysers and hot springs are geothermal. They are heated by the interior of Earth. They produce water that is significantly higher in temperature than the air around them.

Earth's Extremes

Temperatures vary from state to state and around the world. The people of San Antonio, Texas, have a different idea of summer than those in Reykjavik, Iceland. Spring in Thunder Hawk, South Dakota, is not the same as it is in Tokyo, Japan. Scientists track and record temperature, wind, and other weather extremes around the world.

So far the hottest place on Earth is Al Aziziyah, Libya. The temperature reached 57.3°C (136°F) on September 13, 1922. The coldest temperature ever recorded is –89.2°C (–128.6°F). This occurred in Vostok, Antarctica, on July 21, 1983.

Ice can be found around the world. There are glaciers on every continent except Australia. About three-fourths of the world's fresh water is frozen in glaciers. The Bering Glacier is the longest in the United States. It's more than 204 kilometers (127 miles) long.

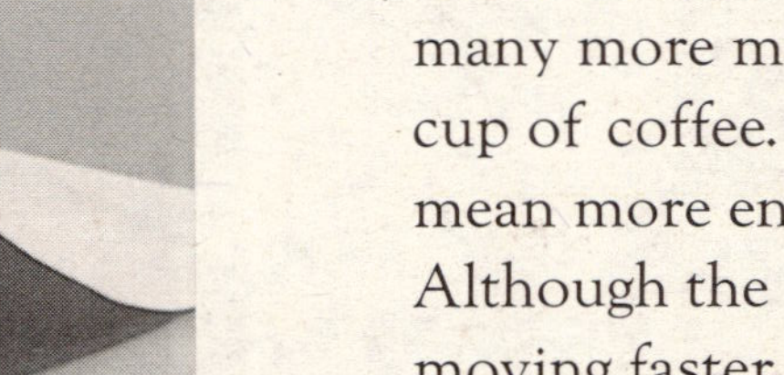

Death Valley, California, is the second-hottest location on Earth. In 1913, a temperature of 56.67°C (134°F) was recorded there.

cup of coffee

Which has more heat: an iceberg or a cup of coffee? It's easy to figure out that the iceberg has a lower temperature than a cup of coffee. Now think about the definition of heat. Did you figure out that the iceberg also has more heat? An iceberg is much larger than a cup of coffee. Therefore it contains many more molecules than the cup of coffee. More molecules mean more energy of motion. Although the molecules are moving faster in the coffee, there are more molecules that have energy in the iceberg. So the iceberg has more heat!

Moving Molecules

Ice is a solid. Its molecules are close together. They move only slightly and in fixed positions. Water is a liquid. Its molecules easily flow past each other. Molecules of a liquid are packed less closely than molecules of a solid.

ice molecules

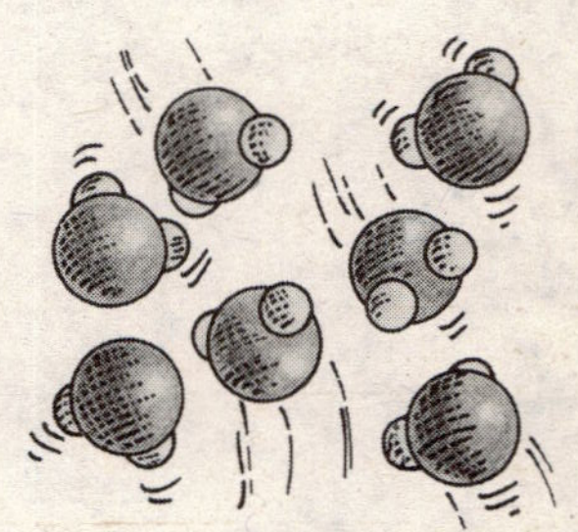

water molecules

Measuring Temperature

Thermometers are used to measure temperature. There are different types of scales used in thermometers. The Celsius and Fahrenheit scales are most common. The temperature on the Fahrenheit scale at which water freezes is 32°F. Water boils at 212°F. On the Celsius scale, water freezes at 0°C. It boils at 100°C.

Thermometers measure temperature in different ways. A digital thermometer uses a heat-sensitive electronic probe to detect temperature. Other thermometers use a column of liquid—generally alcohol or mercury—in a sealed tube. They have a scale showing degrees.

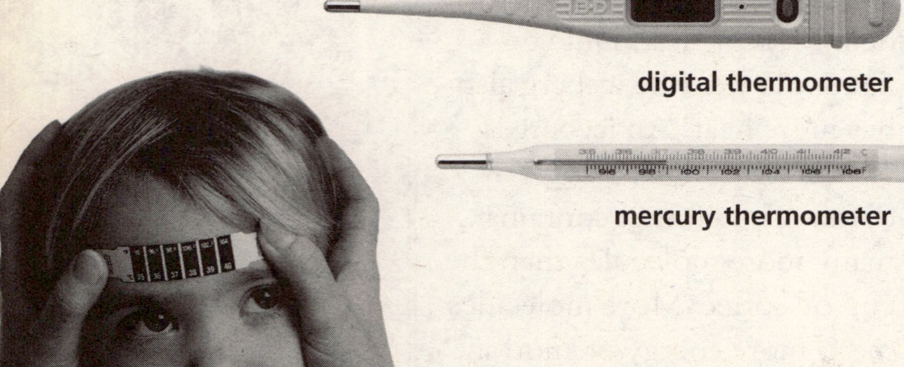

digital thermometer

mercury thermometer

Liquid crystal thermometers are put on a person's forehead. They indicate temperature by color.

Inuit children dress in insulating clothes to keep warm in Alaska's cold climate.

Heat conducts through some materials better than others. Poor conductors, such as wood and air, are called insulators. These materials help to trap or hold heat rather than transferring it. This is called insulation. Multiple layers of cold-weather clothing help people keep warm in very cold temperatures. The layers of clothing and the air pockets in them trap and hold warm air next to the body. Dressing in layers helps you stay warm when you are outside in very cold weather.

Buildings need insulation too. Heating and cooling expenses are usually more than half of a home's energy costs. Adding insulation to the attic of a home can greatly reduce the cost of energy. When it is cold outside, insulation helps keep warm air inside a building. It does the reverse in hot weather. Then it helps keep a building cool.

Conduction and Insulation

Conduction is another kind of heat transfer. Conduction occurs when vibrating molecules bump and then transfer energy to the molecules next to them. An example of heat transfer by conduction begins when a metal wok, such as the one below, is placed over a flame. In a short time the flame causes the temperature of the metal wok to increase. This, in turn, speeds up the movement of the molecules in the wok. Soon the temperature of the entire wok increases. Metal is a good conductor of heat, so the wok will conduct heat from the flame below it to the food inside it.

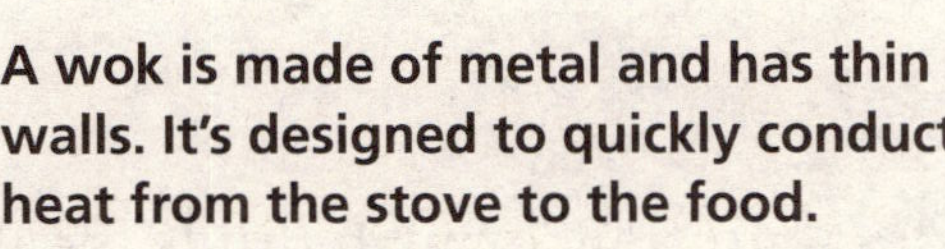

A wok is made of metal and has thin walls. It's designed to quickly conduct heat from the stove to the food.

Celsius and Fahrenheit

You've already learned that water freezes (and ice melts) at 0°C. You also know that water boils (and steam becomes a liquid) at 100°C. Celsius is part of the metric system. Most of the world uses Celsius to measure temperature. However, the United States uses Fahrenheit. Frozen water that is 32°F is just as cold as ice that's 0°C. Boiling water that is 212°F is just as hot as boiling water that is 100°C. The only difference is in the scales that were used to indicate and measure the two readings.

ice

steam from boiling water

The National Aeronautics and Space Administration, or NASA, uses a thermometer with a different scale to measure temperatures in space. Scientists measure temperature with the Kelvin scale. The Kelvin scale measures greater temperature extremes than we need to measure in everyday life.

The scale you use to measure temperature depends on what and where you are measuring. For example, a veterinarian might measure your dog's temperature using the Fahrenheit scale. Many people in the world use the Celsius scale to measure air temperature.

Heat on the Move

Heat generally flows from matter at a higher temperature to matter at a lower one. A warm dish removed from a heated oven will gradually cool down. The dish passes its heat to the cooler air around it and to the surface on which it's resting. The dish then becomes cooler.

Radiation is one form of heat transfer. Radiation is heat that moves in rays or waves. Although we can't see it without the use of instruments, all objects and materials emit infrared radiation. Infrared radiation is an energy similar to light. We can use special infrared cameras to produce pictures or images that show this radiation. This is called thermographic imagery. Thermographic images show changes in surface heat. Different levels of heat show up as different colors.

Blue shows coldest area.

Red shows hottest area.

A thermographic image shows variations in heat given off by different parts of the body.

Hang gliders soar on convection currents.

Heat transfer through fluids is called convection. Convection is another way that heat travels. A convection current is produced when heat moves in a pattern. When the Sun heats an area on the ground, the air near the ground is also heated. This warm air expands and rises. Thermal columns, or columns of rising hot air, develop. The moving air within these columns allows hang gliders to soar through the sky. Pilots of gliders and hang gliders look for places on the ground that the Sun will heat well, such as areas covered with blacktop. These areas will be good sources of thermal columns.

Genre	Comprehension Skill	Text Features	Science Content
Nonfiction	Cause and Effect	• Captions • Labels • Text Boxes • Glossary	Electricity and Magnetism

Scott Foresman Science 4.13

PEARSON Scott Foresman
scottforesman.com
ISBN 0-328-13897-5
9 780328 138975 90000

Science

Physical Science

Poles Apart

by Patricia Walsh

What did you learn?

1. How does a maglev train use magnets to move?
2. Where on Earth are you most likely to see auroras in the sky?
3. Think about a room in your home. Make a list of the things in that room that use electricity.
4. **Writing** in Science You have read about electricity and magnetism in this book. What do you think is the most important tool we have that uses these invisible forces? Why do you think so? Include details from the book to support your answer.
5. **Cause and Effect** When you stroke a bar of steel with a magnet, what causes the bar to become magnetized? What effect might this magnetized bar have on other metal objects?

Vocabulary	Extended Vocabulary
electric current	aurora
electromagnet	foundry
magnetic field	maglev train
magnetism	magnetic north
parallel circuit	magnetite
resistance	magnetosphere
series circuit	MRI
static electricity	solar prominences

Picture Credits
Every effort has been made to secure permission and provide appropriate credit for photographic material. The publisher deeply regrets any omission and pledges to correct errors called to its attention in subsequent editions.

Photo locators denoted as follows: Top (T), Center (C), Bottom (B), Left (L), Right (R), Background (Bkgd).

7 (CR) James Leynse/Corbis; 12 Per-Magnus Hedén/pixonnet.com/Alamy Images; 13 (TR) ©SOHO (ESA & NASA)/NASA; 16 profimedia/Alamy Images; 21 (CR) Rubberball Productions; 23 Lester Lefkowitz/Corbis.

Scott Foresman/Dorling Kindersley would also like to thank: Opener: Stephen Oliver/DK Images.

ISBN: 0-328-13897-5

2 3 4 5 6 7 8 9 10 V004 13 12 11 10 09 08 07 06 05

Glossary

aurora	a display of different colors of light in Earth's magnetosphere
foundry	a place where metal is melted and made into a shape
maglev train	a high-speed train propelled by electromagnetism
magnetic north pole	the northernmost point of the magnetic field that surrounds Earth
magnetite	iron ore that is magnetic
magnetosphere	an area around Earth affected by Earth's magnetic field
MRI	magnetic resonance imaging, used by doctors to diagnose illness or injury
solar prominences	explosions of hot gas from the Sun

Poles Apart

by Patricia Walsh

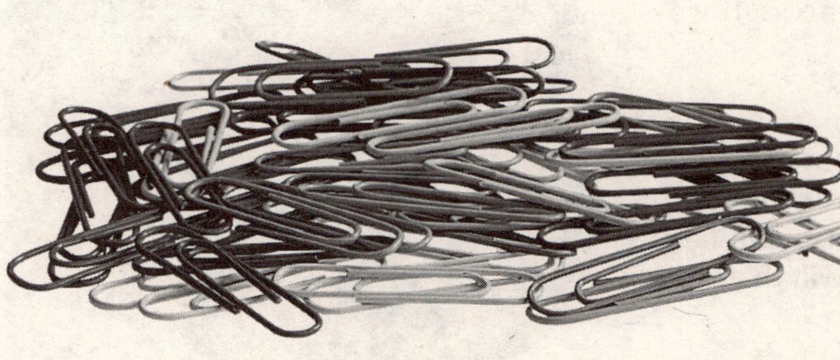

PEARSON Scott Foresman

What You Already Know

Objects are made of tiny, electrically charged atoms. The particles that make up atoms can have a positive or negative charge, or no charge at all. Static electricity comes from electrical charges moving between atoms. This causes both powerful lightning and clinging socks.

An electrical force can develop between objects that have opposite charges. The space around electrically charged objects is an electric field.

When an electric charge is in motion, it is an electric current. An electric charge does not move easily through an insulator. It moves more easily through a conductor. A material with resistance does not allow an electric charge to flow easily through it.

You can cause static electricity by rubbing balloons against your hair. The balloons will then stick to things.

Electromagnets are used in our health care instruments. An MRI machine uses powerful electromagnets to produce images of the inside of a patient's body. The patient lies still while the machine takes pictures from many angles. The letter M in MRI stands for "magnetic."

Electromagnetic power can be found everywhere. Can you imagine a world without it?

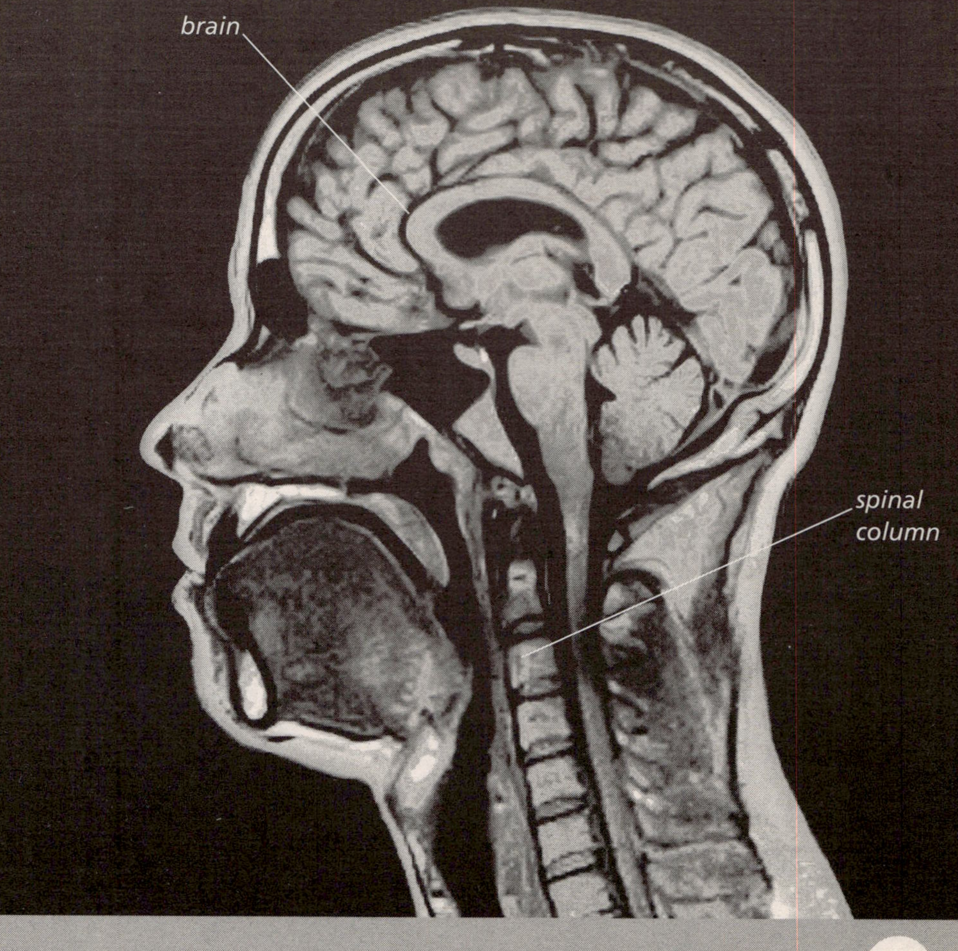

There are electromagnets in the motors in our cars as well. The driver's seat might be adjusted by as many as seven electric motors. Power windows are run by an electric motor. The windshield wipers and the starter are just a few more places that you will find motors with electromagnets.

Computers use electromagnets in order to store information in memory. You can find electromagnets in electric clocks, DVD players, CD players, and calculators. Many battery-operated toys have electromagnets. Our transportation also depends on electromagnets. Buses, motorcycles, and airplanes cannot travel very far without the help of electromagnets.

Computers use electromagnets.

Most electricity flows through a circuit. A series circuit has one path for the electric charge to follow. Everything along this path receives the same amount of energy. A parallel circuit has two or more paths. It can handle devices that need different amounts of current.

Magnetism is the force that pushes or pulls magnetic materials near a magnet. A magnet has an invisible magnetic field around it. This field is strongest at the magnet's poles. Earth is similar to a huge magnet, with a magnetic field and poles. The needle of a compass points to Earth's magnetic north pole.

An electromagnet is a coil of wire wrapped around an iron core. It transforms electrical energy into magnetic energy. We can find electromagnets in many objects we use every day. Magnetism can also be used to make electricity.

horseshoe magnet

Electricity and magnetism are related in many ways. In this book we'll take an in-depth look at the invisible world of electricity and magnetism that surrounds us, works for us, and makes our lives easier.

An Invisible Force

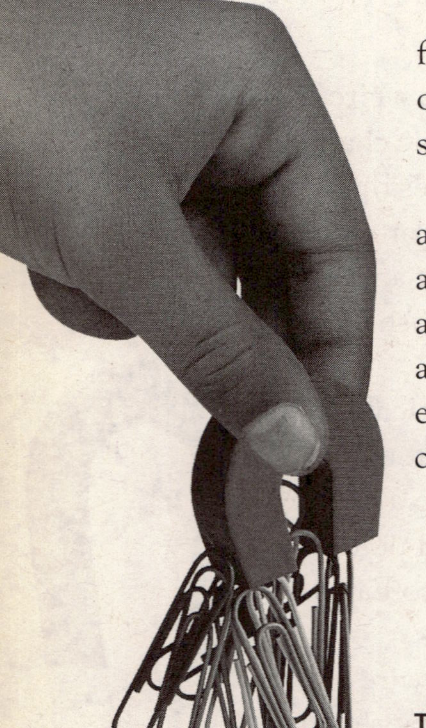

Magnetism is an invisible force that is strongest at the poles, or ends, of a magnet. A magnet is surrounded by a magnetic field.

The paper clips in this picture are made of metal. Metal objects are often attracted to the poles of a magnet. The magnetic field around this magnet is powerful enough to pull some of the paper clips toward it.

The force of this magnet pulls the paper clips to its poles.

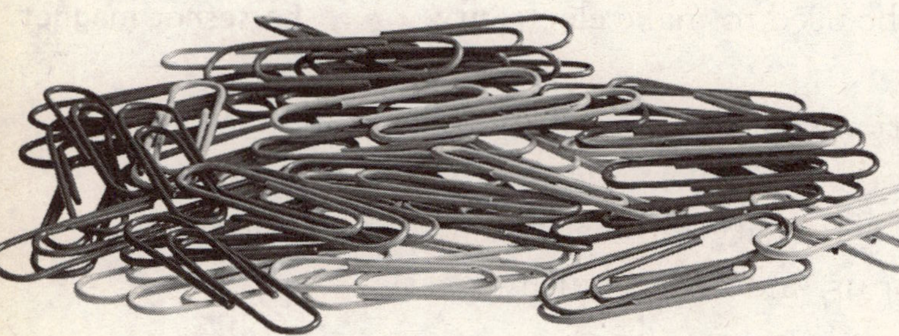

Electric guitars use electromagnets to make the sound you hear. The strings on an electric guitar vibrate when they are plucked. The guitar has magnetic pickups that sense these vibrations electronically. A pickup is a bar magnet with wire wrapped around it. An electric guitar can have several pickups or just one. The pickup sends the electronic vibrations as an electronic signal to a speaker. You hear the sound from the guitar.

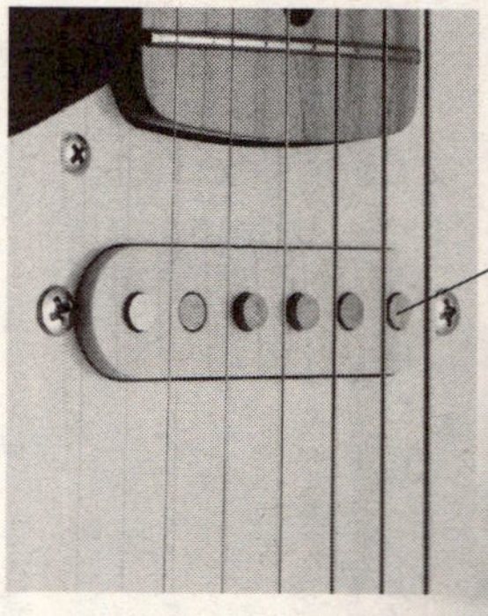

pickups

Guitar pickups turn sound vibrations into electricity.

Using Electromagnets

You'll find that electricity and magnetism have many uses in our daily lives. We depend on electric power for light at night, sounds from the radio, and cool air in the summer. Electric power also cooks our food and keeps it cold.

Electromagnets are used to make doorbells ring. Current flows to a device that controls just how much current reaches the electromagnet in the bell. Electricity that is flowing in the coil of the wire magnetizes the electromagnet.

This causes the hammer to strike the bell, which makes the sound we hear.

Bells use electromagnets to make a ringing sound.

The magnetic field of an object can be very strong. Iron and steel objects placed within a magnetic field will be pulled toward the magnet. The pattern made by the iron filings shows the bar magnet's magnetic field.

A compass needle points north. However, when a magnet is placed near the compass, the magnet has a strong pull on the needle. This makes the needle point in the direction of the magnetic field.

The pattern of iron filings and the compass needles show the magnetic field of the bar magnet.

Pushes and Pulls

The end of a bar magnet is either a north pole or a south pole. When placed near each other, opposite magnetic poles attract. This means they try to pull together. If you turn one of the magnets around and place the same magnetic poles together, such as two south poles, they repel each other. This means they push apart.

One use for this property of magnetism is maglev trains. Maglev is short for magnetic levitation. Today most trains roll on wheels along steel tracks. Maglev trains use magnets to make the train float over a magnetized track.

Electric motors don't stop there. A part of the motor called the commutator reverses the magnetic field of the electromagnet. Its north pole becomes its south pole, and its south pole becomes its north pole. When this happens, the poles of the bar magnets and the electromagnet repel each other and are attracted to the opposite poles. This makes the electromagnet rotate. This movement makes machinery run.

You might be surprised to learn how many electric motors power the things you see and use each day. Elevators, refrigerators, vacuum cleaners, hair dryers, and fans are some items that use electric motors.

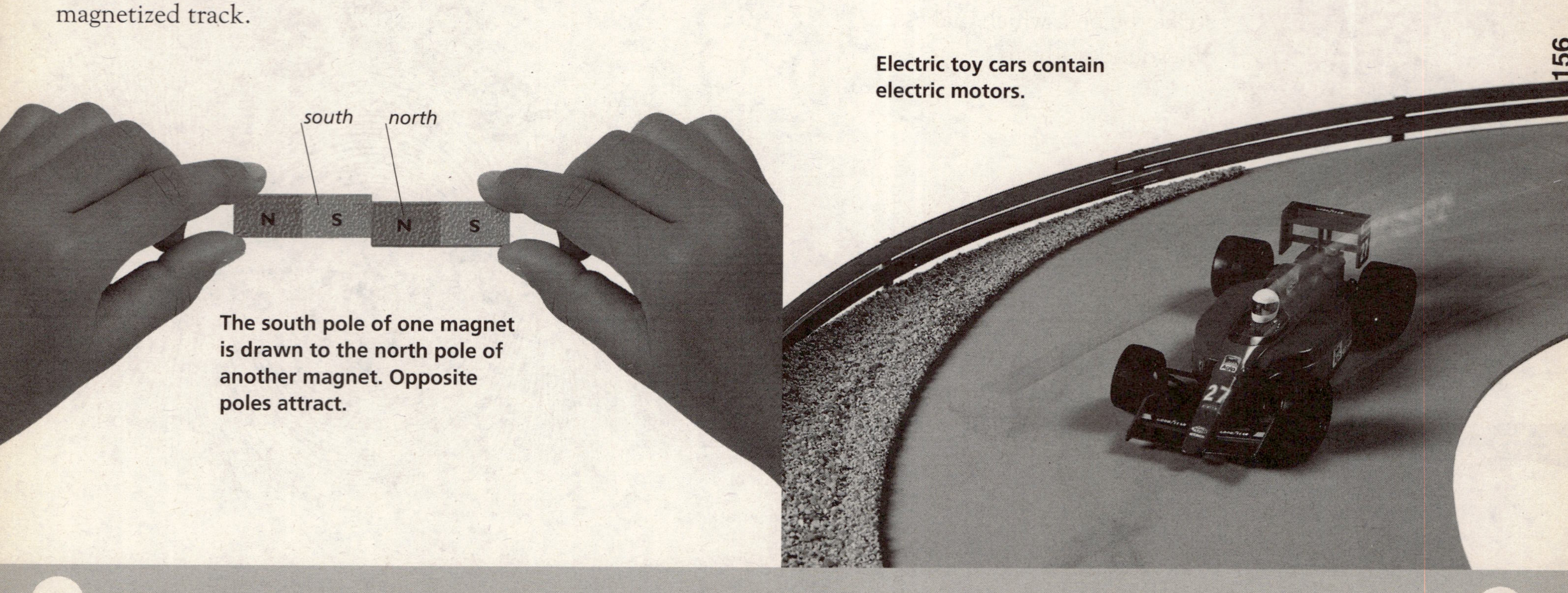

The south pole of one magnet is drawn to the north pole of another magnet. Opposite poles attract.

Electric toy cars contain electric motors.

Electric Motors

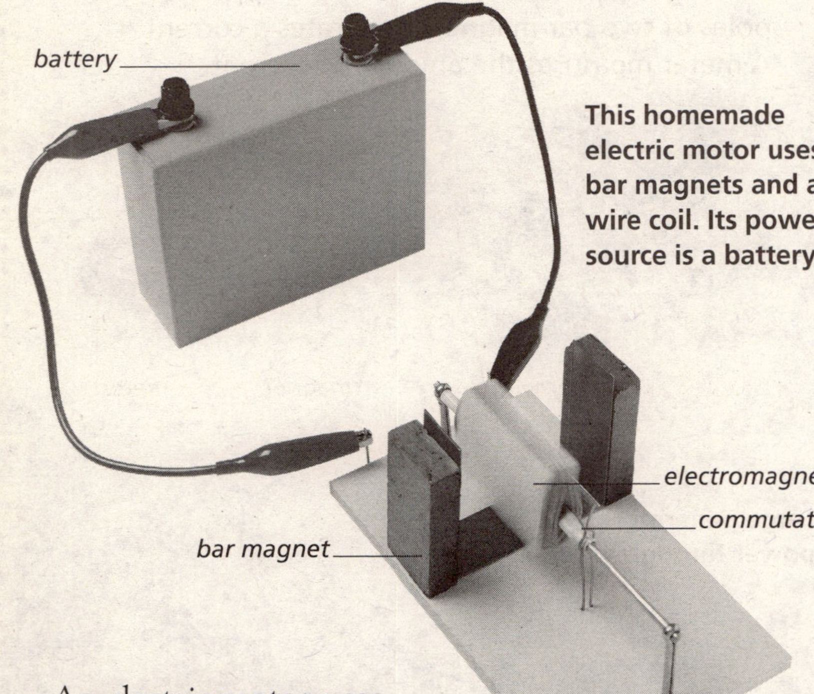

This homemade electric motor uses bar magnets and a wire coil. Its power source is a battery.

An electric motor uses magnets and electromagnets to make motion. It has a wire coil and permanent magnets, such as bar magnets, on each side. One bar magnet has its north pole facing up, and the other one has its south pole facing up. When electricity from a power source flows into the wire coil, it makes an electromagnet. The north pole of the electromagnet is attracted to the south pole of the bar magnet, and the south pole of the electromagnet is attracted to the north pole of the bar magnet.

Two south poles push away from each other. Similar poles repel.

The maglev train makes use of magnets and electromagnets in order to move.

Large magnets are attached to the underside of a maglev train. The magnets on the track and the magnets on the train repel each other. This makes the train move above the track. Electromagnets push and pull the train along the track. Maglev trains have reached speeds of more than 300 miles per hour. Scientists think maglev trains could travel even faster.

The technology is ready, but it is still very expensive to build a maglev transportation system. Do you think one day you will step into a maglev train?

What makes a magnet?

Some stones found in Earth's crust can attract iron. These stones are natural magnets. They are pieces of magnetite, or lodestone, a mineral rich in iron.

The magnets that you may put on your refrigerator are probably not natural magnets. Refrigerator magnets are usually manufactured in a foundry, or a place where metal is melted and molded into a shape. The metal is then magnetized.

Magnetite with iron filings

Magnets are being cast in a foundry.

Generating Electricity

Moving a copper wire between the opposite poles of two bar magnets generates a current. A meter measures the amount of current.

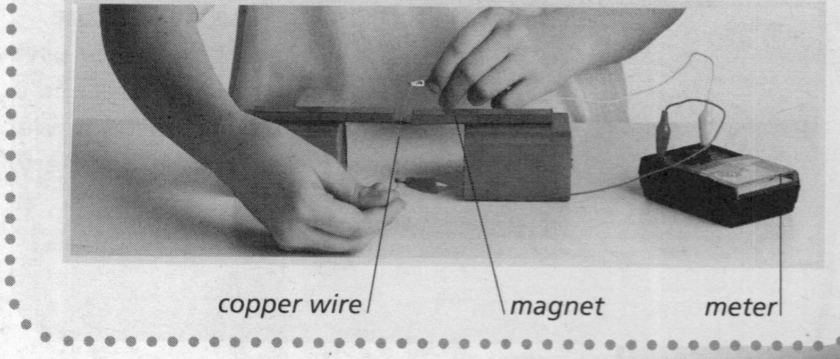

Large generators send power through wires.

Generating Current

You now know that electricity and magnetism are often used together. Just as electric currents can make a magnetic field, magnets can be used to make electric current. Magnetism plays an important part in powering the appliances and lights in our homes. Most of our electric power comes from large generators that may be miles away.

In a generator, a coiled wire is surrounded by a spinning magnet. When the magnet spins, it pushes electric current through the coiled wire. A turbine keeps the magnet moving. A turbine is a machine that has a rotating wheel with paddles attached to it. Steam, moving air, or moving water is usually used to power the turbine. The generator sends out current that travels through wires, often over many miles.

Magnetize a Steel Bar

Rubbing a magnet over a steel bar organizes the magnetized areas in the bar. Striking the bar mixes those areas and weakens the magnet.

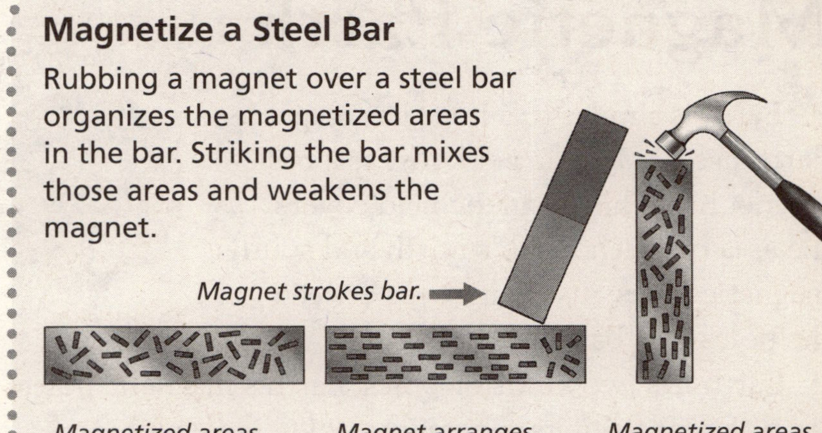

The bar and horseshoe magnets used in classroom experiments are also made in a foundry. Manufactured magnets are similar to natural magnets in that they contain iron, cobalt, or nickel. These metals can be magnetized. They are made up of tiny crystals whose atoms line up in a regular order. Each crystal acts as a tiny magnet with a north and south pole.

A magnetized material, such as a steel bar, is stronger when the north poles on all of the crystals point in one direction and the south poles all point in the opposite direction. When this happens, there is just one north pole and one south pole.

Magnetic Earth

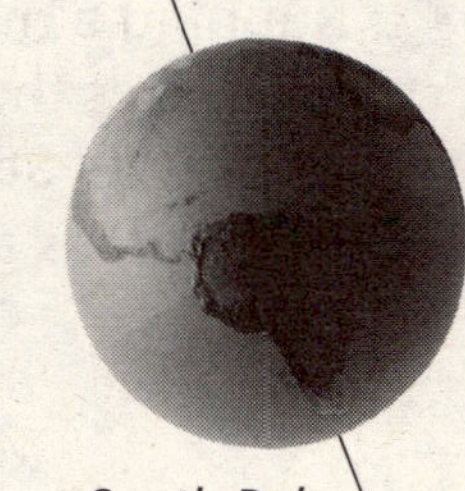

Earth is similar to a huge bar magnet. Earth has a magnetic field, just as a bar magnet has. This magnetic field covers the area between Earth's north and south magnetic poles, just as it does between the poles of a bar magnet.

Earth has two kinds of poles. Earth's magnetic poles are different from its geographic poles. Geographic north is the area in the Arctic Ocean called the North Pole. The magnetic north and south poles are found near the geographic North and South Poles.

How to Make a Compass

Rub a bar magnet over a needle. Then float the magnetized needle on a piece of cork in water. It will point north.

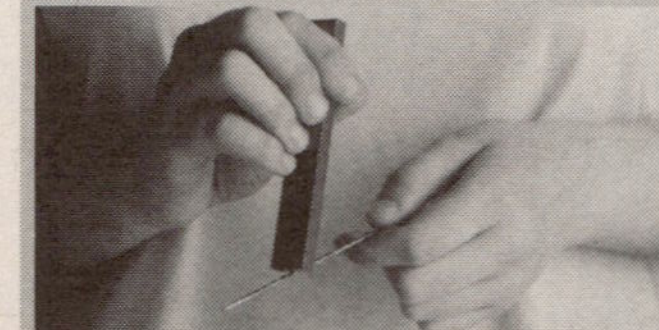

magnetizing a needle

needle on cork floating in water

Electromagnets are so powerful that they can lift and transport very heavy pieces of metal. That is why electromagnets are valuable pieces of equipment at construction sites and recycling centers. The electromagnet is turned on to pick up pieces of metal. Once the pieces are placed in their new location, the magnet is turned off.

The electromagnet will drop the pieces of metal when the electric current stops flowing.

Electromagnetism

Electric and magnetic forces are used together to produce electromagnetism. An electromagnet begins with a power source, such as a battery or a generator. Electric current can flow through a wire. This makes a magnetic field around the wire. If you coil the wire, you'll make the magnetic field stronger. The more turns in the coil, the stronger the magnetism. To make an even stronger electromagnet, you can wind the wire around an iron bar. Using a larger iron bar will make the electromagnet stronger.

An electromagnet is similar to a bar magnet because it also has a north and south pole. But unlike a bar magnet, which is always magnetic, an electromagnet is a temporary magnet. The magnetic field exists only when electric current flows through the wire. If the electric current stops flowing, the magnetic field disappears.

Magnets can be used to make a compass. The needle inside a compass is a small magnet, often made of steel. The needle is attracted to Earth's magnetic north. It swirls around so it points in that direction.

Earth's magnetic field attracts more than just compass needles. It can also attract charged particles in space. The area around Earth that is affected by Earth's magnetic field is called the magnetosphere. It extends far into space.

You can use a compass to help you find a specific direction.

Magnetism in Space

Earth's magnetism interacts with tiny charged particles that come from the Sun. The positive and negative particles in Earth's magnetosphere collide with gases in the atmosphere. The collisions cause an amazing display of different colors of light. This display is called an aurora. You are most likely to see auroras in the night sky near Earth's magnetic poles. This glowing light show lasts from a few seconds to a few hours.

The Sun also has a magnetic field. The Sun has great explosions of hot gas. These explosions, or solar prominences, erupt from the surface of the Sun into its atmosphere. The Sun's magnetism pulls the gas back to the surface, creating vast loops of burning gas.

Other planets in the solar system also have magnetic fields. Jupiter's magnetic field is about twenty thousand times stronger than Earth's. Uranus and Neptune experience great changes in the strength of their magnetic fields. Some planets have weaker magnetic fields than Earth. Venus is not magnetized.

Hot gas erupts from the Sun in a solar prominence. The Sun's magnetic field pulls it back.

The aurora borealis can be seen in parts of the Northern Hemisphere.

Genre	Comprehension Skill	Text Features	Science Content
Nonfiction	Draw Conclusions	• Captions • Call Outs • Text Boxes • Glossary	Sound and Light

Scott Foresman Science 4.14

ISBN 0-328-13900-9
9 780328 139002
90000

scottforesman.com

Science

Physical Science

Movie Science

by Sam Brelsfoard

What did you learn?

1. What were some early machines that led to the first movie cameras?

2. How did early film cameras record images in color?

3. What is the role of the sound engineer on a movie?

4. **Writing** in Science A praxinoscope showed images that appeared to be moving. Describe how this machine worked. Include details from the book to support your answer.

5. **Draw Conclusions** Why do editors and directors have to edit a movie?

Vocabulary	Extended Vocabulary
absorption	animation
compression	blue screen
frequency	boom
opaque	cel
pitch	praxinoscope
reflection	shutter
refraction	splicing
translucent	sprockets
transparent	
wavelength	

Picture Credits
Every effort has been made to secure permission and provide appropriate credit for photographic material. The publisher deeply regrets any omission and pledges to correct errors called to its attention in subsequent editions.

Photo locators denoted as follows: Top (T), Center (C), Bottom (B), Left (L), Right (R), Background (Bkgd).

4 (BR) Science Museum, London/DK Images; 5 (BR) Science Museum, London/DK Images; 16 Dreamworks LLC/The Kobal Collection; 18 (B) Getty Images; 21 (T) Bravo Post Production, London; 22 Touchstone/Jerry Bruckheimer Inc./The Kobal Collection; 23 The Cinema Museum/Ronald Grant Archive.

Scott Foresman/Dorling Kindersley would also like to thank: 4 (BL) Science Museum/DK Images; 20 (BL, BCL, BCR, BR) ©Hibbert/Ralph/DK Images; 21 (BL, BC, BR) ©Hibbert/Ralph/DK Images.

ISBN: 0-328-13900-9

2 3 4 5 6 7 8 9 10 V004 13 12 11 10 09 08 07 06 05

Glossary

animation the production of the illusion of moving images

blue screen technology in which subjects are filmed in front of a blue-colored screen that can be replaced with other images

boom a mechanical arm that holds a microphone

cel a clear piece of film on which a character is drawn and then placed over a background illustration

praxinoscope an early device that gave the illusion of images in motion

shutter part of a camera that opens and closes to control how much light comes through the lens

splicing joining two objects together, such as pieces of film

sprockets gearlike wheels with teeth that fit into the small holes on the sides of film

Movie Science

by Sam Brelsfoard

PEARSON
Scott Foresman

What You Already Know

Sound is a form of energy that travels in waves. Sound is produced when objects vibrate. When sound vibrations travel through air, they cause the air particles to form a pattern. The area of the wave where the particles are bunched together is a compression.

Some waves move in transverse waves. Sound moves in longitudinal waves. The frequency of a wave is the number of waves that pass a point in a certain amount of time. The faster the wave moves, the higher the frequency is. A wavelength is the distance between a point on one wave and a similar point on the next wave. Sound can move through solids, liquids, and gases. Sound cannot move through a vacuum, or empty space.

One characteristic of sound is loudness. Loudness measures how strong a sound seems. Pitch is another characteristic. Pitch is what makes a sound seem high or low. Objects that vibrate slowly have a low pitch, and those that vibrate quickly have a high pitch. Musical instruments can produce sounds with different pitches.

Light is also energy that moves in waves. White light passing through a prism splits into the colors of the visible spectrum. Radio waves, microwaves, and infrared waves are invisible light waves.

People have been going to the movies for many years. What will movies of the future be like?

Many films use computer-generated imagery, or CGI, to make special effects. CGI can be used to make it seem as if one character turns into another. Combining CGI and regular film footage can make it seem as though almost anything were possible.

The way we make and watch movies changes all the time. Computers and special effects have changed the way films are made. Digital projectors and DVDs are changing the way we watch movies. We can only guess what's in store for the future of moviemaking. One thing we can count on is that the science behind moviemaking will keep developing and changing to make movies even more entertaining.

Special Effects

New technology is being developed in the movie industry every day. The blue screen is a technique that caught people's attention when it was first invented. By filming characters in front of a large blue screen, movie editors can later replace the image of the blue screen in the background with anything they want. By replacing the blue screen with stars and planets, for example, filmmakers can make it seem as though characters are flying through space. This sort of technology allows us to see things that seem impossible.

Blue screens enable many special effects.

Light reflection occurs when light rays bounce off a surface. Absorption occurs when an object takes in light, and the light becomes heat energy.

A transparent material lets light rays pass through it. A translucent material lets only some light rays pass through. An opaque material does not let any light rays pass through.

Light bends when it moves at an angle from one medium to another. This bending is called refraction. Lenses are curved pieces of glass or plastic that refract light that passes through them. Light bends toward the middle of a convex lens. Light spreads out when it passes through a concave lens.

Light and sound energy can be used in many ways. In this book, you will learn about an entertaining use for light and sound—movies!

Prisms split white light into different colors.

Light Pictures

The technology needed for making the movies we see today would not have been possible without the invention of the camera. A camera lens takes in beams of light that bounce off objects. The beams bend as they enter the lens, and an upside-down image is projected onto the camera's film. Chemicals in the film react to light and form an image.

By reversing the process of taking a photograph, an image can be projected on a screen. To do this, light is shone through the film and then through a lens. The lens projects the image from the film onto a screen.

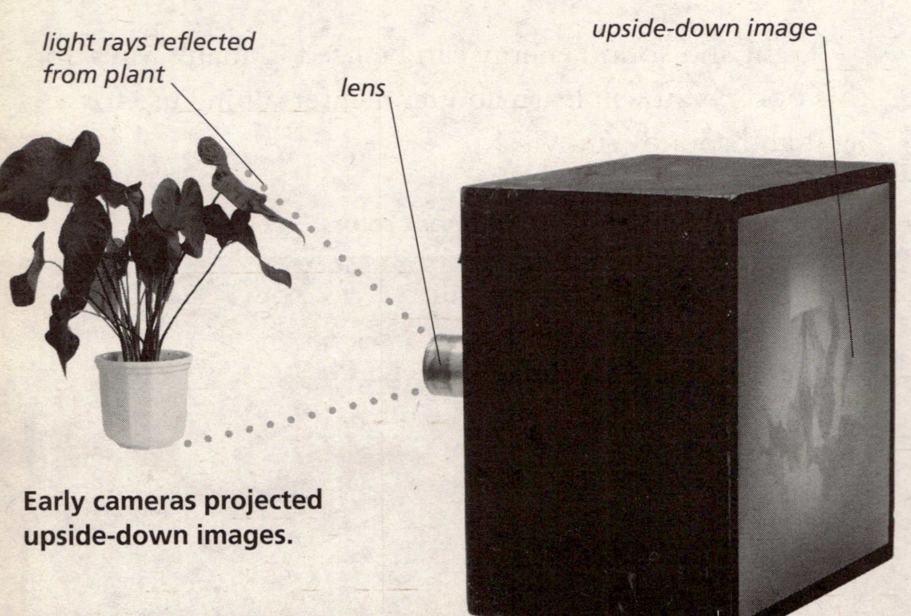

Early cameras projected upside-down images.

Many animated movies now use computers to create 3-D digital animation.

Most of today's animated films are made using computers. Much of the drawing is done on computers, so animators are free to concentrate on other areas of the film. This does not mean that computer animation is any easier. It is simply a different approach to an old idea. Computer animators are skilled technicians who understand the many uses of very advanced software that can help them make animated movies.

Animation

An animated film contains thousands of drawings. In early animated movies, every drawing that you saw on the screen had been drawn by hand. Every scene in an animated movie is carefully planned before any drawing is done. To reduce the amount of drawing each artist has to do, scenes are planned where the backgrounds stay the same. The detailed background is drawn once, and the animated characters are placed on top of it. To do this, the characters that will be placed on top of the background are drawn on a clear piece of film known as a cel. Each action that the character makes is drawn on a fresh cel. The cels are then placed on top of the background and photographed individually. When the film is played back it looks as if the character and the background are the same drawing. The different layers of animation help make the film appear three-dimensional, or 3-D, instead of flat and two-dimensional. It looks more realistic.

Animation is made up of many layers.

The magic lantern was invented in the 1600s. Images were drawn and painted by hand on small pieces of glass. The magic lantern projected these images onto a large screen using light from an oil lamp.

Toward the end of the 1800s, the magic lantern was being used to entertain huge crowds in the United States. The hand-drawn pieces of glass were replaced with photographs. For many years, this was the only kind of projection equipment available. As photography became more popular, it became easier to produce these images. Eventually motion pictures, or movies, took the place of the magic lantern.

Magic lanterns provided early picture shows.

Images in Motion

When you watch a movie, what you are really watching is a series of thousands of images flickering in front of your eyes. This rapid flickering happens so quickly that you do not see each individual image. Your brain puts the images together. You see the illusion of movement on the screen. This illusion is known as animation. This technology was used in many devices in the nineteenth century. One of these devices was known as the praxinoscope.

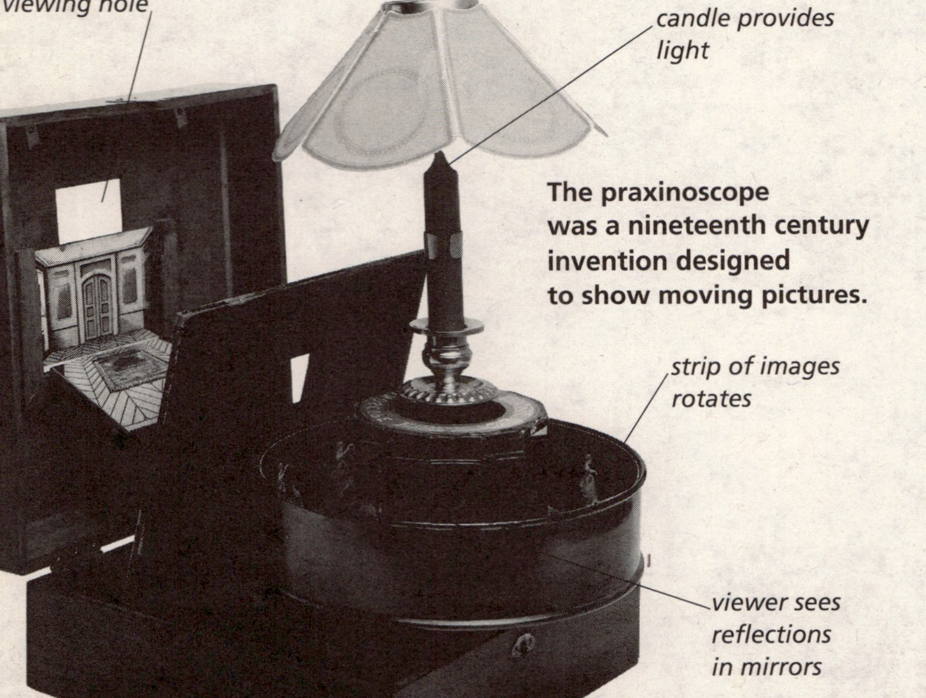

The praxinoscope was a nineteenth century invention designed to show moving pictures.

Sometimes many different versions of the same scenes are recorded. The director and the editor spend many hours watching the film and choosing the best versions from what they recorded. They put the scenes in order, cut out the unnecessary parts, and assemble the film. When they are finished, a new roll of film is made that holds the final version of the movie. It is wound onto spools and sent to theaters.

Today computers are used to edit films. Unedited film is fed into a computer. Editors can use the computer to change the film however they wish. The use of computers is a relatively new tool in editing. In the past, editors worked with the actual pieces of film. In order to cut a scene, an editor used a film splicing machine. This machine cut the film at the desired spot and reconnected the pieces that were left. The editors then threw away the unwanted pieces of film. This was a very time-consuming process. Computers make it much easier for editors and directors to edit their movies.

The final film is wound onto spools.

Editing the Film

Once all of the movie has been filmed and all of the sound has been recorded, the director and the film editor must edit the film. Often, the scenes in a movie have been filmed out of order. This means that when filming is completed, the director and editor have many rolls of film that must be placed in the right order to make the movie.

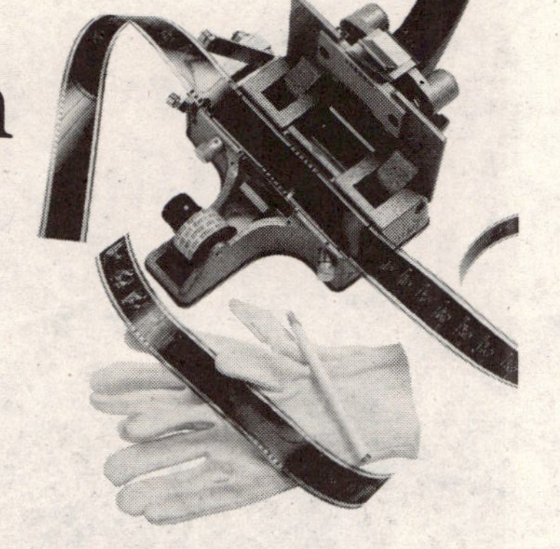

Film editors once used a machine called a film splicer.

Today film is fed into computers and edited digitally.

How to make a flip book

Take a small stack of paper. On the top page, draw a picture you would like to animate, such as a bird in the sky. On the next page, draw the same picture but make it slightly different. The bird could be in a different position on this page. After you've drawn on each page in the stack, flip through the pages very quickly. The picture will seem to move!

The praxinoscope was a device that produced images that seemed to move. It had a short, wide tube that revolved. On the inside wall of the tube was a series of images. In the middle of the tube was a series of mirrors. The number of mirrors in the praxinoscope equaled the number of images. As the tube rotated, the drawings passed in front of the mirrors. When the tube spun fast enough, the images seemed to move. A candle above the tube supplied light. The viewer looked through a hole on one side to see the series of images forming an animation.

This technology would soon merge with the technology of cameras. This led to the invention of cameras that could record movement.

Movie Cameras

The first movie cameras were surprisingly small and lightweight. The film in a movie camera winds from one reel onto another reel. Film is a long strip of very strong, thin plastic that is coated with light-sensitive chemicals. The film is threaded through the camera. It is guided by sprockets. Sprockets are gearlike wheels. Their teeth fit into the small holes along the sides of the film. Many early cameras, including the Debrie Parvo camera, used a crank to turn the film once it was threaded.

The Debrie Parvo camera was used by many filmmakers in the early 1900s.

The audio technician sits at a control panel to put together the final sound for the film.

Once all the sounds have been recorded, it is the work of the audio technicians to mix the sounds together. They use special audio equipment to do this. The technicians' main job is to adjust the volume and quality of the sound to make it work well with the movie. They make sure that all the sounds are heard at exactly the right moments.

When the technicians have finished mixing the sounds, they record the complete, final version. This is then added to the side of the final version of the film as a series of magnetic stripes. When the film is played in movie theaters, the sound and the images match up.

Mixing Sound

Most movies have many sounds: dialogue, sound effects, music, and background noises. All of these sounds must be combined to play along with the movie. Usually each sound is recorded separately. What the actors say, the dialogue, is recorded on the set during filming or later in a sound studio. The background sounds can be recorded with or without the actors being present. The sound effects are usually recorded after the scene has been filmed. The music for the movie is often the last part to be recorded.

Dialogue recorded after filming is called a voice-over.

How cameras work

A shutter is a device on a camera that opens and closes. It controls how much light comes through the lens. When the shutter closes, a claw moves forward and catches the holes on the side of the film. This pulls the film down. The shutter then opens again.

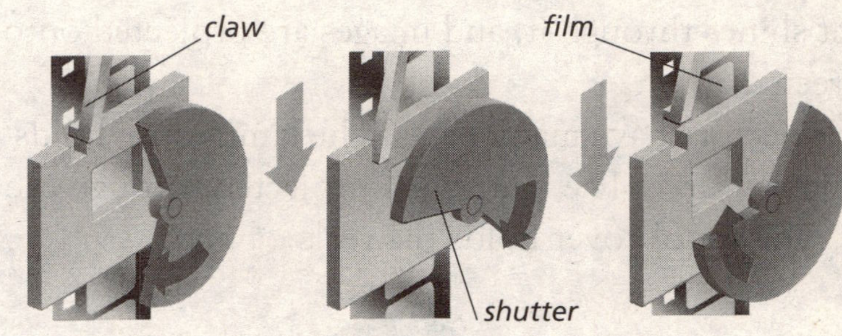

Rotating sprockets move the film through the camera. The film passes in front of the lens. The film is divided into sections called frames. A shutter opens as each frame passes in front of the lens. When the shutter opens, light can reach the film. Twenty-four images per second are captured on the film. Just as you saw in the flip book, each image is slightly different than the one that came before it. This causes the illusion of movement.

frame

sprocket hole

At the Movies

A modern film projector in a movie theater uses very powerful electric lamps to generate light. The projector uses sprockets to push and pull the film, just as a movie camera does. The film passes in front of the shutter. Light shines through it, and images are projected onto a screen.

Projectors have many parts. The lamphouse holds the light source. The images are projected through the lens. The spool cover holds the reels of film.

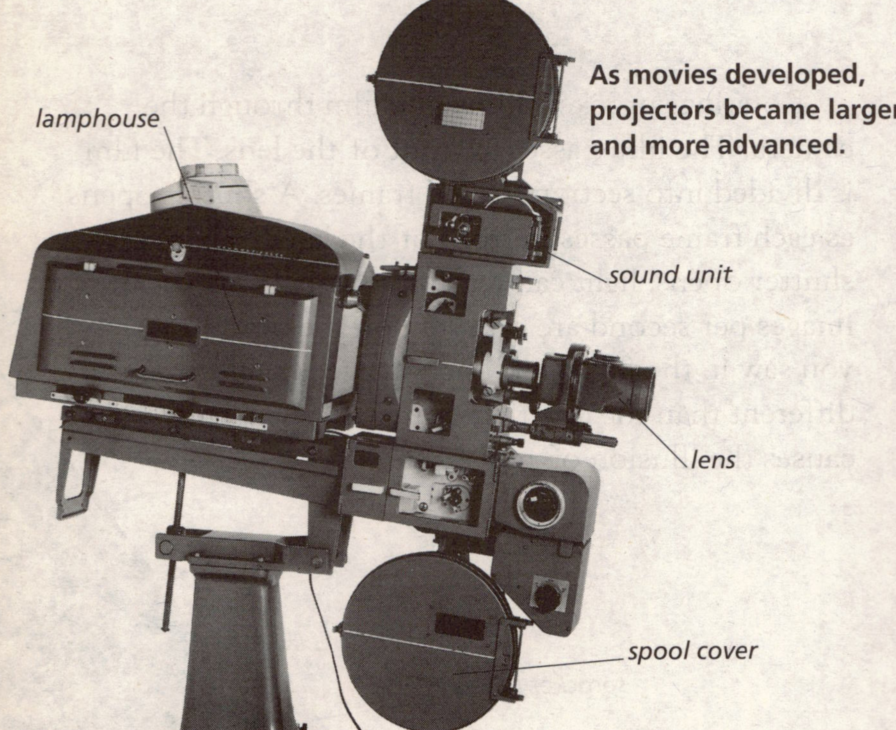

As movies developed, projectors became larger and more advanced.

Microphones pick up sound waves in the air and change them into electric signals. These sound signals travel through wires in the microphone to the sound engineers' portable recording device. There they are stored. Later they are carefully lined up with the images that the camera has recorded.

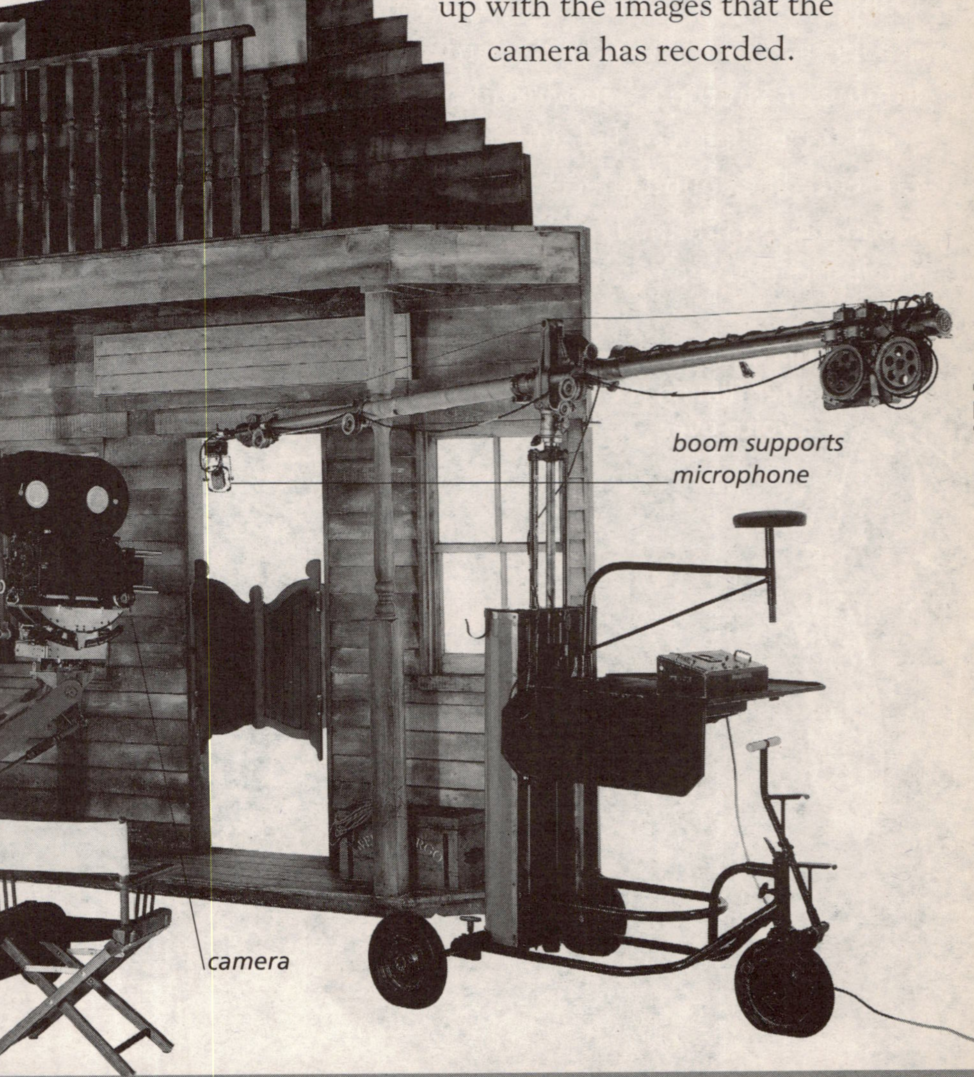

Sound

Sound engineers are the people on a movie set who record the actors' voices, as well as any other sound that is in the movie. The engineers use a large, powerful microphone to capture sound. The sound is then saved on a portable recording device. Usually when engineers are recording sound on a movie set, they will put the microphone at the end of a long mechanical arm called a boom. This keeps the microphone out of the view of the camera while still recording the necessary sounds. Sometimes, if the sound the engineers are trying to capture comes from something that moves throughout the scene, they use a hand-held microphone. This is a microphone that is attached to the end of a pole. It is moved to follow the sound source.

Sound is sometimes recorded with a hand-held microphone.

On a film set, sound is recorded using a long mechanical arm known as a boom.

How a projector works

Inside a movie projector, a light beam shines past the shutter through a moving strip of film. The lens projects the series of images onto a screen.

film spool
magnified image
shutter blocks light
lamp
lens focuses light

A strip of film holds more than just the images it has recorded. It often contains the sound for the movie as well. The sound is located on the side of the film next to the images. A sound unit on the projector picks up the sounds. It changes the sound information into electrical signals and sends them out to the speakers in the movie theater. The speakers turn those signals into the sound that you hear. Because the sound information and the images are on the same piece of film, you hear the sound and see the images at the same time.

Cinema in Color

The primary colors of light are red, blue, and green. When you mix these colors in specific amounts, you can make any other color you want. White light is all colors of the visible spectrum put together. In order for movie cameras to properly record the images in front of them, the film must be able to record all of the right color information. Modern movie cameras use film with layers of chemicals that are sensitive to red, blue, and green light. This ensures that the camera will record every color combination of light that enters the lens.

White light is made up of all the colors in the spectrum.

blue light
green light
cyan
magenta
red light
white light
yellow

Early film cameras were not able to record different colors. So the movies they recorded were black and white. Soon the technology became available to make movies in color. Some of the first color cameras that were invented used a prism to record all of the color information on the film. When white light enters a prism, it splits into all its different colors. The prism in the camera caused light to split and enter the lens as three separate colors: red, blue, and green. Each color was put on its own reel of film. In order to show the film in theaters, the colors had to be combined again. The three rolls of film were processed to make one final full-color reel that could be projected with regular projectors.

Early color cameras recorded colors using a prism.

Genre	Comprehension Skill	Text Features	Science Content
Nonfiction	Sequence	• Captions • Labels • Diagram • Glossary	Motion

Scott Foresman Science 4.15

ISBN 0-328-13903-3
9 780328 139033 90000

PEARSON Scott Foresman
scottforesman.com

Science

Physical Science

Newton AND GRAVITY

by Stephanie Wilder

Vocabulary	Extended Vocabulary
force	elliptical
frame of reference	gravitational pull
friction	prism
gravity	reflecting telescope
kinetic energy	spectrum
potential energy	tides
relative motion	white light
speed	
velocity	
work	

Picture Credits
Every effort has been made to secure permission and provide appropriate credit for photographic material. The publisher deeply regrets any omission and pledges to correct errors called to its attention in subsequent editions.

Photo locators denoted as follows: Top (T), Center (C), Bottom (B), Left (L), Right (R), Background (Bkgd).

1 Erich Lessing/AKG London Ltd.; 2 Jennifer Broadus/Index Stock Imagery; 4 (TR) Erich Lessing/AKG London Ltd., (B) NTPL/Nick Meers/The Image Works, Inc.; 6 (BR) Science Museum, London/DK Images; 7 NASA; 10 Galen Rowell/Corbis; 12 Plainpicture/Alamy Images; 13 (B) Keith Pritchard/Alamy Images.

Scott Foresman/Dorling Kindersley would also like to thank: 5 (T) Trinity College/DK Images; 8 NASA/DK Images; 11 (B) NASA/DK Images.

ISBN: 0-328-13903-3

2 3 4 5 6 7 8 9 10 V004 13 12 11 10 09 08 07 06 05

What did you learn?

1. In addition to his theory of gravity, what are some of Sir Isaac Newton's other achievements?

2. What are Newton's three laws of motion?

3. What is the difference between weight and mass?

4. **Writing** in Science Newton studied laws of gravity. Write to explain how gravity relates to the Moon orbiting Earth. Include details from the book to support your answer.

5. **Sequence** What discoveries did Newton make after seeing an apple fall?

Glossary

elliptical having the shape of an oval

gravitational pull the pull on an object caused by gravity

prism a transparent solid that can separate white light into all colors

reflecting telescope a powerful telescope that uses mirrors instead of glass lenses

spectrum a band of colors formed when a beam of light passes through a prism

tides the alternate rise and fall of the surface of the oceans connected and bodies of water

white light light that is made up of all the colors of the spectrum

Newton AND GRAVITY

by Stephanie Wilder

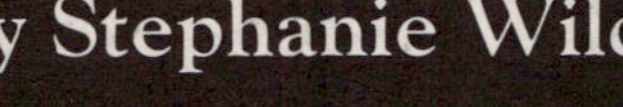

What You Already Know

Relative motion is a change in one object's position compared to another object's position. You can judge relative motion based on your frame of reference. Suppose you are riding in a car. You pass houses and trees. You can tell that you are moving by the objects you pass. Houses do not move relative to you in the car. Your position in the car is your frame of reference.

Speed is a measure of how quickly an object moves. Velocity is a measure of both the speed of an object and the direction in which it moves.

A force is any push or pull. Force can make an object stand still or move forward or backward. The object moves in the same direction as the force acting on it. All forces have size and direction.

Sir Isaac Newton grew up to be one of the most important scientists of all time. His laws of motion and his theory of gravity have helped scientists understand the universe better. Without his scientific contributions, we would not be able to explore space. Newton would be proud to know that his work has allowed future generations to explore the galaxy that he was only able to see through a telescope.

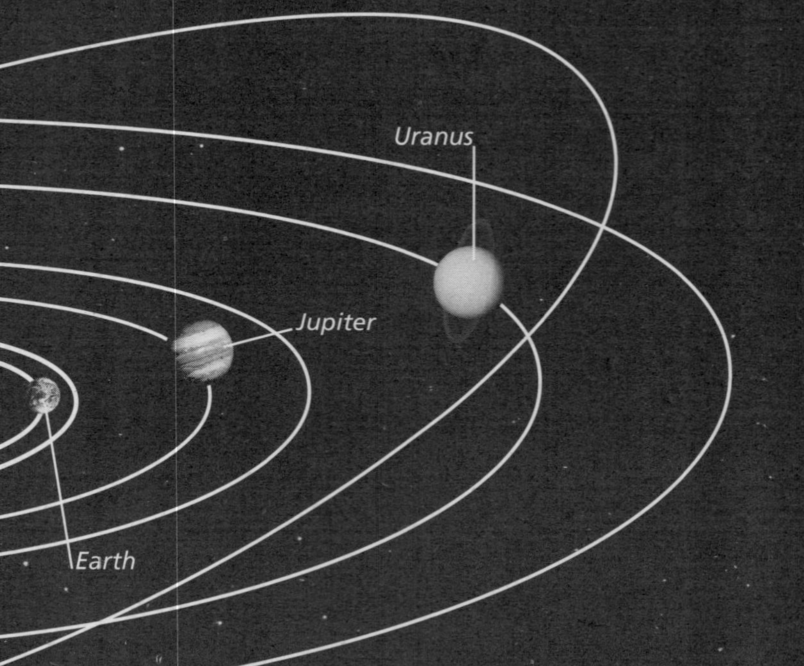

The sizes and distances in this diagram are not true to scale.

The Sun and Planets

All planets in the solar system orbit around the Sun. The Sun holds them in orbit, just as Earth holds the Moon in orbit. Gravity keeps the planets in their orbits. Without gravity, the planets might go hurtling off into space. Newton used his theory of gravity to explain why the planets go around the Sun in an elliptical, or oval, path.

The Sun and planets are controlled by gravity.

An object that is not moving will not start moving unless a force acts on it. Inertia is an object's resistance to any change to its motion.

Friction can play a role in the movement of an object. The more friction there is between objects, the more energy is needed to make them move. Smooth objects don't need a lot of force to move, but rough ones do. Objects with less mass move more easily than objects with more mass.

Work is the ability to move something. Work requires energy. Kinetic energy is the energy of motion. All moving things have kinetic energy. Potential energy is stored energy.

Gravity is the force that pulls two objects toward each other. Gravity is stronger if objects are closer together.

The study of gravity is just one scientific area in which Isaac Newton made a contribution. He made many discoveries that are still used by scientists today.

Newton's study of gravity has made rides such as roller coasters possible.

Isaac Newton

Isaac Newton was born at Woolsthorpe Manor in England on January 4, 1643. Newton was a clever child. He loved to build model windmills and mechanical toys.

Newton was not very good at looking after the family farm. So when he was old enough, Newton went to Trinity College at the University of Cambridge to study.

Isaac Newton

Newton's birthplace

Newton applied his theory of gravity to the tides he saw every day. The part of the ocean that is underneath the Moon is pulled up by the Moon's gravity. This causes high tides. At high tide, water levels rise and more water moves onto the shore. As the water moves toward the Moon, it is pulled away from other areas. These areas experience low tide. At low tide, water levels drop and water moves away from the shore.

During high tide, water is pulled toward the shore.

During low tide, water is pulled away from the shore.

Earth and Moon

Earth pulls on the Moon, keeping it on its path around Earth. The force of gravity keeps the Moon in its orbit. Suppose you are swinging around a ball on a string. You are Earth. The ball is the Moon, and the string is gravity. If you keep holding the string, the ball must keep moving around you. In the same way, as long as there is gravity, the Moon will keep moving around Earth. What if you let go of the string? The ball would fly away from you. The same thing would happen if gravity weren't holding the Moon in place. The Moon would spin away from Earth.

At the same time as Earth is pulling on the Moon, the Moon pulls on Earth. This causes the daily tides in the ocean.

Newton studied at Trinity College in Cambridge, England.

At Cambridge, Newton was an average student. He had trouble understanding the works of the ancient Greek scientists he studied in his classes. But on his own, Newton read books by more modern scientists.

In 1665, a terrible disease swept across England. The University of Cambridge was closed to keep the students from getting sick. In the eighteen months that Newton stayed home from Cambridge, he made his three greatest scientific discoveries. He invented a new kind of math, made discoveries about the relationship between light and color, and came up with the beginning of his theory of gravity. Although Newton would continue to do important work for the rest of his life, these were his greatest achievements.

Scientific Genius

Isaac Newton studied many areas of science. He studied the science behind rainbows. He discovered that white light is made up of all the colors of the spectrum. He also found that white light can be separated into these colors using a prism. When white light goes through a prism, or even a raindrop, you can see all of its colors.

Newton's experiments with prisms contributed to his knowledge of the spectrum.

Newton used all that he had learned from his study of prisms to build the first reflecting telescope. This was a telescope that used mirrors instead of glass lenses. It was more powerful than other telescopes of the time. Now people could study the stars more closely than ever before.

Newton invented the first reflecting telescope.

Gravity also depends on an object's mass. Objects with more mass have more gravity. Earth has much more mass than the Moon. The force of gravity on the Moon is much less than the force of gravity on Earth. If you went to the Moon, your mass would not change. But your weight would change. The Moon's weaker gravity would not pull on you as hard as Earth's strong gravity does. This means you would weigh less.

Your weight is less on the Moon, but your mass stays the same.

Weight and Mass

Mass is the amount of matter in an object. Gravity pulls on mass and makes it move toward the center of Earth. Weight depends on gravity. Weight is the measure of gravity's pull on an object.

If you climb to the top of a tall mountain, your weight will be a tiny bit less than it was at the foot of the mountain. This is because gravity gets weaker as objects get farther apart. At the foot of the mountain, you are fairly close to Earth's gravitational pull. At the top of the mountain, you are a little farther away from that pull. Think about a small magnet and a paper clip. The magnet can move the clip when they are close together. But from across the room, the magnet isn't strong enough to move the clip. The magnet's pull decreases with distance.

You weigh slightly less at the top of a mountain.

Newton described three laws of motion. His first law of motion is that an object in motion will stay in motion unless acted on by an outside force. That means a ball rolling across the floor will keep rolling until a force, such as friction, makes it stop.

The second law of motion explains how force, mass, and movement are related. If two balls have the same mass but one is moving faster, the faster ball will have more force. If the balls are moving at the same speed but one has more mass, the ball with more mass will have more force.

Newton's third law states that when you use force on an object, it uses an equal but opposite force on you. If you stub your toe on a rock, your toe will hurt. This is due to the force of the rock pushing back.

According to Newton's third law, the space shuttle moves up with the same amount of force as that of the rocket engines pushing down.

What is gravity?

Newton stated that gravity is a force that pulls two objects together. Every object has gravity. The pull of an object's gravity depends on the mass of the object and the distance between it and another object. Newton put this idea into his famous book, *Principia*.

The gravitational pull of Earth is very strong. It is this force that pulls you and everything around you toward the center of Earth.

Earth has a powerful gravitational pull.

Perhaps Newton came up with the idea for the theory of gravity after watching an apple fall to the ground from a tree.

Though not recorded officially, many claim that Newton discovered gravity while observing an apple tree. An apple fell from the tree and hit the ground. Newton wondered what made that apple drop to the ground instead of float away.

Then he started to think about the force that keeps the Moon orbiting Earth. Newton knew that objects tend to move in straight paths. So why didn't the Moon move in a straight line off into space? Newton realized that Earth has to be pulling on the Moon to keep it from flying away. This pulling force is gravity. Newton used his math skills to prove that the force that makes the apple fall to the ground is the same force that keeps the Moon in its orbit of Earth.

Science

Genre	Comprehension Skill	Text Features	Science Content
Nonfiction	Summarize	• Captions • Labels • Text Boxes • Glossary	Simple Machines

Scott Foresman Science 4.16

PEARSON Scott Foresman
DK
scottforesman.com
ISBN 0-328-13906-8
9 780328 139064 90000

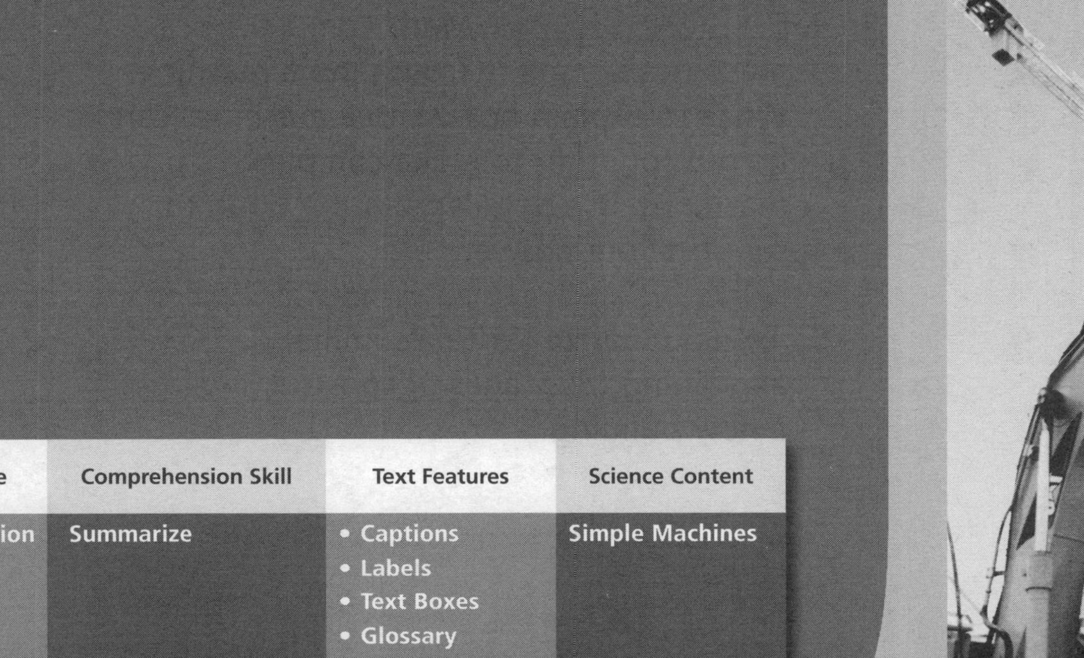

Science

Physical Science

On the Building Site

by Marilyn Greco

Vocabulary	Extended Vocabulary
effort	auger
fulcrum	excavator
inclined plane	foundation
lever	gears
load	jib
pulley	shaft
screw	trenches
wedge	
wheel and axle	

Picture Credits
Every effort has been made to secure permission and provide appropriate credit for photographic material. The publisher deeply regrets any omission and pledges to correct errors called to its attention in subsequent editions.

Photo locators denoted as follows: Top (T), Center (C), Bottom (B), Left (L), Right (R), Background (Bkgd).

Opener: Albert Normandin/Masterfile Corporation; 4 Albert Normandin/Masterfile Corporation; 8 Leslie Garland Picture Library/Alamy Images; 11 (BR) Niall MacLeod/Corbis; 13 (B) Getty Images.

ISBN: 0-328-13906-8

2 3 4 5 6 7 8 9 10 V004 13 12 11 10 09 08 07 06 05

What did you learn?

1. How does an excavator use a simple machine to do work?

2. Why do mobile cranes need special legs?

3. What work does a bulldozer do, and what simple machine does it use?

4. **Writing** in Science Many complex machines are made from simple machines. Write to explain how simple machines can be put together to make complex machines. Use details from the book to support your answer.

5. **Summarize** Write a summary explaining the stages of constructing a new building.

Glossary

auger a large tool for making holes

excavator a large tool that loosens, scoops, and lifts loads of soil and rock

foundation the part of a building that supports all the other parts

gears wheels with teeth that fit into the teeth of other wheels so that when one wheel turns, so do the others

jib the arm of a crane on which a load is placed

shaft a bar that supports the turning parts of a machine

trenches ditches; deep grooves

by Marilyn Greco

What You Already Know

In science, work means using force to push or pull an object or to cause a change. Machines make work easier. Some simple machines help you use less force. Others change the direction of the force you use. Simple machines include the lever, the wheel and axle, the pulley, the inclined plane, the wedge, and the screw.

The lever is a long bar that rests on a support called the fulcrum. A lever is used to lift a load. The effort is the push or pull that makes the load move. Levers are put into groups based on where the fulcrum, effort, and load are.

The wheel and axle is a special kind of lever. It turns or moves objects. The axle is a rod that goes through the center of the wheel. The handle of a screwdriver is a wheel. The blade is the axle. You use force to turn the handle.

The screwdriver is a wheel and axle.

A pulley is a wheel with a rope, a wire, or a chain around it. You can pull on the rope or chain to make the wheel move. A pulley can change the direction of force.

Gears are important parts of construction machinery and are used for many purposes. Gears can make a giant vehicle move faster or slower or change direction. In a cement mixer, gears also direct power from the engine to turn the mixer full of heavy cement.

There is plenty of work at a building site! Bulldozers, saws, cranes, drills, and cement mixers all use simple machines to get the job done.

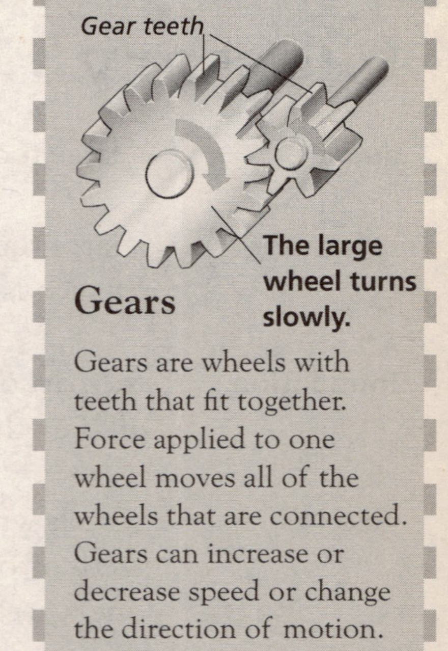

Gears

Gears are wheels with teeth that fit together. Force applied to one wheel moves all of the wheels that are connected. Gears can increase or decrease speed or change the direction of motion.

Gears send power from the engine to mix the cement.

Wheels in Action

The wheel and axle is used in many places on a building site. The axle is a shaft that is joined to a wheel at its center. Turning the wheel also turns the axle.

A wheel and axle can lift heavy loads. A cable is used to connect the load to the axle. Turning the wheel requires less force than turning the axle. As the wheel turns, the cable winds around the axle and moves the load.

The wheel and axle can be used to move a vehicle. The engine of a vehicle is powerful enough to move the axle. The moving axle then moves the wheel. The larger rim of the wheel covers a greater distance than the turning axle. Some construction equipment moves on wheels that are taller than the workers driving them!

The Wheel and Axle

A wheel and axle can be used to lift heavy objects. A load is attached to the axle by a cable. The load is lifted with less effort by turning the wheel. It takes less effort to turn the wheel than it takes to turn the axle.

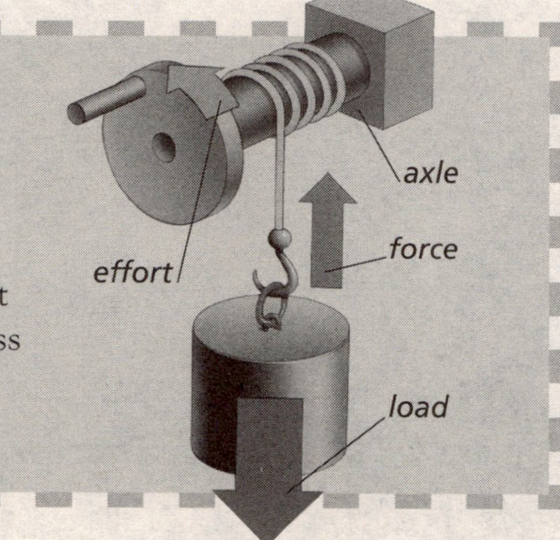

A ramp is an example of an inclined plane. It helps you apply less force to move an object over a greater distance.

A wedge is similar to two inclined planes put together. A force at one end of a wedge moves the other end of the wedge forward.

A screw is a kind of inclined plane. The slanting ridges that wrap around a screw are called threads. Screws can fasten things, lift things, and hold things together.

Simple machines can be put together to make complex machines. A can opener is a complex machine. It uses a wedge, levers, and wheels and axles.

Many complex machines are used for building. Let's see some of the machines we might find on a construction site.

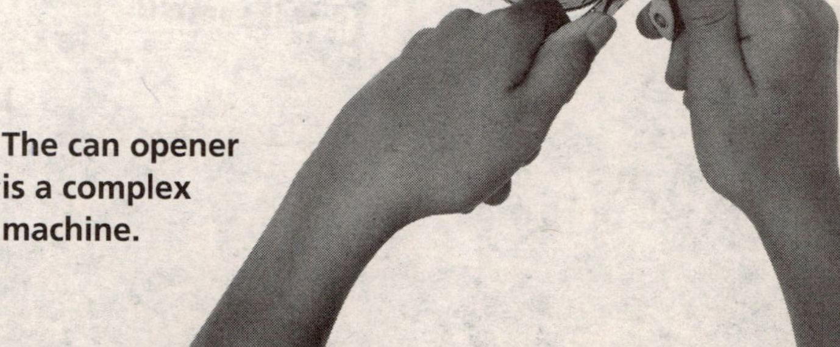

The can opener is a complex machine.

Construction Site

Construction of new buildings is a common sight. People build new malls, apartments, houses, schools, factories, and skyscrapers. There are four stages in the construction of a new building. In the first stage, the ground is prepared and the foundation is laid. Next, workers build the frame of the building. Then the frame is covered with glass, metal, or wood. Finally, the interior is completed.

Very large machines are used mostly in the first stages of building construction. Complex machines such as bulldozers, excavators, cranes, and cement mixers use simple machines to do work.

On a building site, machines help people do work.

A crane is made of many pulleys. The pulleys make heavy objects easier to lift. A crane lifts objects with an arm called a jib. Because cranes lift extremely heavy objects, balance is very important. The jib of a tall crane has many openings that allow wind to pass through it. Without the open frame, a strong wind might push the entire crane over.

Tower cranes are not mobile. The open frame of the jib keeps the crane steady.

The Pulley

Pulleys are grooved wheels with a cable running over them. Pulling on one end of the cable raises a load at the other end. Pulleys reduce the effort needed to lift objects.

Lifting Heavy Loads

Many buildings are supported by steel beams and parts made of concrete. Such building materials are very strong, but they are also extremely heavy. The machine most often used to lift heavy materials and place them in precise locations is the crane.

Some cranes can easily move from one location to another. Mobile cranes are those that can move around. They have special legs that extend to keep them steady while they work. These legs also help the crane support the weight of heavy loads. Tower cranes are those that are used to build skyscrapers. They are fixed in one place and do not move.

Big cranes lift very heavy materials.

The Inclined Plane

A ramp is an example of an inclined plane. Pushing an object up a ramp is easier than lifting it straight up.

A construction site is a busy place. Workers do many different kinds of work, and they use many kinds of machines to help them. Heavy equipment and other machines reduce the effort required to turn plans into a finished building.

Workers who operate heavy equipment must know how their machines work. Machine operators understand how the different kinds of simple machines help them to dig, lift, turn, pour, and haul heavy loads.

Perhaps the simplest of the simple machines is the inclined plane. It has no moving parts! Other simple machines are a bit more complicated, but they all help us do work with less effort. The inclined plane is used in the ramp and in other simple and complex machines. Simple machines help get work done at a building site.

Digging and Shifting

Before a building can be built, the ground must be prepared so the foundation can hold the building's tremendous weight and keep it stable. To make these preparations, a worker uses an excavator. The work of the excavator is to loosen, scoop, and lift many loads of dirt. The excavator drops the dirt into a dump truck, which takes it to another site. The excavator digs out trenches, or ditches, that will be used for the building's concrete foundation.

This excavator uses levers that are joined together to dig and lift dirt.

The Wedge

The wedge is a type of inclined plane. The wedge shape of an axe blade makes it an excellent tool for splitting wood. The blade starts with downward force as it enters the wood. This changes to sideways force that splits the wood apart.

The force splits wood.

The blade is a wedge.

Wedges can be used on building sites in other ways. One simple wedge is a saw. A saw has small grooves on it that are called teeth. If you move a saw back and forth on material such as wood, the teeth cut into the wood and push it apart. The saw acts as a wedge by forcing pieces of the wood to separate.

A nail is another wedge. It is similar to a screw. A hammer pounds the flat head of the nail into a surface. The pointed end of the nail makes a hole as it is pushed in deeper.

The teeth of a saw are sharp wedges that reduce the effort needed to cut wood.

Pushing and Cutting

The bulldozer uses the same simple machine that the ramp and the screw use. It uses the inclined plane. The blade of the bulldozer is a special type of inclined plane known as a moving wedge.

On the bulldozer, force pushing on the wider end of the wedge pushes the thinner edge against the ground. This edge can slice into the ground or scrape the surface. A bulldozer can also pick up dirt and rocks. The inclined plane changes some of the forward-moving force into upward force. By using a wedge, the effort needed to move heavy dirt and rocks is reduced.

The blade of a bulldozer is a wedge. It is used to cut and push.

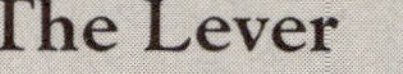

The Lever

A lever is a bar resting on a fulcrum. Force pushing down on one end of the bar lifts a load at the other end.

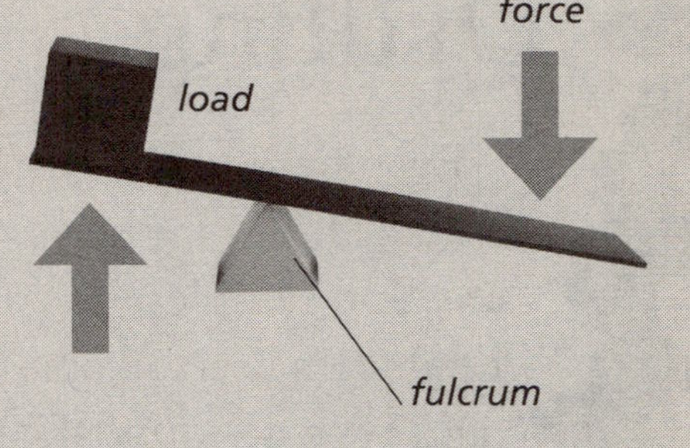

On the building site, an excavator digs and lifts using a simple machine. The arm of the excavator is a series of levers. Each joint of the arm is a fulcrum. The load at the end of each lever is raised when force is applied in the opposite direction at the other end.

Levers change the direction of force. They also allow more work to be done while using less force. The closer the fulcrum is to the load, the less force is required to do the job.

A wheelbarrow is a complex machine. It is a lever. The wheel at the front is the fulcrum. The wheel is also a wheel and axle.

Drilling

Even before any digging starts, drills are used to make holes in the ground at a construction site. Soil samples are collected for analysis. Engineers use soil analysis to decide the depth and type of foundation that will be needed.

Tall buildings require special foundations that will support their weight. An auger is a piece of equipment used to drill large holes in the ground. These holes will hold underground columns that help support the buildings. Smaller hand drills are used to finish work inside the buildings.

Workers use a giant auger to dig holes for underground columns.

The Screw

A screw works much like a drill. The head of the screw has a slot to hold a screwdriver. The screwdriver turns the screw around and around. The spiraling threads of the screw are a kind of inclined plane. The screw makes a hole as it pushes deeper and deeper.

force

motion

A drill uses an inclined plane wrapped around a bar called a shaft. The tip of the shaft narrows to a point. Force is applied to push the pointed end of the drill into the material to be cut. The sharp edge cuts a hole in the material. The spiral design of the drill allows this machine to continue cutting deeper and deeper. Drills and augers are designed so that they can be removed from the holes they make.

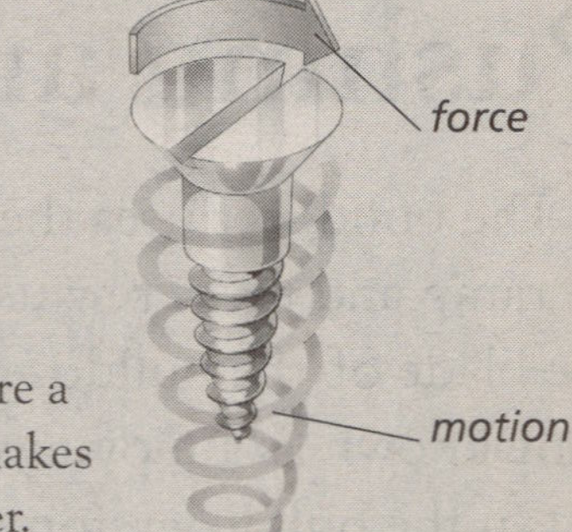

Power drills can be used to make small holes.

Science

Genre	Comprehension Skill	Text Features	Science Content
Nonfiction	Cause and Effect	• Captions • Diagrams • Call Outs • Glossary	Earth Cycles

Scott Foresman Science 4.17

scottforesman.com

ISBN 0-328-13909-2
90000
9 780328 139095

Science

Space and Technology

ECLIPSE

by Kelly Kong

Vocabulary	Extended Vocabulary
axis	annular eclipse
constellation	corona
eclipse	diamond ring effect
ellipse	partial eclipse
lunar eclipse	penumbral shadow
orbit	total eclipse
revolution	umbral shadow
rotation	zone of totality
solar eclipse	

Picture Credits
Every effort has been made to secure permission and provide appropriate credit for photographic material. The publisher deeply regrets any omission and pledges to correct errors called to its attention in subsequent editions.

Photo locators denoted as follows: Top (T), Center (C), Bottom (B), Left (L), Right (R), Background (Bkgd).

Opener: Getty Images; 1 Getty Images; 4 Reuters/Corbis; 7 Getty Images; 8 William H. Mullins/Photo Researchers, Inc.; 9 (TR) Frank Zullo/Photo Researchers, Inc.; 10 (T) Reinhard Krause/Reuters/Corbis; 11 (BR) Roger Ressmeyer/Corbis; 13 Reuters/Corbis; 15 Getty Images.

Scott Foresman/Dorling Kindersley would also like to thank: 6 (TC) NASA/DK Images.

ISBN: 0-328-13909-2

2 3 4 5 6 7 8 9 10 V004 13 12 11 10 09 08 07 06 05

What did you learn?

1. Compare total and partial solar eclipses. How are they different?

2. Describe the diamond ring effect. When and why does this occur?

3. Total solar eclipses and lunar eclipses do not occur every month. Why not?

4. **Writing** in Science There are many good and bad ways to view solar and lunar eclipses. Explain some ways in which you would and would not observe eclipses. Use examples from the book to support your answer.

5. **Cause and Effect** Occasionally, the Moon looks red during a lunar eclipse. Describe what causes this glowing effect.

Glossary

annular eclipse an eclipse that occurs when the Moon is at the farthest point from Earth in its orbit and is directly between the Sun and Earth

corona the Sun's outer atmosphere that looks like a halo of light around the Sun

diamond ring effect a bead of light resembling a diamond, which shines through a valley of the Moon during an eclipse

partial eclipse an eclipse that occurs when part of the Moon's shadow passes over part of Earth's surface

penumbral shadow faint, outer shadow

total eclipse an eclipse that occurs when the Moon completely blocks the light of the Sun from reaching Earth

umbral shadow dark, inner shadow

zone of totality the areas on Earth from where a total solar eclipse can be seen

ECLIPSE

by Kelly Kong

PEARSON Scott Foresman

What You Already Know

Earth spins around an imaginary line called an axis. The spinning motion is called rotation. As Earth rotates, it also moves around the Sun. The movement of one object, such as Earth, around another object, such as the Sun, is called a revolution. Earth moves around the Sun in a path called an orbit. Earth's orbit is an ellipse, or an oval shape.

Earth's axis is always tilted in the same direction. This tilt causes the different seasons. At different points in the orbital path, some parts of Earth are closer to the Sun than others. The half of Earth that is tilted toward the Sun receives more light and heat. The daylight in this half of Earth lasts longer.

The Sun is the star closest to Earth. Trillions of other stars occupy the sky. Stars often appear in many shapes and patterns in the sky. These patterns are called constellations. People in different regions do not see the same star patterns. As Earth moves, the stars appear to move across the sky.

Just as Earth revolves around the Sun, the Moon moves around Earth. The Moon rotates on its own axis as it revolves around Earth. It does not produce light. We see the sunlight that reflects off the Moon's surface.

total solar eclipse

Predicting eclipses is relatively easy due to the regular orbits of the Sun, the Moon, and Earth. The map to the left predicts total eclipses through 2020.

A total solar eclipse occurs about every one and a half years somewhere in the world. However, these eclipses often fall over the ocean or in areas where only a few people live. Lunar eclipses occur more frequently. They may happen several times a year.

We know a great deal about the Sun, the Moon, Earth, and their orbits. This information helps scientists predict eclipses far into the future. The time and place of past eclipses are also easy to calculate. Some people go on special trips just to watch eclipses happen. Where would you go if you took a trip to see an eclipse?

Predicting Eclipses

If the Moon's orbit were not tilted, solar and lunar eclipses could happen each month. A solar eclipse would occur every time the Moon was new, and a lunar eclipse would take place every time the Moon was full. However, due to the Moon's tilt, eclipses take place only when the Sun, the Moon, and Earth are perfectly in line with each other. This does not happen very often.

total solar eclipses to 2020

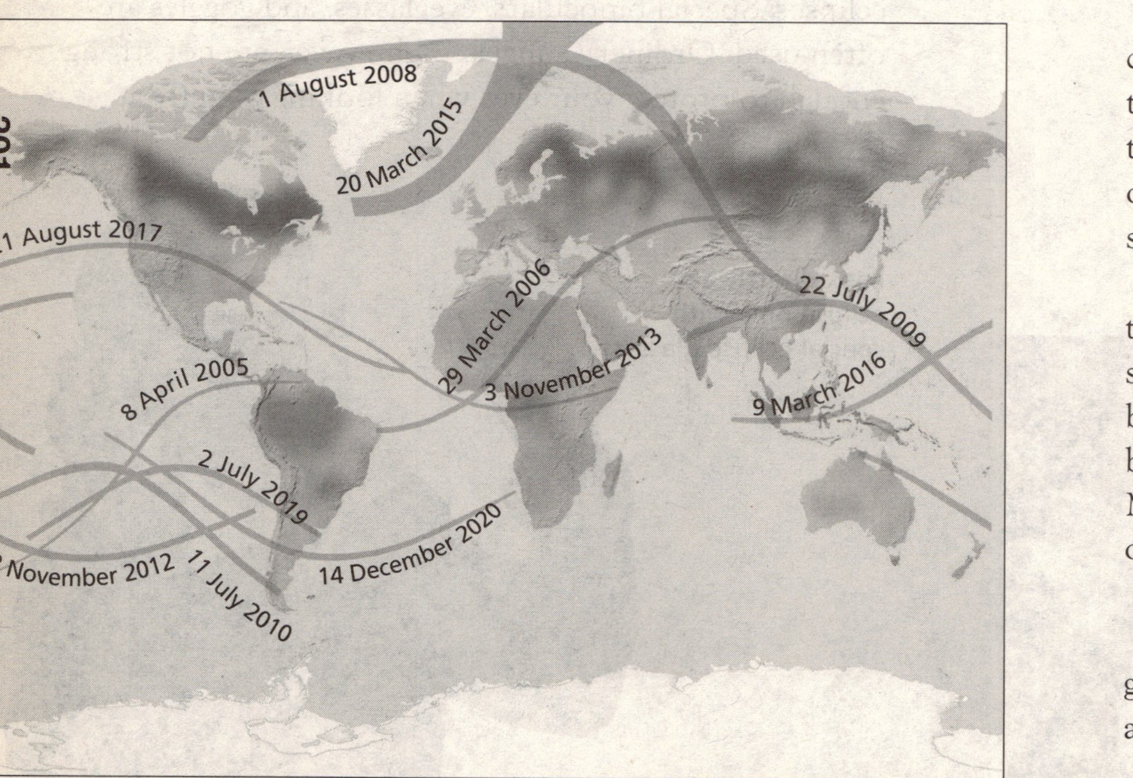

phases of the Moon

Sometimes the entire lighted side of the Moon directly faces Earth. Other times, only a small part of the lighted section is visible from Earth. The shape of the Moon appears to change depending on how much of the lighted part can be seen from Earth. The different shapes that we see are called the phases of the Moon.

An eclipse occurs when an object moves between the Sun and another object and casts a shadow on the second object. A lunar eclipse takes place when Earth is between the Sun and the Moon. The Moon is covered by Earth's shadow. A solar eclipse occurs when the Moon is between the Sun and Earth. The Moon blocks our view of the Sun.

The movement of the Sun, the Moon, and Earth greatly affect each other. To learn more about eclipses, as well as the Sun, the Moon, and Earth, keep reading!

The Power of the Sun

The closest star to Earth is the Sun. It provides energy and light to all of Earth's living things. The Sun plays an important role in all life cycles.

The Sun, however, can also be harmful. It is so powerful that if you look at it directly, it can cause permanent damage to your eyes. It can even blind you. It is important never to look directly at the Sun without protective eyewear, even when the Sun is covered by an eclipse.

Eclipses do not occur only with Earth and the Moon. They can occur with other planets in the solar system. One of Jupiter's moons can move into Jupiter's shadow, causing a lunar eclipse. But we are most familiar with eclipses that take place between Earth and the Moon.

These students are using protective eyewear to watch a solar eclipse.

An example of an indirect method to observe solar eclipses is using the pinhole camera method. With this method, the Sun's image is projected onto a light-colored board or sheet of paper.

First, take a sheet of paper and prop it up or place it on the ground. Then, use another sheet of paper and poke a small hole in it. Attach this paper to a pair of binoculars. Stand with the Sun behind you and look at the first sheet of paper. The image of the eclipse will be visible on the paper.

Other instruments can also be used to view solar eclipses. Special binoculars, eyeglasses, and goggles are often used. Ordinary sunglasses, however, are not strong enough to protect your eyes when looking directly at the Sun.

Look directly at an eclipse only with special eclipse glasses.

Watching Eclipses

> **DANGER!**
> You need proper equipment to watch an eclipse safely. You can use filters that have aluminum, chromium, or silver to view an eclipse.

Even though you may want to stare directly at the Sun during eclipses, it is important to protect your eyes. Lunar eclipses are easier to observe than solar eclipses. The Sun is incredibly bright and powerful. As a result, solar eclipses are harmful to your eyes. Solar eclipses are best viewed indirectly.

You can watch an eclipse by projecting the Sun through binoculars onto a sheet of paper or a board.

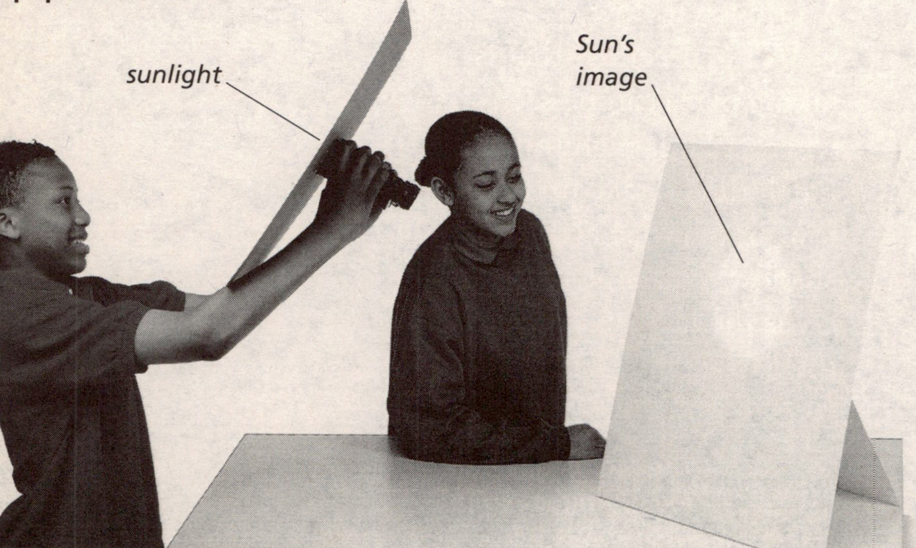

As the Moon travels in its orbit, it can move between Earth and the Sun. This keeps sunlight from reaching Earth. The Moon's shadow is cast on Earth. This is a solar eclipse.

How a Solar Eclipse Occurs

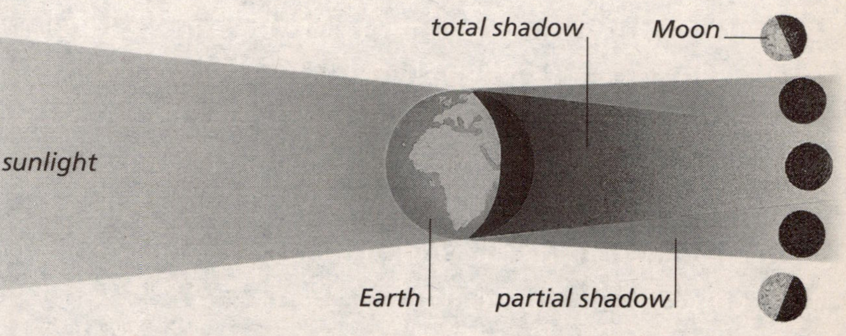

As the Moon continues its orbit, Earth may move between the Sun and the Moon. Earth is in the path of sunlight to the Moon. This prevents the Sun's light from reaching the Moon. This is a lunar eclipse.

How a Lunar Eclipse Occurs

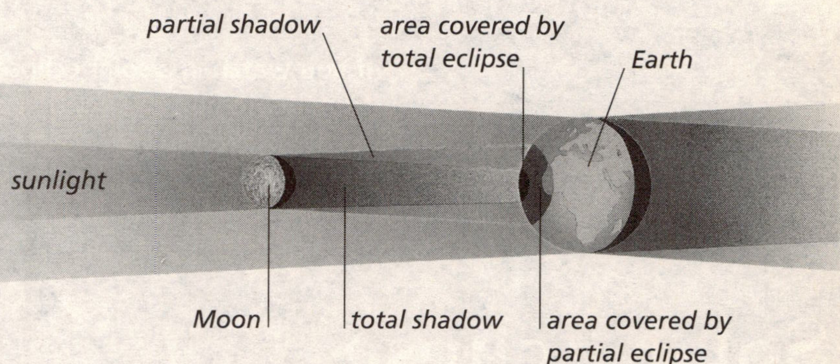

Corona

If you watched a solar eclipse from beginning to end, this is what you would see.

Solar Eclipse

There are three different kinds of solar eclipses: total eclipses, partial eclipses, and annular eclipses. A total eclipse is the rarest kind of eclipse.

In a total solar eclipse, the Moon completely blocks the light of the Sun. The eclipse begins as the Moon slowly makes its way between the Sun and Earth. It appears to cover more and more of the Sun. A total solar eclipse occurs when the Moon is between the Sun and Earth. The Sun is completely blocked by the Moon. The Sun's corona becomes more visible than it usually is to those on Earth. The corona is a glowing halo of light that surrounds the Sun. You can see the corona in the center of the image above.

When only part of the Moon crosses the umbral shadow, a partial lunar eclipse takes place. If the whole Moon crosses Earth's umbral shadow, a total lunar eclipse takes place. A total eclipse may last more than an hour.

When the Moon is in Earth's umbral shadow, some sunlight still manages to reach it. This sunlight, however, first passes through the Earth's atmosphere, which filters out some colors in the light. The light that reaches the Moon can be deep red or orange. This can give the Moon a red glow.

A lunar eclipse that is taking place can be seen wherever it is night on Earth. It can take up to four hours for Earth's shadow to completely cross the face of the Moon.

The Moon may look red during an eclipse.

This is the sequence the Moon follows during a lunar eclipse.

Lunar Eclipse

In addition to being elliptical, the Moon's orbit is also tilted. This tilt usually keeps the Moon out of Earth's shadow. But sometimes the Moon crosses Earth's shadow. A lunar eclipse occurs when a full Moon passes through Earth's shadow.

Earth's shadow is made of two parts. The first part is the outer, or penumbral, shadow. In this part of the shadow, Earth blocks part of the Sun's light from reaching the Moon. Penumbral shadows are faint partial shadows. They cause penumbral lunar eclipses, which are difficult to see.

The second part, which is located in the middle of the penumbral shadow, is the inner, or umbral, shadow. This full shadow blocks all sunlight from reaching the Moon.

Just before the eclipse reaches its peak, a diamond ring effect may form for a few seconds. This effect is caused by the Sun's light shining through very short valleys, or craters, on the uneven surface of the Moon. A bead of light that sparkles and looks like a diamond may be visible from Earth. The bead of light, combined with the Sun's corona, makes a diamond ring effect during the eclipse.

A solar eclipse cannot be seen from everywhere on Earth. The area from which a solar eclipse can be seen is called the zone of totality. This zone is ten thousand miles long but only one hundred miles wide. An eclipse is usually not visible at any one point for more than eight minutes.

The small bead of light shining past the Moon's surface shows the diamond ring effect.

Partial Eclipse

Another kind of solar eclipse is called a partial eclipse. Partial eclipses are much more common than total eclipses. A partial solar eclipse happens when part of the Moon's shadow passes over part of Earth's surface. The center of the Moon does not pass directly over the center of the Sun. The Moon appears to cover only part of the Sun.

Partial eclipses are more dangerous to the human eye than total eclipses. During a partial eclipse, a large portion of the Sun can still be seen. The brightness of the Sun can harm the eyes of anyone who looks at it.

During a partial solar eclipse, the Moon covers only some of the Sun.

Annular Eclipse

Just like a total eclipse, an annular eclipse occurs when the Moon is directly between Earth and the Sun. But the Moon must also be farthest from Earth in its orbit. The great distance between the Moon and Earth means the Moon can't block all of the Sun. Some of the darkest parts of the Moon's shadows will not reach Earth. Because of this, a bright ring of Sun remains, as shown photo.

During an annular eclipse, many places only see a partial eclipse.

How an Annular Eclipse Occurs

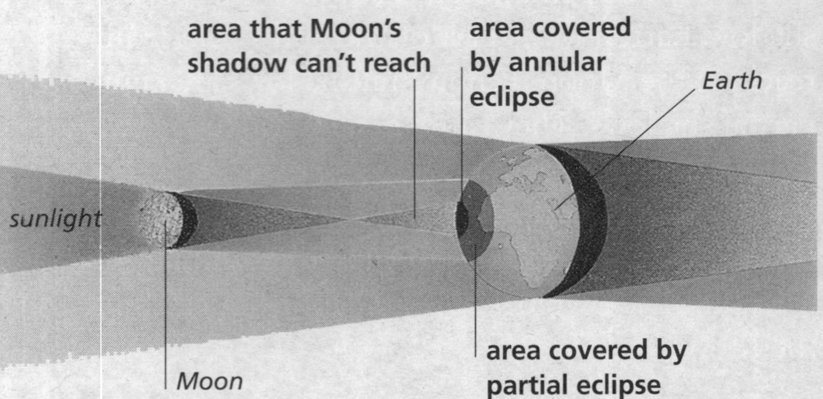

Genre	Comprehension Skill	Text Features	Science Content
Nonfiction	Predict	• Captions • Diagrams • Text Boxes • Glossary	Solar System

Scott Foresman Science 4.18

PEARSON
Scott Foresman
scottforesman.com

DK

ISBN 0-328-13912-2
9 780328 139125 90000

Science

Science

Space and Technology

The Red Planet

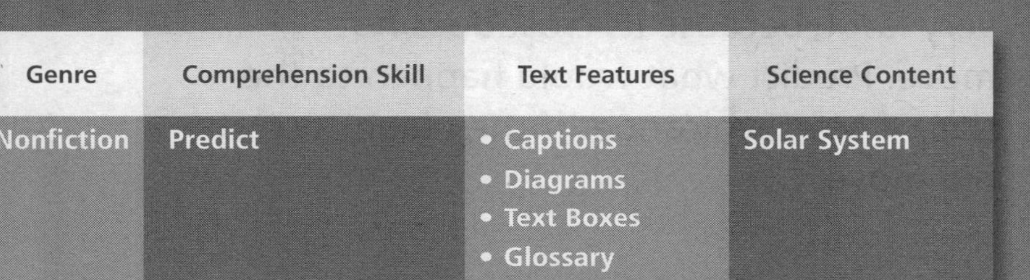

by Jean Szeto

Vocabulary	Extended Vocabulary
astronomy	asteroids
craters	gullies
galaxy	ozone layer
satellite	polar caps
solar system	rover
space probe	spectrometer
universe	terrain

Picture Credits
Every effort has been made to secure permission and provide appropriate credit for photographic material. The publisher deeply regrets any omission and pledges to correct errors called to its attention in subsequent editions.

Photo locators denoted as follows: Top (T), Center (C), Bottom (B), Left (L), Right (R), Background (Bkgd).

Opener: USGS/NASA; 1 NASA; 5 NSSDC/NASA; 9 SPL/Photo Researchers, Inc.; 10 (B) NASA; 12 NASA; 15 USGS/NASA; 16 The Hubble Heritage Team (STScI/AURA)/NASA; 17 Jet Propulsion Laboratory/NASA; 18 ©Galaxy Picture Library; 19 (TR) NASA Headquarters-Greatest Images of NASA /NASA; 20 NASA/Photo Researchers, Inc.; 21 NASA; 22 NASA; 23 NASA.

Scott Foresman/Dorling Kindersley would also like to thank: 6 (CR) NASA/DK Images; 7 (BR) Natural History Museum, London/DK Images.

ISBN: 0-328-13912-2

2 3 4 5 6 7 8 9 10 V004 13 12 11 10 09 08 07 06 05

What did you learn?

1. What are some ways in which Mars and Earth are different?

2. When space probes are sent into space, what do they do?

3. Can you breathe the air on Mars? Why or why not?

4. **Writing** in Science The water supply on Mars has changed. Explain what has changed about the planet's water supply and what evidence suggests these changes. Use examples from the book to support your answer.

5. **Predict** Volcanoes on Mars become very large because its crust does not move. Predict what would happen to the size of Mars' volcanoes if the planet's crust did move.

Glossary

asteroids small, rocky objects too small to be considered planets

gullies deep ditches made by running water

ozone layer a region of the upper atmosphere that blocks ultraviolet rays

polar caps areas permanently covered with ice

rover a vehicle used to explore the surface of objects in space

spectrometer an instrument used for measuring wavelengths of light

terrain the physical features of an area of land

The Red Planet

by Jean Szeto

PEARSON Scott Foresman

DK

What You Already Know

The universe is composed of millions of galaxies. A galaxy is a system of stars, gases, and dust. We live in the Milky Way galaxy. The study of the Sun, the Moon, and the objects in space is called astronomy.

The solar system includes the Sun, the planets, and other objects. The Sun is a medium-sized star and the largest body in the solar system. Its gravity pulls planets toward it. Planets move around the Sun in curved paths.

Mercury, the closest planet to the Sun, is covered with dents called craters. A space probe is a vehicle that carries cameras and other tools for studying objects in space. Space probes have been sent to many planets in our solar system, including Mercury.

Venus is nearly the same size as Earth. Its atmosphere is very hot and made up of poisonous gases.

Earth is the only planet that has liquid water on its surface. Earth has one large moon. A moon is a satellite, or an object that orbits another object in space.

Jupiter is the largest planet in our solar system. It has many moons and rings. Jupiter's atmosphere is mostly hydrogen and helium.

Saturn has rings made of ice and ice-covered rocks of different sizes. It has more than thirty moons. Its atmosphere is mainly hydrogen and helium.

Humans may one day travel to Mars. Technological improvements must happen to make sure that astronauts can travel to Mars, roam and explore the planet, and safely return to Earth. This kind of exploration is very dangerous but it is also an exciting adventure. Perhaps one day, you will be the first astronaut to visit Mars!

Life on Mars?

Scientists and other people around the world are curious about this mysterious planet. Information gathered by recent missions shows that Mars currently has a freezing environment without liquid water. Long ago, Mars may have been a warm, wet planet that supported life. The search for life on Mars continues.

In the future, new technologies will help us explore Mars in more detail. For example, scientists have developed ways to capture better quality pictures and to land space probes more accurately.

A 4.5 billion-year-old rock named Rock ALH84001 was found on Antarctica. Scientists think it came from Mars.

Rock ALH84001 viewed with a microscope

Uranus also has a ring system and at least twenty-seven moons. It is tilted and rotates on its side. Its atmosphere is mostly hydrogen, helium, and methane.

Neptune is about sixty times as big as Earth and has at least thirteen moons. One of its moons may have the coldest temperature in our solar system.

Pluto is the smallest planet in the solar system. It has one moon. Pluto's orbit is tilted.

In 2003, scientists discovered Sedna, which may be a tenth planet. Sedna is smaller than Earth's moon.

Mars is the fourth planet from the Sun. Read on to learn more about this "red planet."

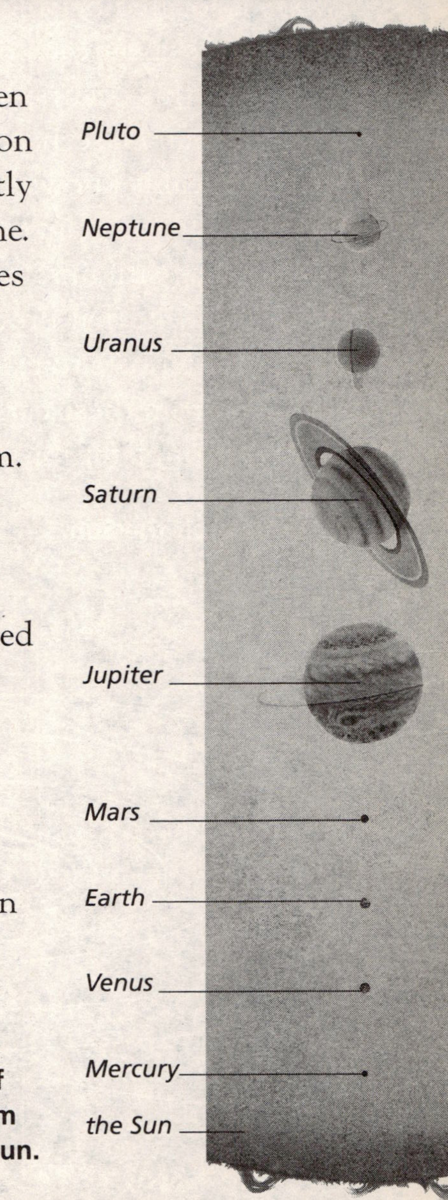

This image shows the sizes of the planets in the solar system compared to the size of the Sun.

Mars

Mars is located between Earth and Jupiter. Mars and Earth pass near each other almost every two years. When this occurs, Mars is one of the brightest objects that can be seen in Earth's night sky.

A great deal is known about Mars because exploration of the planet started as early as 1960. The first successful mission to Mars was in 1964. A probe was sent that produced twenty-one close-up photos for scientists to examine. Scientists learned a great deal from these early photos. They learned even more from later missions to Mars.

The planets orbit the Sun.

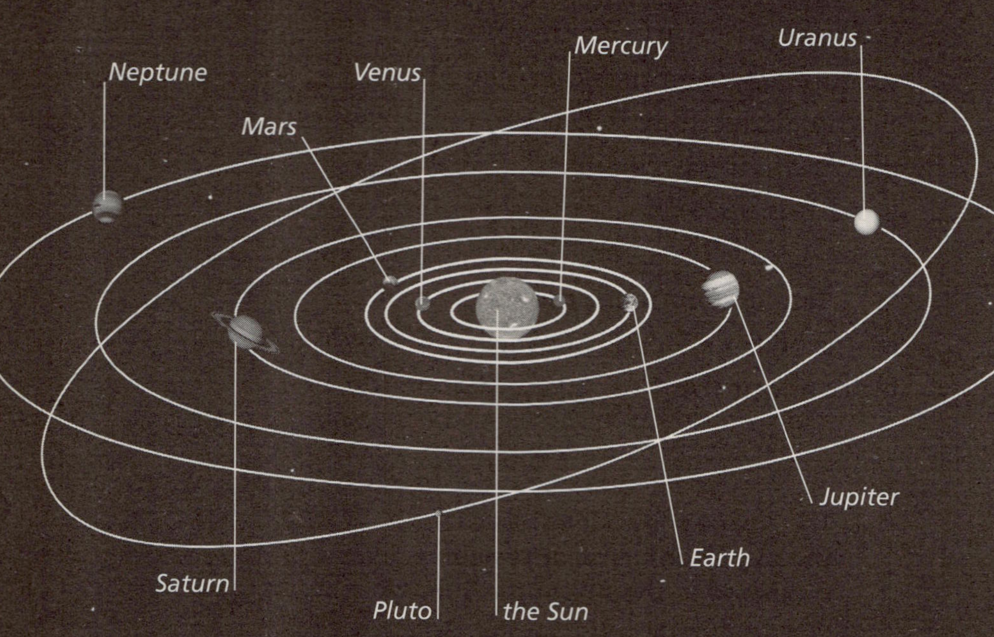

Rovers explored Mars for evidence of liquid water.

The two rovers, *Spirit* and *Opportunity,* produced images of the surface of Mars.

In 2004 two rovers landed on Mars. These Mars Exploration Rovers were named *Spirit* and *Opportunity*. *Spirit* and *Opportunity* were exactly the same kind of rover in design. NASA sent the rovers to explore different sections of the Red Planet at the same time. *Spirit* and *Opportunity* were sent to find evidence of liquid water on Mars.

These two rovers were able to move better and faster than *Sojourner*. *Spirit* and *Opportunity* could cross about 100 meters (328 feet) of land in one day. That's how far *Sojourner* moved during its whole time on Mars.

Many future missions to Mars have already been planned. The Mars Reconnaissance Orbiter is scheduled to launch in August 2005. In August 2007, NASA plans to launch the *Phoenix* spacecraft and lander.

On December 4, 1996, the National Aeronautics and Space Administration, or NASA, launched another probe to Mars. It was called the Mars *Pathfinder.* This mission was unique because it brought a robot named *Sojourner* to explore the landscape of Mars. *Pathfinder* reached Mars on July 4, 1997.

Sojourner had an X-ray spectrometer, or measuring instrument, attached to it. This spectrometer allowed *Sojourner* to identify chemicals within different rocks.

This mission provided thousands of observations about Mars. More than fifteen different chemical analyses of rocks and soil were produced. Instruments on *Pathfinder* also collected data on wind patterns and other weather factors on Mars.

The *Sojourner* rover identified the chemicals in rocks on Mars.

Mars is sometimes called the "Red Planet."

Mars is covered with rocks and soil that contain a mineral called iron oxide. Iron oxide is the chemical that makes up rust. It is reddish-brown in color. This gives Mars its color and is the reason that it is known as the "Red Planet."

Mars is very dry, rocky, and cold. It has the largest known volcano and the deepest known canyon in the solar system. In some ways, Mars is very similar to Earth. In other ways, however, Mars and Earth are very different.

The size and distances shown are not true to scale.

Earth and Mars have ice caps, volcanoes, and canyons. Both Earth and Mars have clouds in their atmospheres and seasonal weather patterns. The tilt of Mars' axis is approximately the same as the tilt of Earth's axis.

It is difficult for scientists to learn about the inner structure of Mars. They have determined that Mars has a thin outer crust, a mantle, and a core. This is similar to the structure of Earth's interior.

The diameter of Mars is about half the diameter of Earth.

Mars

Earth

Mars has a diameter of 6,790 km (4,219 miles).	**Earth has a diameter of 12,755 km (7,926 miles).**
The length of a Mars day is 24 hours and 37 minutes.	**The length of an Earth day is 23 hours and 56 minutes.**
The length of a Mars year is 687 Earth days.	**The length of an Earth year is 365.26 Earth days.**
Temperatures on Mars range from -142°C (-225°F) to 27°C (81°F).	**Temperatures on Earth range from -89°C (-128°F) to 57°C (136°F).**

Viking lander

The Viking missions landed on Mars and produced much clearer pictures.

Spacecraft called *Viking 1* and *Viking 2* were launched in 1975. *Viking 1* was launched on August 20, 1975, and *Viking 2* was launched on September 9, 1975. Both missions were very successful. Both space probes orbited and then landed on Mars. Landing on Mars was a huge accomplishment. No previous mission had come close to meeting such a goal. In fact, *Viking 1* was the first spacecraft ever to land on another planet!

Together *Viking 1* and *Viking 2* produced more than fifty thousand pictures of Mars. By gathering so much scientific data, the *Viking* space probes provided researchers and scientists with an immense amount of new information. A great deal of what we have learned today is based on research and discoveries such as these.

Missions to Mars

To understand more about Mars and its history and to predict what it may look like in the future, different countries send out space probes or launch missions into space. The first successful mission to Mars was launched on November 28, 1964. This United States spacecraft was named *Mariner 4*. In July, 1965 it produced the first close-up pictures of the surface of Mars.

Many other missions to Mars occurred after the success of *Mariner 4*. Some missions produced very little information, if any at all. Other missions were successful and sent back more pictures of the planet's surface. Scientists studied these pictures to learn more about the history of Mars.

Mariner 9 launched on May 30, 1971. The mission produced 7,329 pictures. On November 13, 1971 it became the first space probe ever to orbit Mars. On October 27, 1972, this probe sent information for the last time.

***Mariner 4* produced close-up pictures of Mars.**

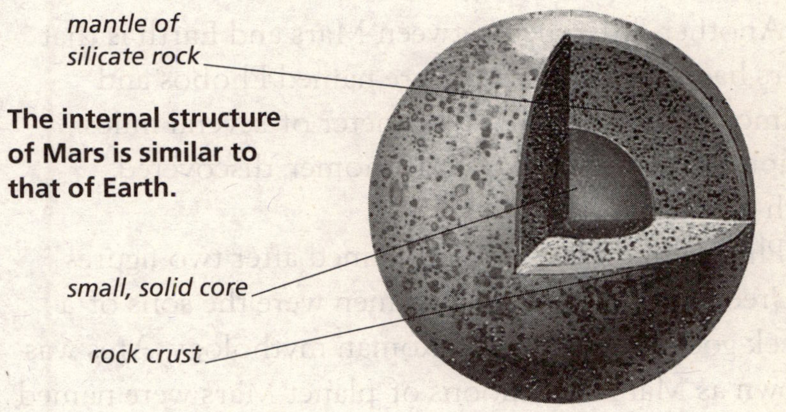

The internal structure of Mars is similar to that of Earth.

The core of Mars is made of iron. Scientists think that Mars has a liquid outer core and a solid inner core. The mantle around the core is made of a mineral called silicate. The crust that covers the mantle is a thin layer of rock.

One difference between Mars and Earth is that Mars is colder and drier than Earth is. The average temperature on Mars is –62° Celsius, or about –81° Fahrenheit. On Earth, the average temperature is 16° Celsius, or 60° Fahrenheit.

This is one of thirty-two meteorites that scientists have identified as coming from Mars.

Two Moons

Another difference between Mars and Earth is that Mars has two moons. They are named Phobos and Deimos. Each moon has a diameter of several miles. Asaph Hall, an American astronomer, discovered both moons.

Phobos and Deimos were named after two figures in Greek mythology. The two men were the sons of a Greek god named Ares. In Roman mythology, Ares was known as Mars. The moons of planet Mars were named after the two sons. *Phobos* means "fear" and *Deimos* means "panic" in the Greek language.

Mars has two moons named Phobos and Deimos.

Phobos

Deimos

When it is summer in a particular hemisphere, the polar cap in that hemisphere shrinks and the dark regions become even darker. In the winter, the polar cap grows and the dark region becomes paler.

Dry gullies and dried-up flood plains show that in the past, Mars may have had flowing, liquid water. Some of the polar caps and rock types contain a kind of ice that can form only when water is present. Today, scientists believe that large amounts of water lie frozen beneath Mars' surface.

Gullies hint that liquid water was once on the surface of Mars.

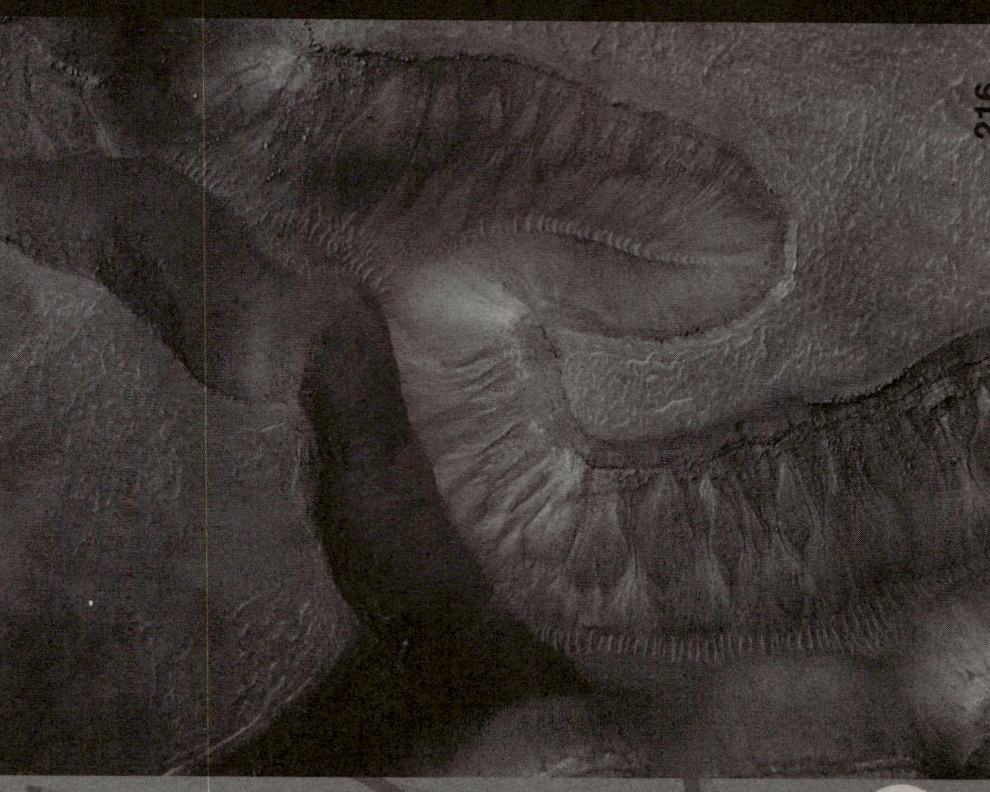

Is there water?

Mars has two large polar caps. Polar caps are white, icy areas that grow and shrink each year. This growing and shrinking shows that Mars has seasonal weather patterns.

The northern polar cap is made mostly of frozen water, or ice, and the southern polar cap is made mostly of frozen carbon dioxide. Frozen carbon dioxide is also known as dry ice. During the winter, some places may have more than a meter of frost.

Mars has polar caps on its north and south poles.

Phobos in its orbit of Mars

Both moons of Mars are relatively small and have surface materials that resemble those of asteroids. Many scientists believe that Phobos and Deimos are actually captured asteroids, or asteroids that have been pulled into the orbit around Mars.

Phobos is closer to Mars than Deimos is. On average, Phobos is 9,377 kilometers (5,826 miles) from Mars. The distance between Deimos and Mars is much greater at 23,436 kilometers (14,562 miles).

Phobos also appears to be spiraling closer to Mars. Some scientists predict that Phobos will eventually break into pieces and hit Mars.

Atmosphere

The atmosphere of Mars is mainly carbon dioxide and some water vapor. This atmosphere is very different from Earth's atmosphere, which is made of nitrogen, oxygen, argon, and other gases. Mars does not have breathable oxygen or an ozone layer. There is nothing to stop the Sun's dangerous ultraviolet rays from reaching the planet's surface.

Large amounts of dust move around in the atmosphere of Mars. Dust storms occur during the Martian spring and summer. These storms are similar to giant tornadoes. Dust storms can cover the entire planet. When the rust-colored dirt and dust are picked up and blown across the planet's surface, the sky of Mars appears to be pink and red. This is because the tiny pieces of fine red dust hang in the atmosphere.

Volcanic Giant

Compare the size of Olympus Mons to Mount Everest, one of the largest mountains on Earth. How small Mount Everest seems next to Olympus Mons!

In 1971 a space probe discovered a fault system in the middle of Mars. This fault system was named the Valles Marineris canyon and is much larger than the Grand Canyon in Arizona. In fact, Valles Marineris is larger than any canyon on Earth!

Valles Marineris is approximately 4,000 kilometers (2,500 miles) long. In some spots, the canyon is more than 600 kilometers (375 miles) wide and 9 kilometers (5.6 miles) deep. Valles Marineris is so long that it would stretch from the Atlantic Ocean across the United States to the Pacific Ocean.

The largest canyon on Mars is named Valles Marineris.

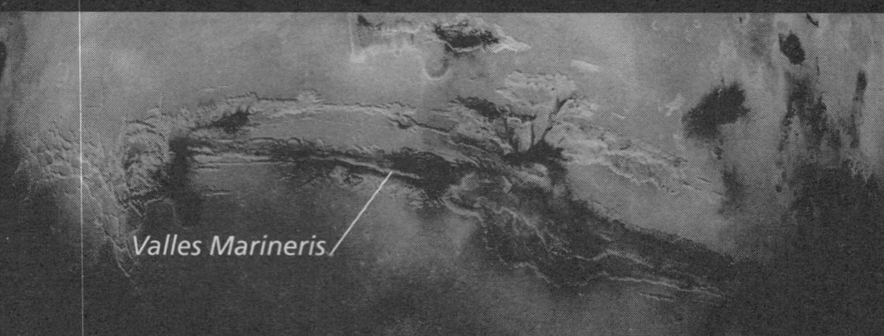

Volcanoes and Canyons

There are many large volcanoes on Mars. One reason that these volcanoes are so large is that the crust of Mars does not move in the same way that Earth's crust moves. Since the crust does not shift around much, lava is able to pile up more than it does on Earth, forming massive mountains and volcanoes.

The biggest volcano on Mars is Olympus Mons. It has a diameter of about 540 kilometers (335 miles). It is approximately 21 kilometers (13 miles) tall. Olympus Mons is the largest known volcano in the solar system.

Olympus Mons is the largest volcano on Mars.

Dust Sky

Mars' sky has different layers. The atmosphere is made mostly of carbon dioxide. The pinkish color in its sky is a result of the red dust, icy water vapor, and frozen carbon dioxide in its atmosphere.

clouds of frozen carbon dioxide

fog of icy water vapor

iron-rich red dust

At the same time, icy water vapor moves between the planet's surface and the atmosphere. This water vapor, combined with dust in the air, also affects the color of the sky. The amount of water vapor in the atmosphere, as well as what the water vapor is mixed with, contributes to the pinkish color of Mars' sky.

Both the surface and the sky of Mars can look red.

Shifting Sands

Long ago, volcanoes erupted, meteors caused deep craters, and flash floods rushed across the surface of the planet. These violent natural phenomena gave the surface of Mars the shape it now has.

Evidence of these events can be found in Mars' landscape. For example, rounded pebbles and rocks on the ground suggest that some kind of moving water was once on Mars. According to some scientists, Mars may have had liquid water in the form of small river systems as long as two billion to four billion years ago. During this time, there may have been large lakes or even oceans on Mars!

Today, however, only wind and sand shape the terrain. Broken rocks and pebbles are scattered across the landscape. Shifting winds and fine sand erode the surface of Mars.

The landscape of Mars changes as wind moves sand and pebbles.

We know that Mars was given the nickname the "Red Planet" due to the color of the sand, rocks, and dust that cover its surface. Scientists know a great deal about the red dust storm that covers a large portion of Mars. They have also learned that the darker areas of the planet's surface come from a buildup of dust. These areas make up almost one-third of its surface. They change as the winds of different seasons blow.

The southern hemisphere of Mars has craters and elevated areas of land. The planet's northern hemisphere is low, flat plains. Between the northern and southern hemispheres is a bulge called the Tharsis rise. It is covered with huge, extinct volcanoes.

Science

Space and Technology

GREAT Inventions

by Patricia Walsh

Genre	Comprehension Skill	Text Features	Science Content
Nonfiction	Main Idea and Details	• Captions • Labels • Text Boxes • Glossary	Technology

Scott Foresman Science 4.19

PEARSON Scott Foresman

ISBN 0-328-13915-7
9 780328 139156 90000

scottforesman.com

Vocabulary	Extended Vocabulary
communication	carbonized
optical fibers	device
technology	filament
telecommunications	graphics
vehicle	hover
	portable
	projector
	transistor

Picture Credits
Every effort has been made to secure permission and provide appropriate credit for photographic material. The publisher deeply regrets any omission and pledges to correct errors called to its attention in subsequent editions.

Photo locators denoted as follows: Top (T), Center (C), Bottom (B), Left (L), Right (R), Background (Bkgd).

Opener: The Science Musuem/©DK Images; 1 ©Bettmann/Corbis; 4 (B, BR) Getty Images; 5 (BR) The Cinema Museum/Ronald Grant Archive; 6 (TL) ©Bettmann/Corbis, (BL) The Science Musuem/©DK Images; 7 (T) Schenectady Museum/Hall of Electrical History Foundation/Corbis, (CR) Brand X Pictures; 8 (TL) ©Bettmann/Corbis, (B) Science Museum, London/DK Images; 9 (TR) Alfred Pasieka/Photo Researchers, Inc.; 10 (TL) ©Bettmann/Corbis; 11 (CR) Reuters/Corbis; 12 (TL) ©Bettmann/Corbis, (B) Science Source/Photo Researchers, Inc.; 14 (TL) Hulton-Deutsch Collection/Corbis.

Scott Foresman/Dorling Kindersley would also like to thank: 11 (TL) Museum of the Moving Image/DK Images.

ISBN: 0-328-13915-7

2 3 4 5 6 7 8 9 10 V004 13 12 11 10 09 08 07 06 05

What did you learn?

1. How is a filament used in a light bulb?
2. How have movies changed over the past one hundred years?
3. What can helicopters do that airplanes cannot do?
4. **Writing** in Science The invention of the transistor changed how computers were made and used. Describe how the transistor did this. Use details from the book to support your answer.
5. **Main Idea and Details** What are some details that help you understand how Alexander Graham Bell's telephone worked?

Glossary

carbonized changed into carbon by burning

device something invented for a particular use or purpose

filament threadlike wire that glows when electric current is passed through it

graphics drawings or pictures

hover to hang or float near the same place in the air

portable easily carried

projector a machine that sends out an image onto a screen

transistor a small device that controls the flow of electricity in electronic equipment

GREAT Inventions

by Patricia Walsh

PEARSON Scott Foresman DK

What You Already Know

Technology helps us solve problems and makes our work easier and more efficient. It also helps us live healthier and safer lives. Technology has helped make a sport such as in-line skating safer. In-line skates are made from materials that people have made from natural resources. Iron ore is a natural resource that is used to make the screws that hold an in-line skate's wheels in place. The plastic found on an in-line skate is made from chemicals found in nature.

Technology has improved medical care. Optical fibers are thin tubes that allow light to pass. They help doctors see inside the body. X-ray machines take pictures of bones in the body. Another diagnostic tool is magnetic resonance imaging, also known as MRI. It also allows doctors to get a detailed look inside the body so they can identify problems.

Radio, TV, the telephone, the Internet, and e-mail help us communicate faster and across greater distances. Communication is any way of sending a message from one place to another. There are many ways to communicate.

In 1955 scientists at Bell Labs designed the first computer that had a transistor. Until then, a computer took up an entire room. This new computer was faster and smaller than the room-sized computer it replaced. Today our computers and handheld devices are even smaller, yet faster and more powerful.

What do you think the next important invention will be? Do you think it will change the world?

The Internet

The Internet is a global network that connects millions and millions of computers and computer users through wires, cables, and satellites. It allows people everywhere to gather and exchange information, news, and opinions.

Today's computers have many uses.

The Computer Age

Charles Babbage

Charles Babbage, a British mathematician, was far ahead of his time. In 1834, he had an idea for a programmable computer that would solve math problems faster than humans could. Although his Analytical Engine was never completed, his idea helped lead to the development of the modern computer.

Many years later, in 1947, three scientists at Bell Telephone Laboratories searched for a way to process information quickly. John Bardeen, Walter Brattain, and William Shockley built on the ideas of earlier scientists and invented a tiny device called a transistor. A transistor controls the flow of electricity in electronic equipment. One of the first uses of transistors was in hearing aids that were small enough to fit into the ear.

Babbage's Analytical Engine was a huge technological advancement.

Telecommunications are communications made electronically over a distance. We can communicate with people around the world, with astronauts, and with spacecraft in outer space.

Today's transportation vehicles include cars, trucks, and airplanes. A vehicle carries people and goods. Transportation technology moves people and goods from place to place. Today through new technology, engineers make transportation safer and more efficient.

Science and technology have improved because many people have been curious about how things work and about ways to make them better. In this book you will read about inventors and their inventions that changed our world.

Changing the World

Technology of our modern age is due to the discoveries and inventions of inventors of the past. Over the past two hundred years, the way we live and communicate with one another has changed so much! The inventions of the telephone and the computer have changed how we send and receive information. Today we can pick up the phone and speak to a friend living on the other side of the world. We can send an e-mail to our next-door neighbor or even to astronauts in space.

How to use electricity was a very important discovery. Think of how important electricity is to our everyday lives! Without electricity, we would not be able to do so many of the things we do each day.

light bulb

telephone

computer

Airplanes have revolutionized the way we travel.

Later that day, Wilbur Wright flew for fifty-nine seconds at a speed of thirty-one miles per hour. The U.S. Army, seeing a future use of this new technology, asked the Wright brothers to build a flying machine that could travel with a passenger at a speed of forty miles per hour.

Now, just over one hundred years later, commercial jet airplanes carry hundreds of passengers and cargo at a speed of six hundred miles per hour. What do you think the Wright brothers would say about today's busy airports?

Helicopters

A helicopter with its rotary blades can be flown almost anywhere. It can do three things an airplane cannot do. It can fly backward, rotate in the air, and hover.

Taking To The Sky

Wilbur and Orville Wright

Wilbur and Orville Wright worked in their Ohio bicycle shop, picturing the day that people would fly. They used their knowledge of mathematics and mechanics to design a vehicle that would fly. From 1900 to 1903, they experimented with gliders and powered aircraft in the windy hills near Kitty Hawk, North Carolina. Then on December 17, 1903, the Wright brothers flew the first ever manned aircraft. Orville Wright was the pilot for the first flight, which lasted just twelve seconds.

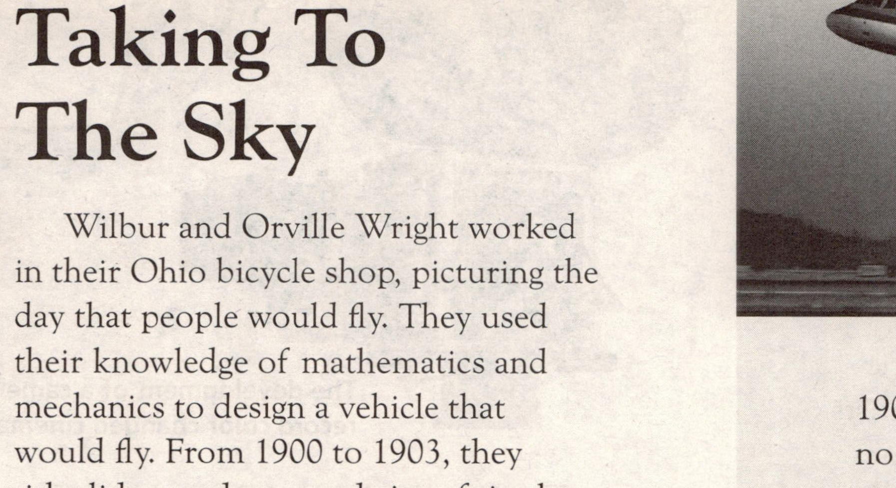

The first powered flight took place at Kitty Hawk, North Carolina.

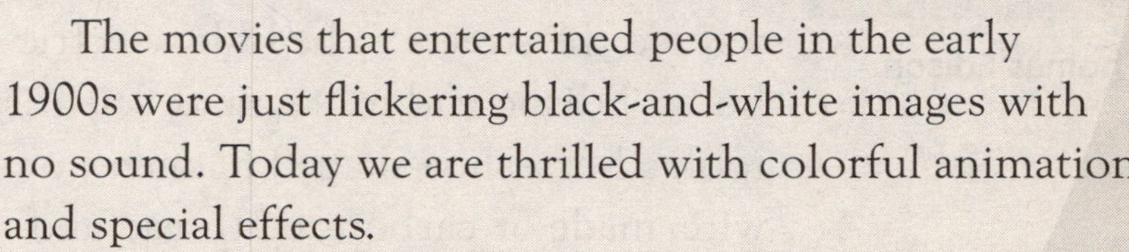

airplane

The movies that entertained people in the early 1900s were just flickering black-and-white images with no sound. Today we are thrilled with colorful animation and special effects.

Pioneers traveled across the country in wagons or on foot. The invention of powered flight and the airplane made big changes in how we travel. Now crossing the United States takes only a few hours instead of a few months. The credit for these advancements goes to amateur and professional scientists and inventors.

movie theater

Thomas Edison

A Bright Idea

Before Thomas Edison and his team of inventors improved the light bulb, city streets were lit with the flicker of gas lamps. Thomas Edison was a scientist and inventor who wanted the streets to be lit by electric bulbs. Edison and his team of scientists took a horseshoe-shaped filament, or wire, made of carbonized thread and heated it with an electric current. They found it would glow for several hours inside a glass globe. Edison had his assistants string up these new electric lights outside his research laboratory in Menlo Park, New Jersey.

The night of December 31, 1879 was Edison's first public demonstration of these lights powered by electricity. A few dozen electric lamps glowed above the heads of three thousand spectators. The people had never seen anything quite like it.

This version of Edison's lamp was made in 1880.

color film

The development of a camera that could record color changed cinema forever.

The Lumière brothers' first movie was titled *Workers Leaving the Lumière Factory*. Can you tell from the title what the film was about?

In just a few months, the *Cinématographe* was in use all over Europe. Soon movies and moviemaking were gaining popularity all over the world. The first movies were black and white. By the 1940s the technology was available for movies to be made in color. Today films are more and more advanced with computer graphics and special effects that entertain and inform us.

Digital Animation

Digital animation is a series of moving images made on a computer screen. It can be as simple as a moving shape or as detailed as the 3-D animation in full-length movies.

The Age Of Film

Auguste and Louis Lumière

In the late 1800s Thomas Edison invented a movie camera that he called a Kinetoscope. It could record images and then reproduce them. French inventors Louis and Auguste Lumière first saw Edison's Kinetoscope in 1894. The Lumière brothers had ideas about how to improve it.

Within a year, they invented a combination movie camera and movie projector. They called it the *Cinématographe*. The first public demonstration of this new technology was in Paris in December 1895. It was more portable than other cameras of the time. It projected images onto a screen using a lens and a light source.

Cinématographe

Pearl Street Power Station provided electricity to homes and businesses in New York.

Edison wanted a safe, affordable, practical system that would bring electricity to people's homes. He invented the electric meter. He planned the Pearl Street Power Station in New York City, the first power plant to generate electricity. By the end of the 1880s, everyone in New York had access to Edison's electricity.

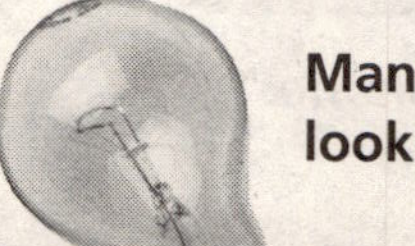

Many light bulbs still look much like Edison's.

Neon Lights

Today neon lights are often used in advertising signs. Neon is a colorless, odorless gas. An electric current passing through tubes filled with neon causes the colored light.

Alexander Graham Bell

The Telephone

Alexander Graham Bell invented the telephone in 1876. He was interested in finding new ways to transmit sound. With Thomas Watson, Bell tried to make electric currents imitate sound waves so people could communicate over long distances. After many experiments, Bell was finally able to speak with Watson using the first telephone. The first words spoken on the telephone were, "Mr. Watson, come here. I want to see you." Bell's invention had used an electric current to send the sound of a voice through wires. His first telephone combined the earpiece and the mouthpiece. It used a magnet to help transfer the sound.

Bell's first telephone was known as the *"Box Telephone."*

Modern telephones don't look like Bell's invention, but they use the same principles.

Optical Fibers

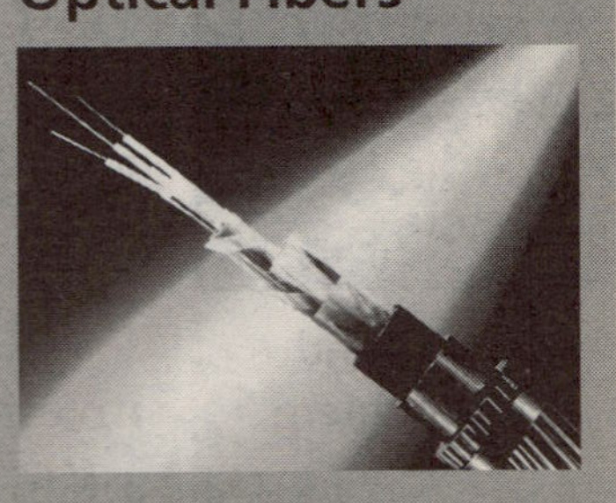

Today many telephone systems use the technology of optical fibers to transmit telephone calls. Information is changed into light pulses that are carried by thin glass or plastic filaments.

In 1915 telephone lines crossing the country connected America's East and West Coasts. After telephone cables were laid under oceans, people on different continents could talk to one another for the first time.

Two technologies are combined to make today's cellular phone. They are Bell's invention of the telephone and Nikolai Tesla's invention of the radio. The scientific principles of these two inventions led to the development of this form of wireless communication.